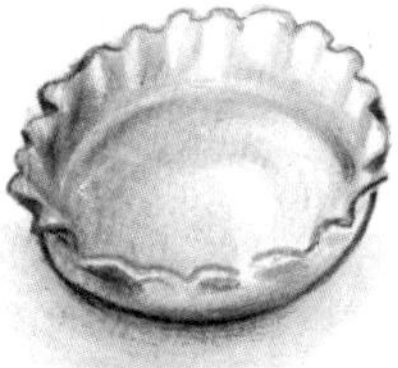
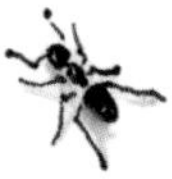
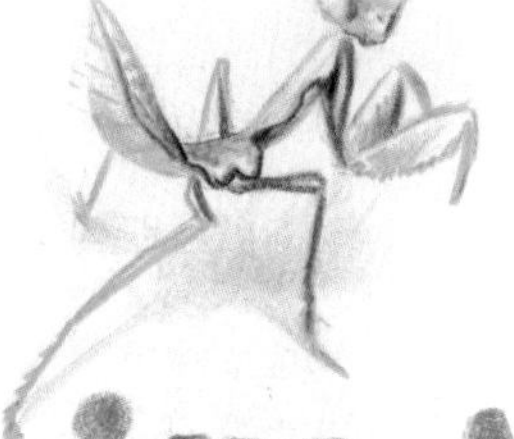
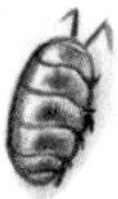

MANABESHIMA ISLAND JAPAN

ONE ISLAND, TWO MONTHS, ONE MINICAR, SIXTY CRABS, EIGHTY BITES AND FIFTY SHOTS OF SHOCHU

FLORENT CHAVOUET

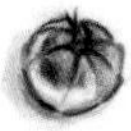
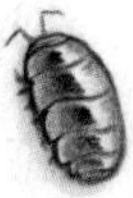
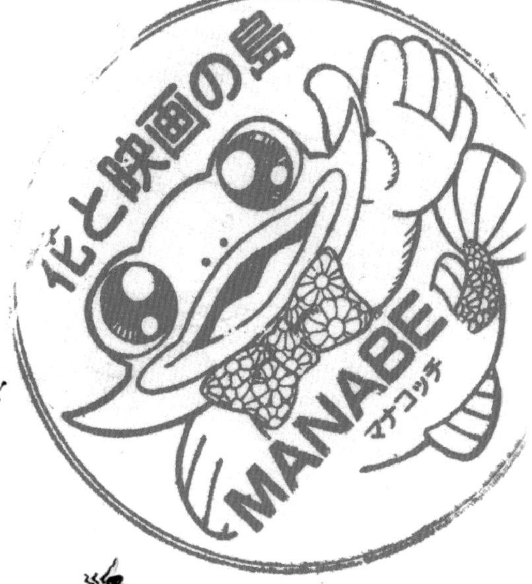
花と映画の島
MANABE
マナコッチ
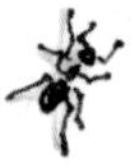
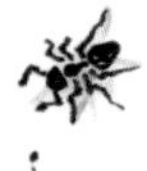
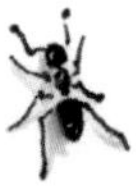
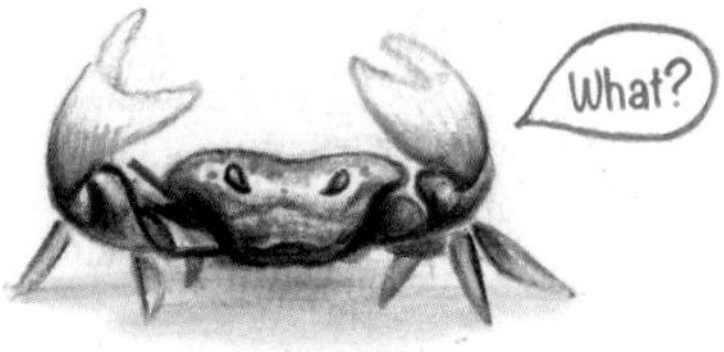
What?

TUTTLE Publishing

Tokyo | Rutland, Vermont | Singapore

The Tuttle Story
"Books to Span the East and West"

Many people are surprised to learn that the world's leading publisher of books on Asia had humble beginnings in the tiny American state of Vermont. The company's founder, Charles E. Tuttle, belonged to a New England family steeped in publishing.

Immediately after WWII, Tuttle served in Tokyo under General Douglas MacArthur and was tasked with reviving the Japanese publishing industry. He later founded the Charles E. Tuttle Publishing Company, which thrives today as one of the world's leading independent publishers.

Though a westerner, Tuttle was hugely instrumental in bringing a knowledge of Japan and Asia to a world hungry for information about the East. By the time of his death in 1993, Tuttle had published over 6,000 books on Asian culture, history and art—a legacy honored by the Japanese emperor with the "Order of the Sacred Treasure," the highest tribute Japan can bestow upon a non-Japanese.

With a backlist of 1,500 titles, Tuttle Publishing is more active today than at any time in its past—still inspired by Charles Tuttle's core mission to publish fine books to span the East and West and provide a greater understanding of each.

Published by Tuttle Publishing, an imprint of Periplus Editions (HK) Ltd.

www.tuttlepublishing.com

Copyright © 2010 by Editions Philippe Picquier

English-language translation copyright © 2015 by Periplus Editions (HK) Ltd.

Library of Congress Control Number: 2015945222

ISBN 978-4-8053-1343-5

First English-language edition
18 17 16 15
5 4 3 2 1
1508TW

Printed in Malaysia

Distributed by

North America, Latin America & Europe
Tuttle Publishing
364 Innovation Drive
North Clarendon
VT 05759-9436 U.S.A.
Tel: 1 (802) 773-8930
Fax: 1 (802) 773-6993
info@tuttlepublishing.com
www.tuttlepublishing.com

Japan
Tuttle Publishing
Yaekari Building, 3rd Floor
5-4-12 Osaki, Shinagawa-ku
Tokyo 141 0032
Tel: (81) 3 5437-0171
Fax: (81) 3 5437-0755
sales@tuttle.co.jp
www.tuttle.co.jp

Asia Pacific
Berkeley Books Pte. Ltd.
61 Tai Seng Avenue #02-12
Singapore 534167
Tel: (65) 6280-1330
Fax: (65) 6280-6290
inquiries@periplus.com.sg
www.periplus.com

Japan is so much an island that it's an archipelago.
And if you count isolated rocks, the country claims
more than four thousand islands.

BUT I ONLY KNOW TWO.

It's a very meager ratio if you compare it to the three cathedrals
that an average japanese tourist visits out of the two hundred that
are in FRANCE. In order to compensate for this lack and to better
my average, I decide to take a Boat or a Bridge and to meet at least
one new island.

YES, BUT WHICH ONE?

In the japanese catalog, islands are many — some are
sacred and some are gated, some are industrial and some
are artificial, some are tropical and some are topical,
some are mountainous and some are scandalous, some
are wild and some are mild, some are atolls and some are
dust bowls, and there are even islands
where people fish and drink.

What Luck: I don't know how to fish.

In order for my decision not to be completely a by-product of chance,
I impose upon myself a few criteria: an island small in size and
in the number of inhabitants, and isolated but still accessible.

In short, a real island. Better still, an island's island.

So the catalog gets shorter, and narrows itself down,
and my choice hones in on the Inland Sea (SETO NAIKAI),
a region where villages are separated not by prairies but
by ocean currents, and where bell towers are lighthouses.

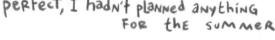

It remains for me to choose between these
crumbs of land the one island that is
the least spoken about and to select among
the four seasons the one where fish grow.

Perfect, I hadn't planned anything
for the summer.

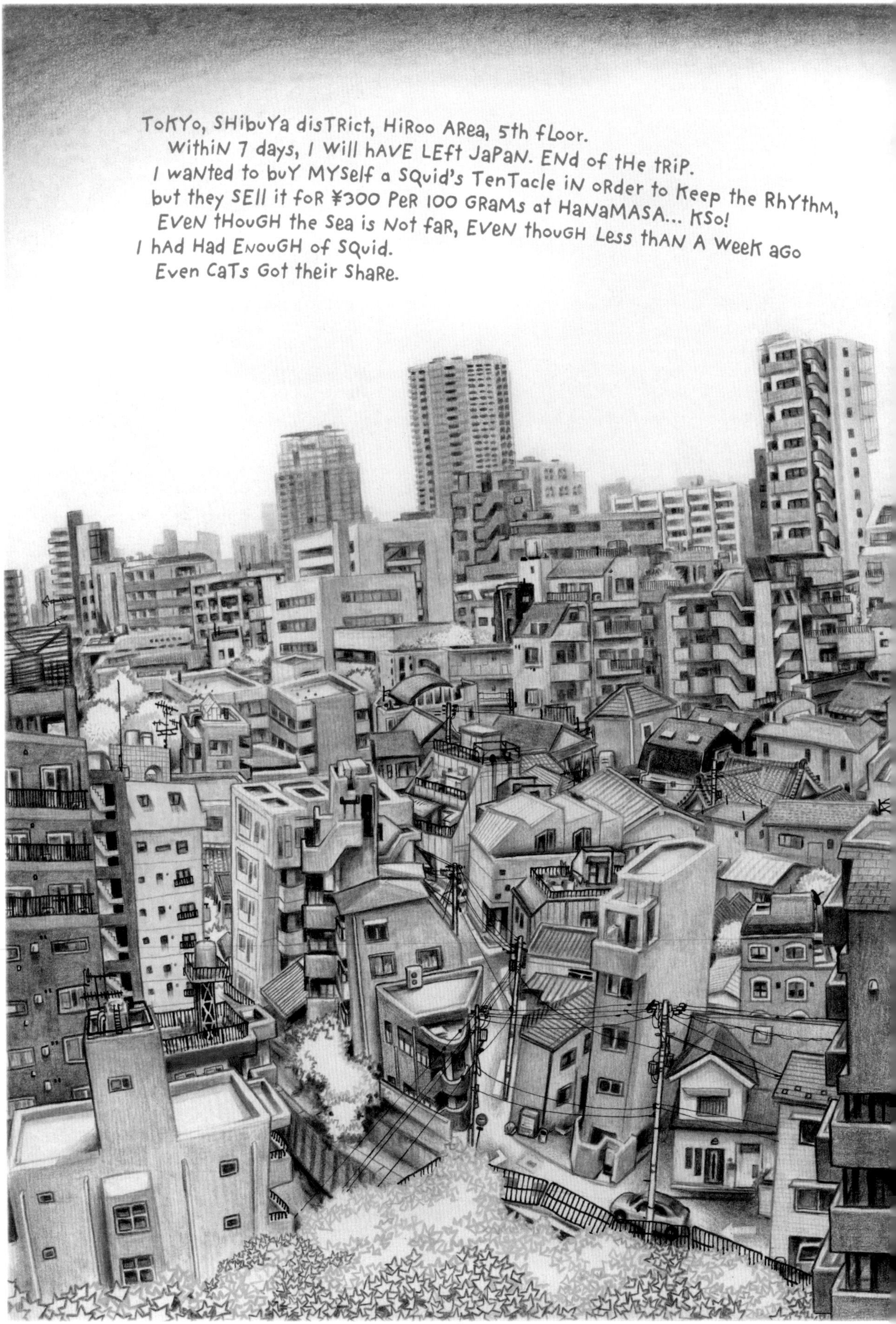
Tokyo, Shibuya district, Hiroo area, 5th floor.
Within 7 days, I will have left Japan. End of the trip.
I wanted to buy myself a squid's tentacle in order to keep the rhythm,
but they sell it for ¥300 per 100 grams at Hanamasa... Kso!
Even though the sea is not far, even though less than a week ago
I had had enough of squid.
Even cats got their share.

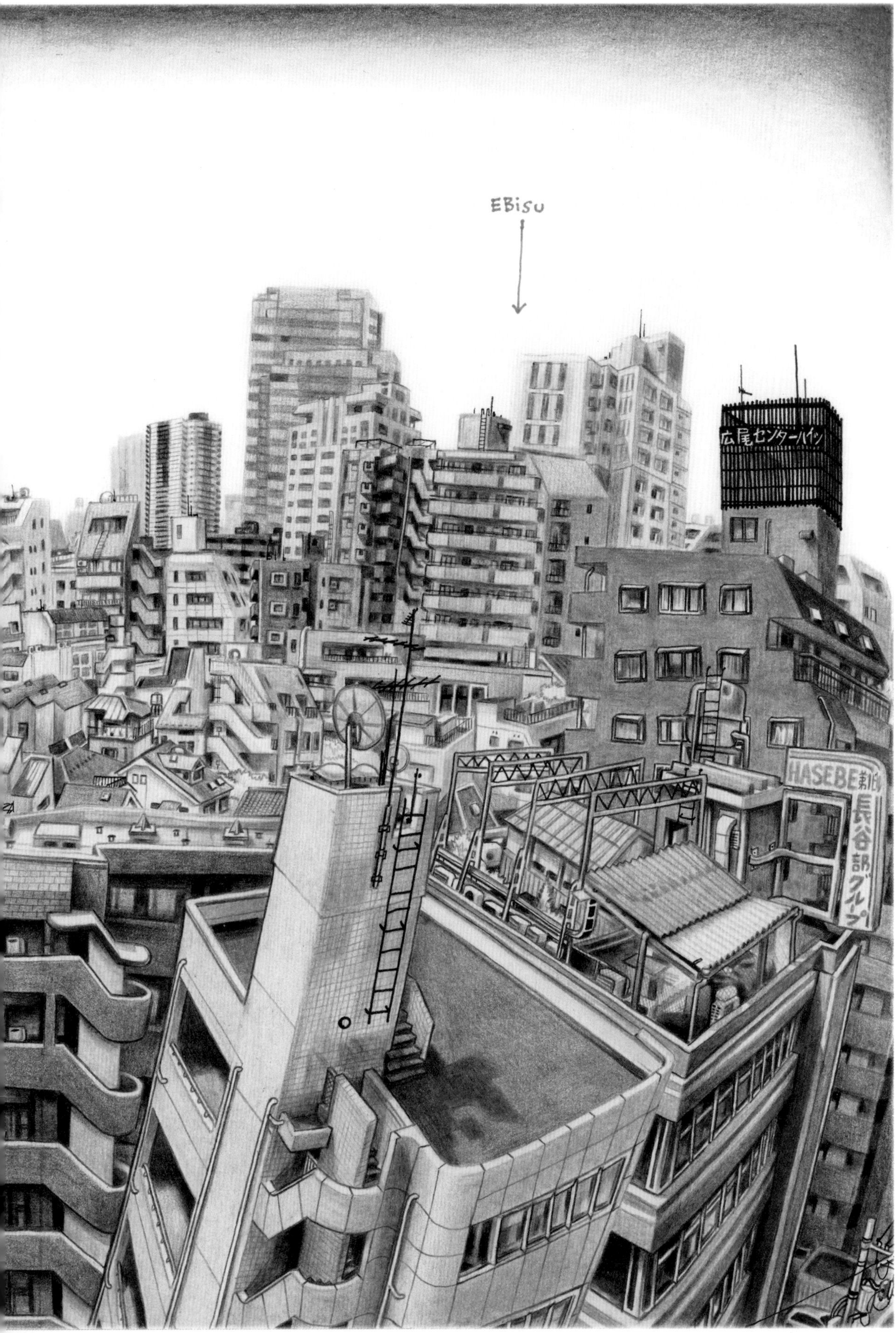
EBISU
広尾センターハイツ
HASEBE第1ビル
長谷部グループ

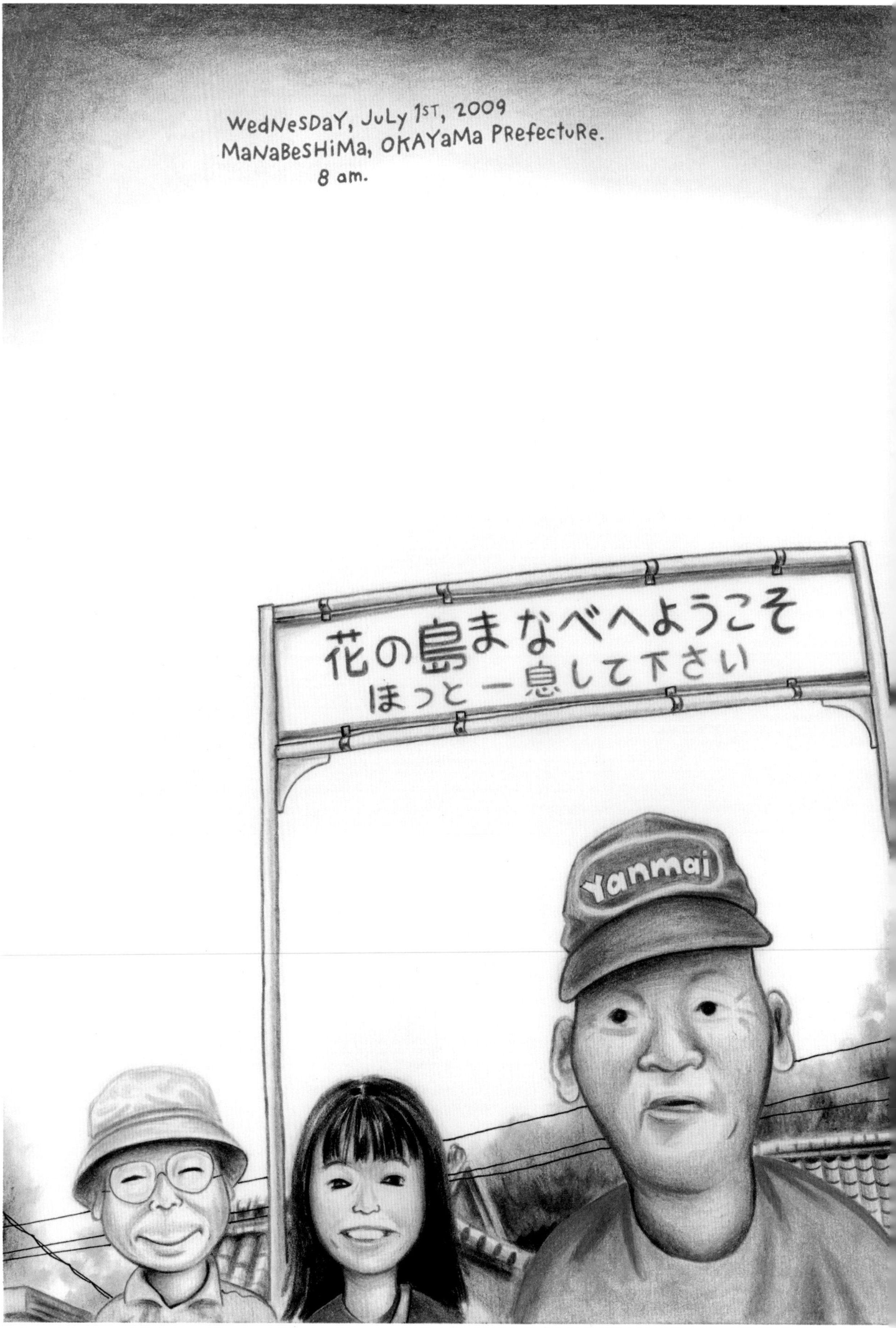
WedNesDaY, JuLy 1ST, 2009
MaNaBeSHiMa, OKAYaMa PRefectuRe.
8 am.
花の島まなべへようこそ
ほっと一息して下さい
Yanmai

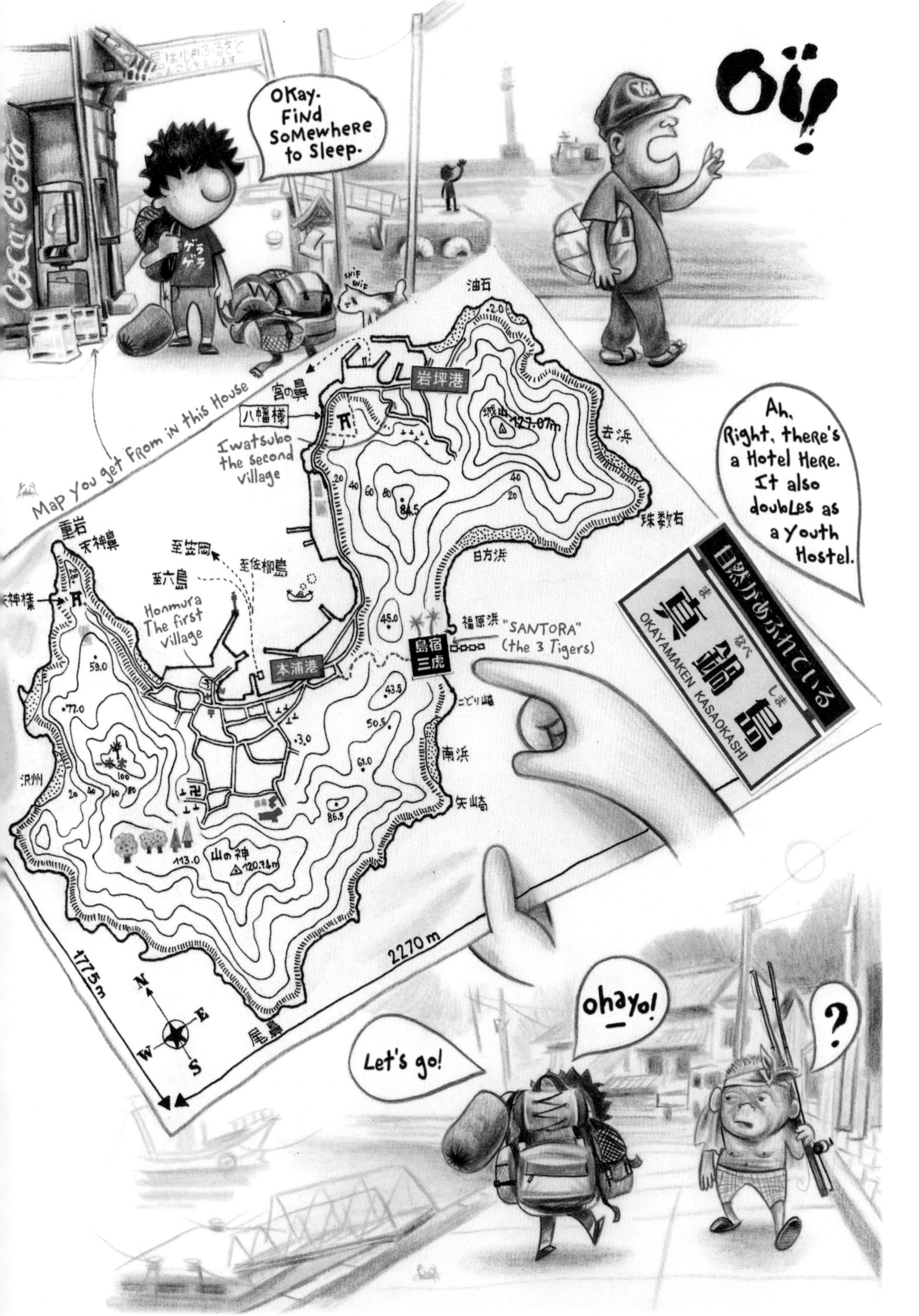
Coca-Cola
Okay. Find Somewhere to Sleep.
ゲラゲラ
SNIF SNIF
Oï!
Map you get from in this House
Iwatsubo the second village
Honmura The first village
油石
岩坪港
宮の鼻
八幡様
城山 127.07m
去浜
珠数石
日方浜
重岩
天神鼻
至笠岡
至六島
至佐柳島
本浦港
島宿 三虎
福原浜
"SANTORA" (the 3 Tigers)
南浜
矢崎
山の神 120.74m
2270 m
1775 m
N
E
S
W
Ah, Right, there's a Hotel Here. It also doubles as a Youth Hostel.
自然があふれている
真鍋島
OKAYAMAKEN KASAOKASHI
ohayo!
Let's go!
?

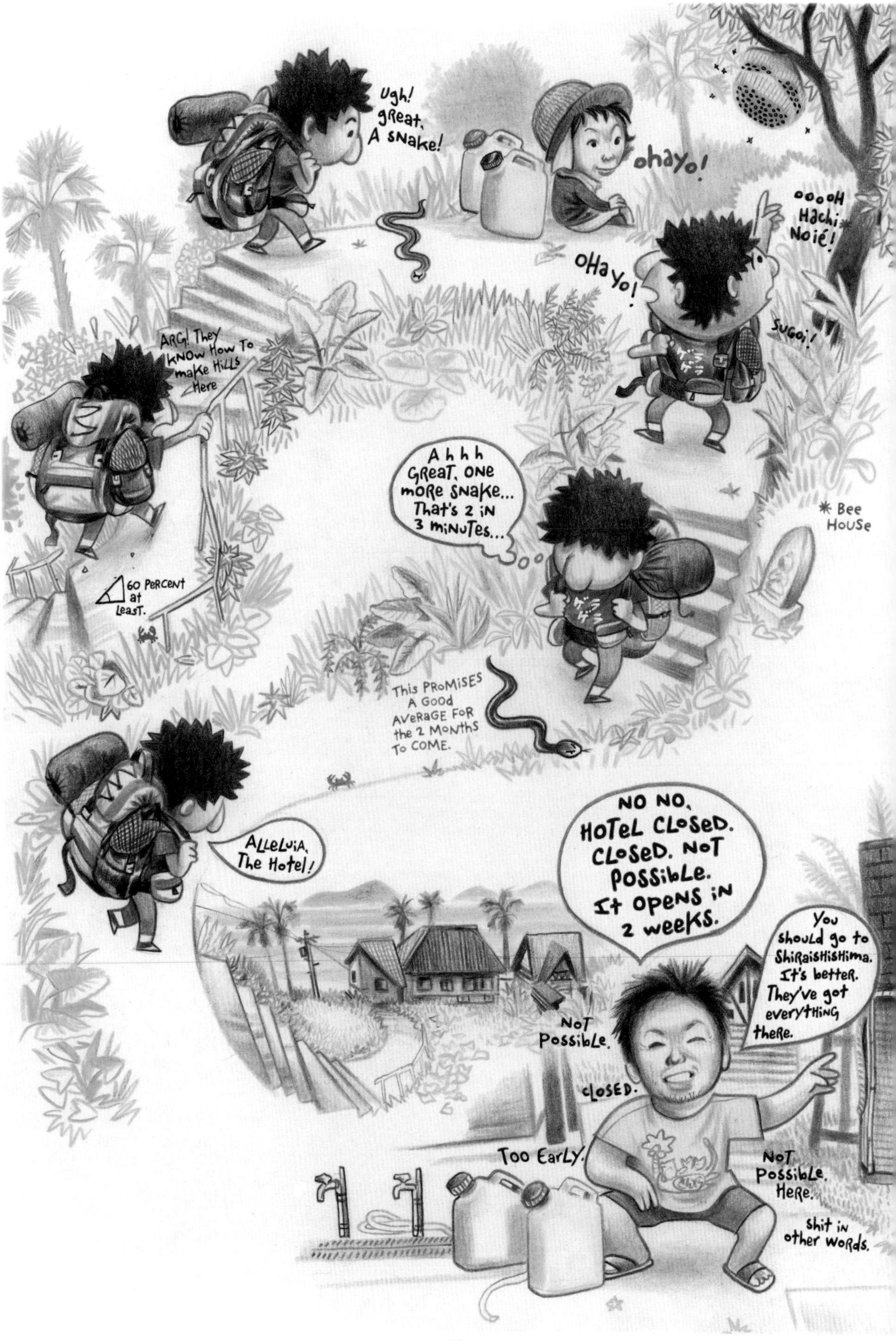
Ugh! great, A snake!
ohayo!
ooooH Hachi Noié!
OHayo!
Sugoi!
ARG! They know how to make Hills Here
Ahhh GReaT, ONE MORE SNAKE... That's 2 iN 3 minuTes...
* Bee House
60 PERCENT at LeasT.
This PROMISES A GOOD AVERAGE FOR the 2 MONTHS TO COME.
Alleluia, The Hotel!
NO NO, HOTEL CLOSED. CLOSED. NOT POSSIBLE. It OPENS IN 2 weeks.
You should go to ShiraishiShima. It's better. They've got everything there.
NoT Possible.
CLOSED.
Too Early.
NoT Possible. Here.
shit in other words.

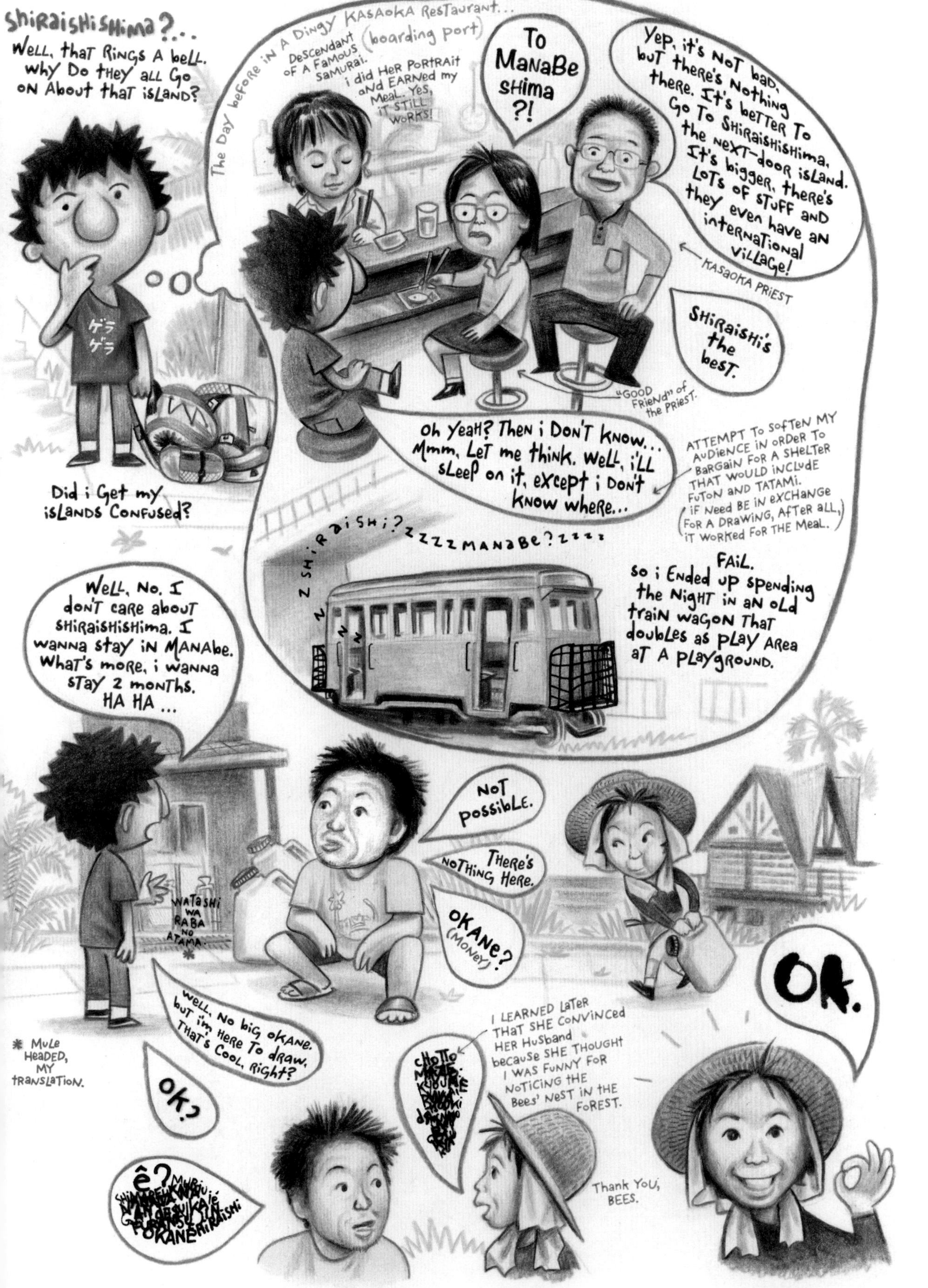

SHiraiSHiSHima?...
WeLL, that RinGs A beLL. why Do tHey aLL Go on About that isLand?
The Day before in A Dingy KASAOKA Restaurant... (boarding port)
DeScendant of A FamouS SamuRai.
i did Her Portrait and EARNed my MeaL. Yes, it STILL works!
To ManaBe sHima?!
Yep, it's NoT bad, but there's Nothing there. It's better To Go To ShiraiShiShima, the next-door island. It's bigger, there's LoTs of stuff and they even have an international viLLage!
KASAOKA PRIEST
ShiRaishi's the best.
"GOOD FRiend" of the PRiEST.
Oh yeaH? Then i Don't know... Mmm, Let me think. weLL, i'LL sLeep on it, except i Don't know where...
ATTEMPT To sofTen MY AUDIENCE iN oRDER To BARGAIN FOR A SHELTER THAT WOULD iNCLUDE FUTON AND TATAMI. iF NEED BE iN EXCHANGE FOR A DRAWING, AFTER ALL, iT WORKED FOR THE MeaL.
Did i Get my isLands Confused?
Z SHiRaiSHi? zzzzMANaBe? zzzz
FAiL. so i Ended up spending the Night in an oLd train wagon That doubLes as pLay Area at A pLaygRound.
WeLL, No. I don't care about ShiraiShiShima. I wanna stay in ManaBe. What's more, i wanna stay 2 months. HA HA...
WATASHi WA RABA NO ATAMA.*
NoT possibLe.
There's NoTHing Here.
OKANE? (Money)
WeLL, No big okane. but i'm Here To draw. ThaT's CooL, Right?
* MuLe HEADED, MY TRANSLATION.
OK?
I LEARNED LaTER THAT SHE CONViNCed HER Husband because SHE THOUGHT I WAS FUNNY FOR NoTiCiNG THE Bees' NesT iN THE FoREST.
OK.
ê?
Thank You, BEES.

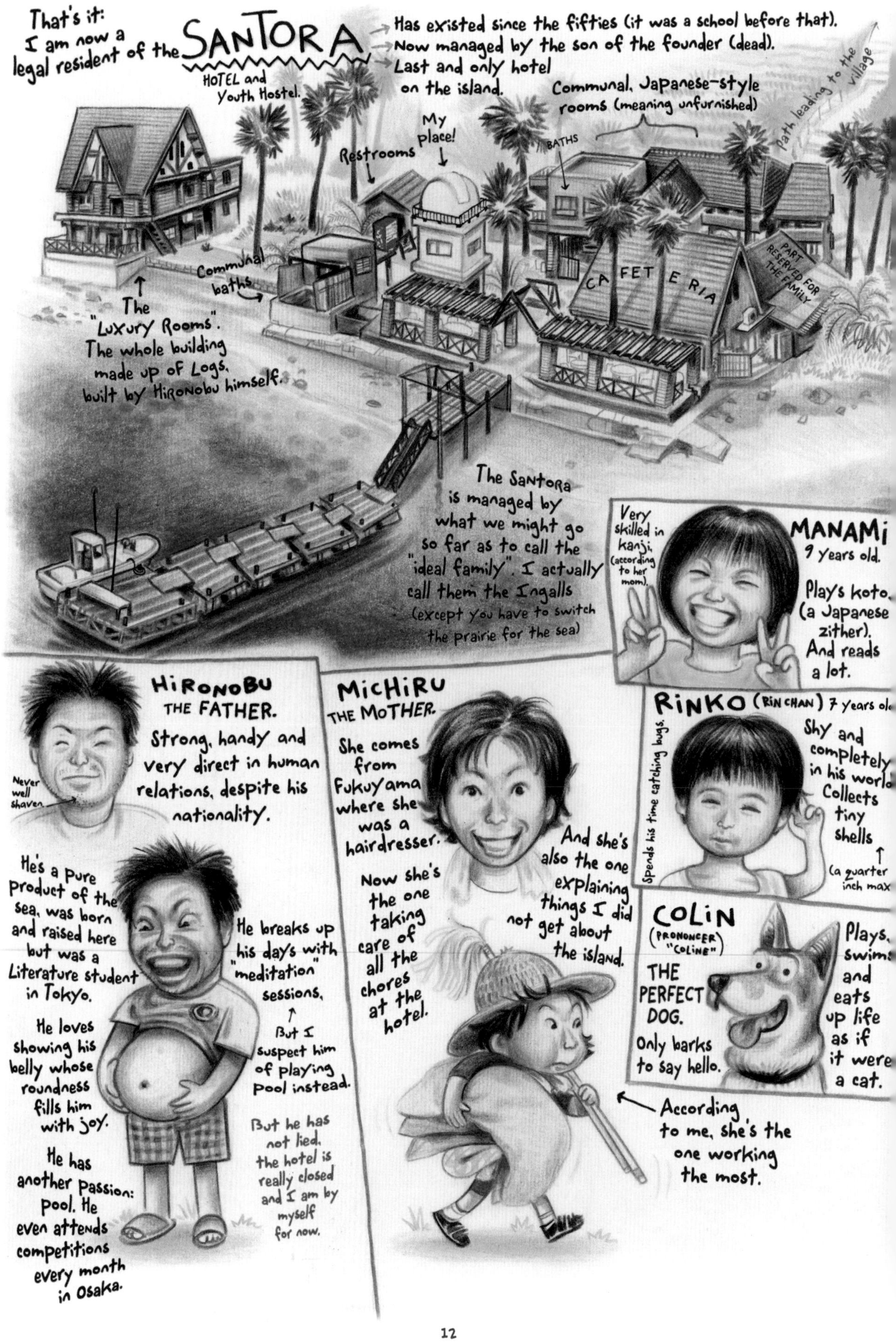
That's it: I am now a legal resident of the SANTORA
HOTEL and Youth Hostel.
Has existed since the fifties (it was a school before that).
Now managed by the son of the founder (dead).
Last and only hotel on the island.
Communal, Japanese-style rooms (meaning unfurnished)
Path leading to the village
My place!
Restrooms
BATHS
Communal baths
CAFETERIA
PART RESERVED FOR THE FAMILY
The "Luxury Rooms". The whole building made up of Logs, built by Hironobu himself.
The Santora is managed by what we might go so far as to call the "ideal family". I actually call them the Ingalls (except you have to switch the prairie for the sea)
Very skilled in kanji (according to her mom).
MANAMI 9 years old.
Plays koto (a Japanese zither). And reads a lot.
HIRONOBU THE FATHER.
Strong, handy and very direct in human relations, despite his nationality.
Never well shaven
He's a pure product of the sea, was born and raised here but was a Literature student in Tokyo.
He loves showing his belly whose roundness fills him with joy.
He has another passion: pool. He even attends competitions every month in Osaka.
He breaks up his days with "meditation" sessions.
But I suspect him of playing pool instead.
But he has not lied, the hotel is really closed and I am by myself for now.
MICHIRU THE MOTHER.
She comes from Fukuyama where she was a hairdresser.
Now she's the one taking care of all the chores at the hotel.
And she's also the one explaining things I did not get about the island.
According to me, she's the one working the most.
RINKO (RIN CHAN) 7 years old
Spends his time catching bugs.
Shy and completely in his world. Collects tiny shells
(a quarter inch max)
COLIN (PRONONCER) "COLINE"
THE PERFECT DOG.
Only barks to say hello.
Plays, swims and eats up life as if it were a cat.

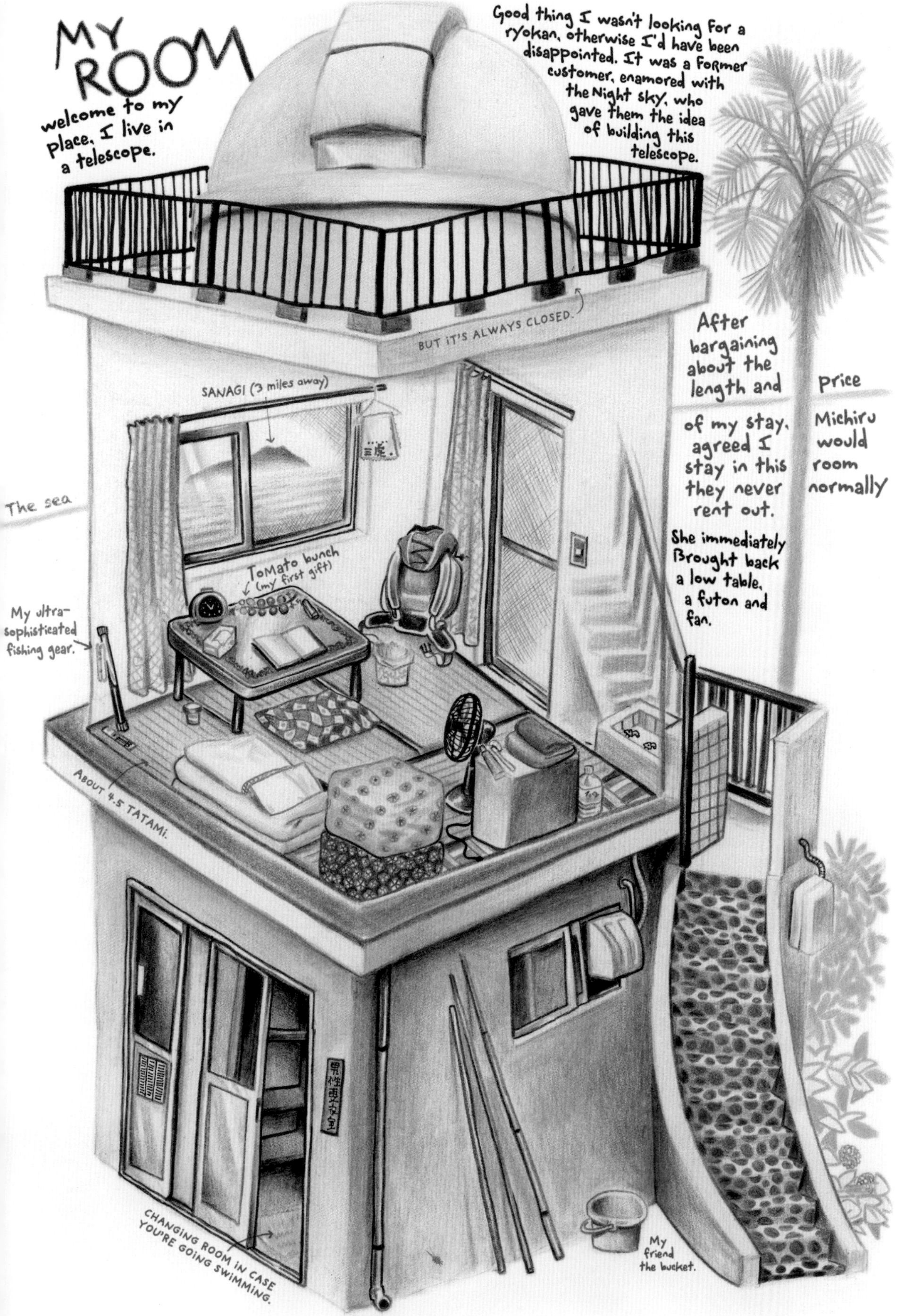
MY ROOM
welcome to my place. I live in a telescope.
Good thing I wasn't looking for a ryokan, otherwise I'd have been disappointed. It was a former customer, enamored with the Night sky, who gave them the idea of building this telescope.
BUT iT'S ALWAYS CLOSED.
After bargaining about the length and
Price
of my stay, agreed I stay in this they never rent out.
Michiru would room normally
She immediately Brought back a low table, a futon and fan.
SANAGI (3 miles away)
The sea
TOMato bunch (my first gift)
My ultra-sophisticated fishing gear.
ABOUT 4.5 TATAMi.
男性更衣室
CHANGING ROOM IN CASE YOU'RE GOING SWIMMiNG.
My friend the bucket.

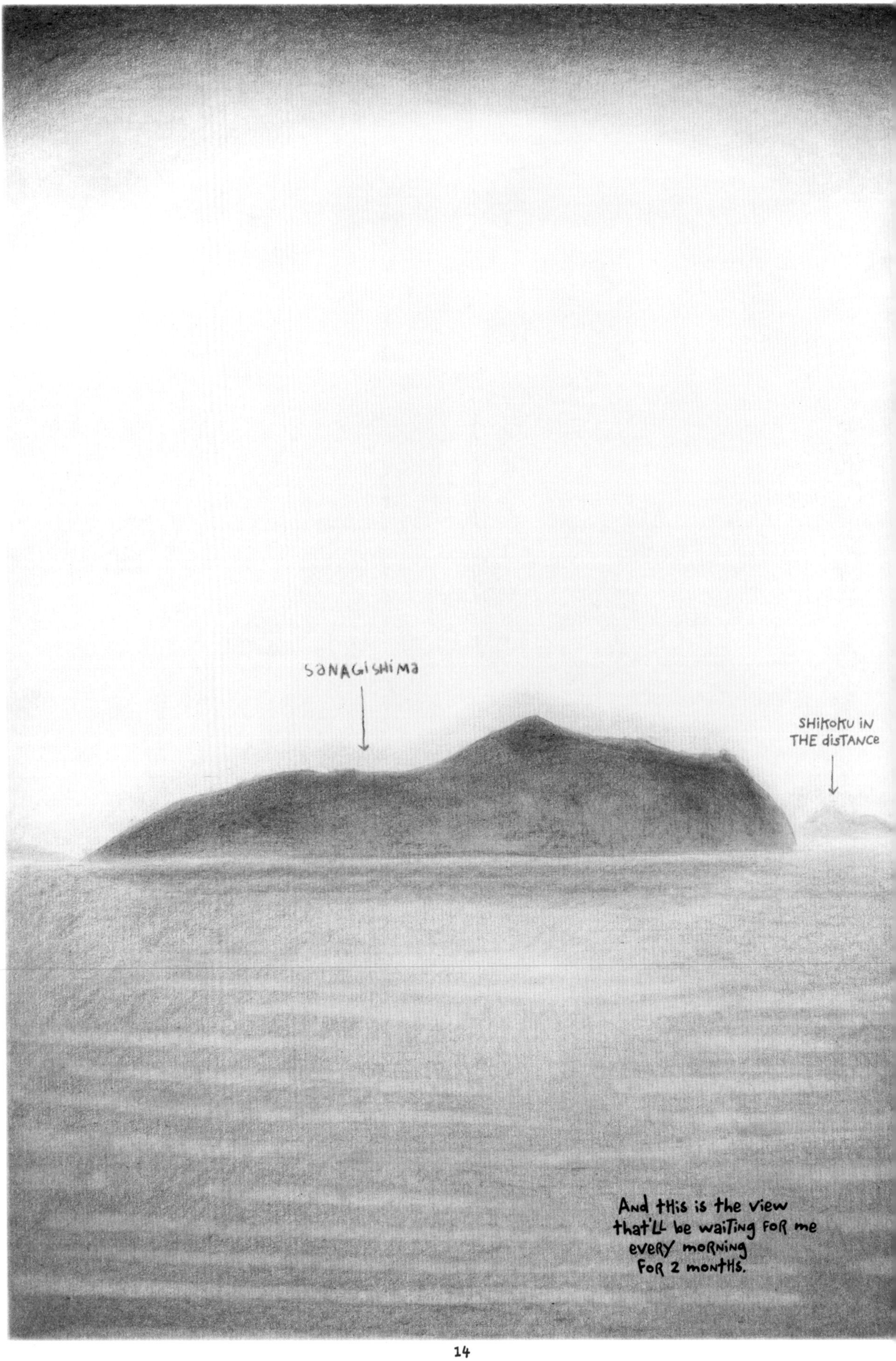
SaNAGISHIMa
SHIKOKU IN THE disTANCe
And tHis is the view that'LL be waiTing FOR me every morning FOR 2 monTHS.

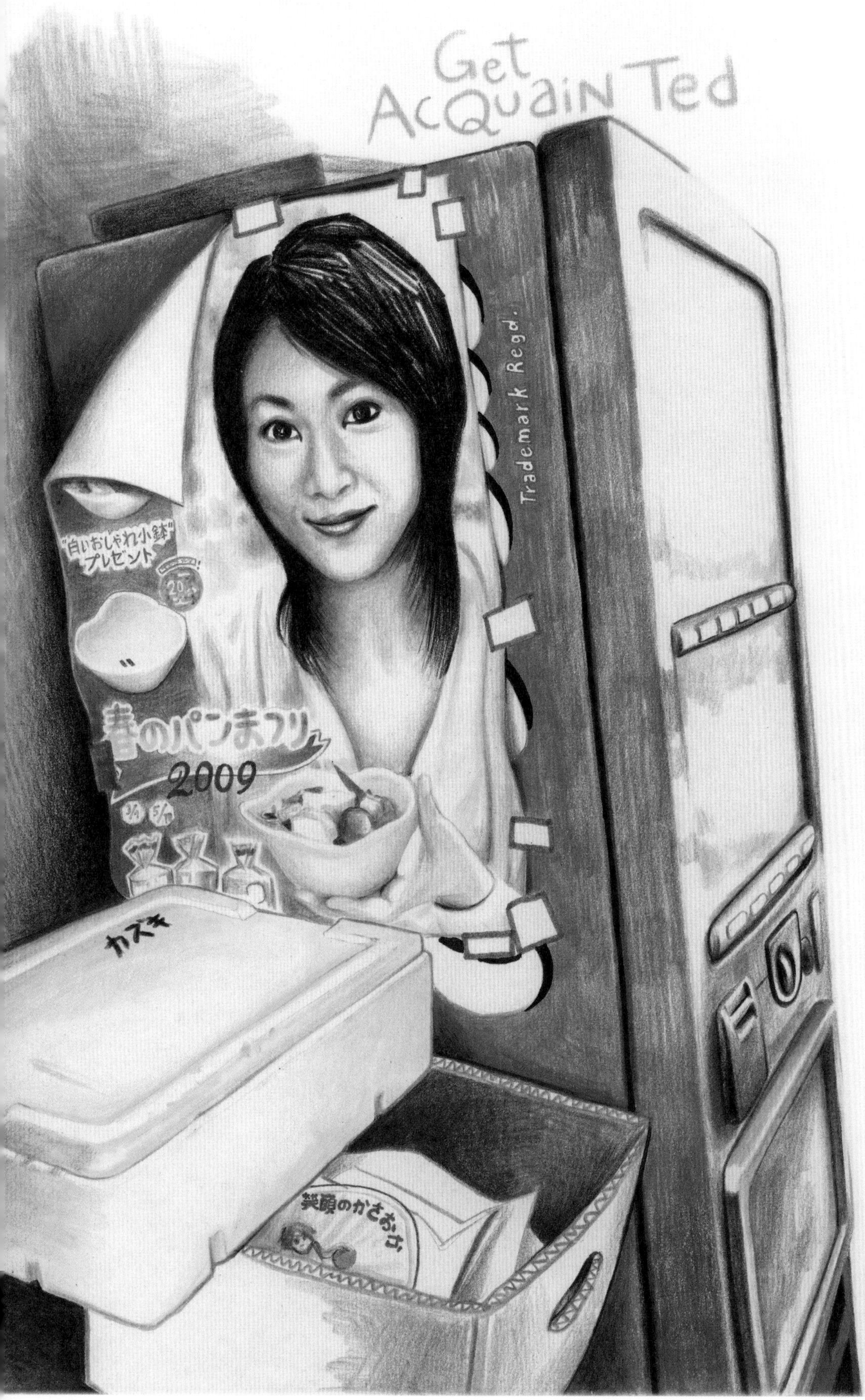
Get
AcQuain Ted
Trademark Regd.
"白いおしゃれ小鉢"
プレゼント
春のパンまつり
2009
カズキ

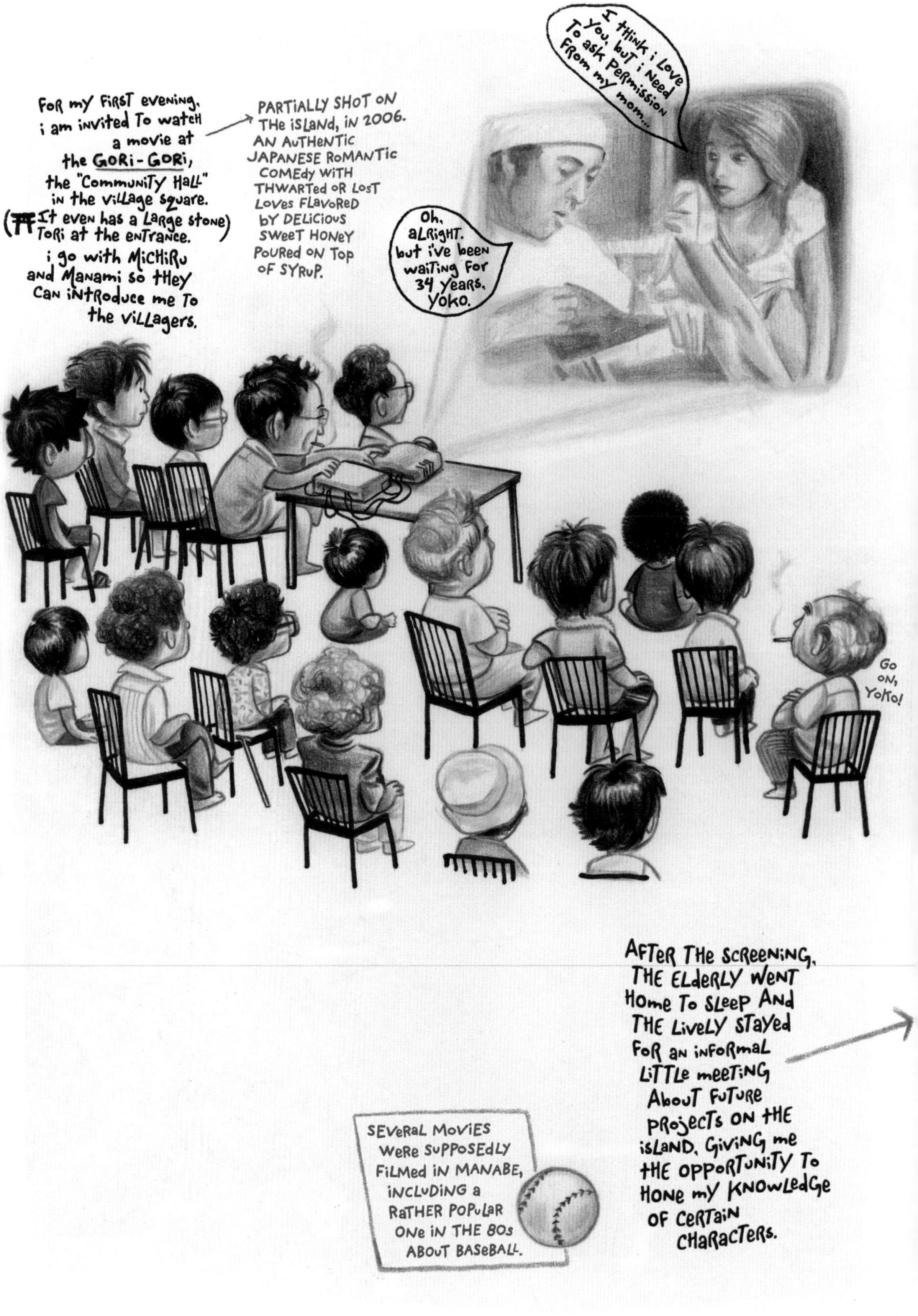

For my first evening, i am invited to watch a movie at the GORI-GORI, the "Community Hall" in the village square. (It even has a Large stone Tori at the entrance.) i go with Michiru and Manami so they can introduce me to the villagers.
PARTIALLY SHOT ON THE ISLAND, IN 2006. AN AUTHENTIC JAPANESE ROMANTIC COMEDY WITH THWARTED OR LOST LOVES FLAVORED BY DELICIOUS SWEET HONEY POURED ON TOP OF SYRUP.
I think i love you, but i need to ask permission from my mom...
Oh, alright. but i've been waiting for 34 years, Yoko.
Go on, Yoko!
After the screening, the elderly went home to sleep and the lively stayed for an informal little meeting about future projects on the island, giving me the opportunity to hone my knowledge of certain characters.
Several movies were supposedly filmed in Manabe, including a rather popular one in the 80s about baseball.

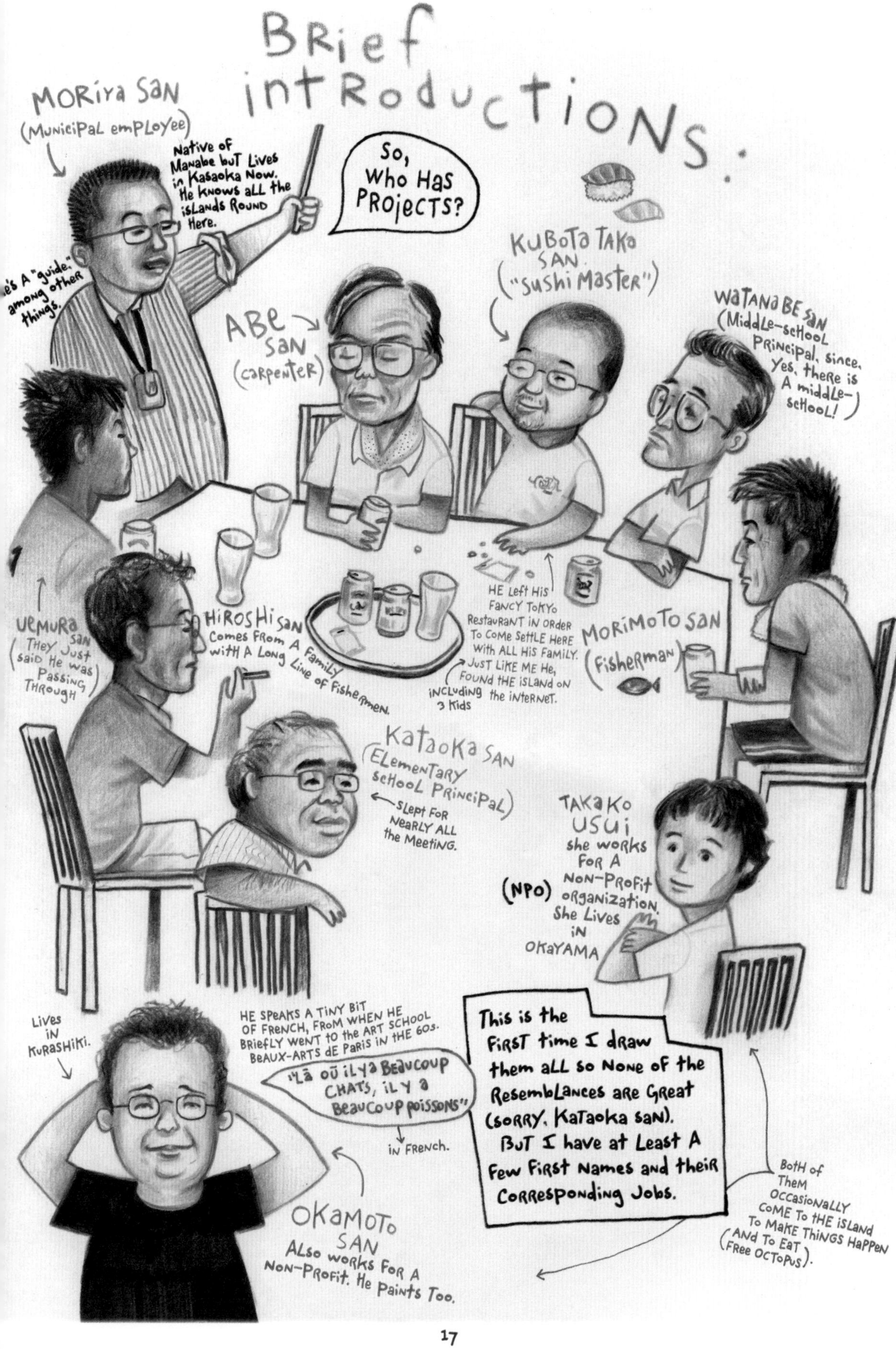

Brief introductions.
MORiya SAN (MuniciPaL empLoyee)
Native of Manabe buT Lives in Kasaoka Now. He KNOWS aLL the iSLands Round Here.
e's A "guide." among other things.
So, Who Has PROjecTS?
ABe SAN (caRpenTeR)
KUBoTa TAKo SAN ("SushiMaster")
WaTANaBE SAN (Middle-school PRincipal, since, yes, there is A middle-school!)
UeMURa SAN THEY Just said He was Passing Through
HiROSHi SAN Comes FRom A Family with A Long Line of Fishermen.
HE Left HiS FANCY ToKYo Restaurant in ORder To Come SettLE HERE with ALL HIS FAMILY. JUST LIKE ME He, FOUND THE iSLAND ON the interNET.
iNCLUDiNG 3 Kids
MORiMoTo SAN (Fisherman)
KaTaoKa SAN (ELementary schooL PRinciPaL)
SLept FOR NeaRLY ALL the MeeTING.
TAKaKo USUi she works FOR A NON-PRofit organization. She Lives iN OKaYAMA
(NPO)
Lives iN KuRaSHiKi.
HE SPEAKS A TINY BIT OF FRENCH, FROM WHEN HE BRIEFLY WENT TO the ART SCHOOL BEAUX-ARTS dE PARIS IN THE 60s.
"Là où iLya Beaucoup CHATS, iLy a Beaucoup poissons"
iN FRENch.
This is the FiRST time I draw them aLL so None of the ResembLances are GReat (SORRY, KaTaoka saN). BuT I have at Least A Few FiRst Names and theiR CoRResponding Jobs.
BoTH of Them OCCasionaLLY come To tHE iSLand To Make THiNGS HaPPen (And To EaT Free OCTopus).
OKaMoTo SAN ALso works FoR A NON-Profit. He Paints Too.

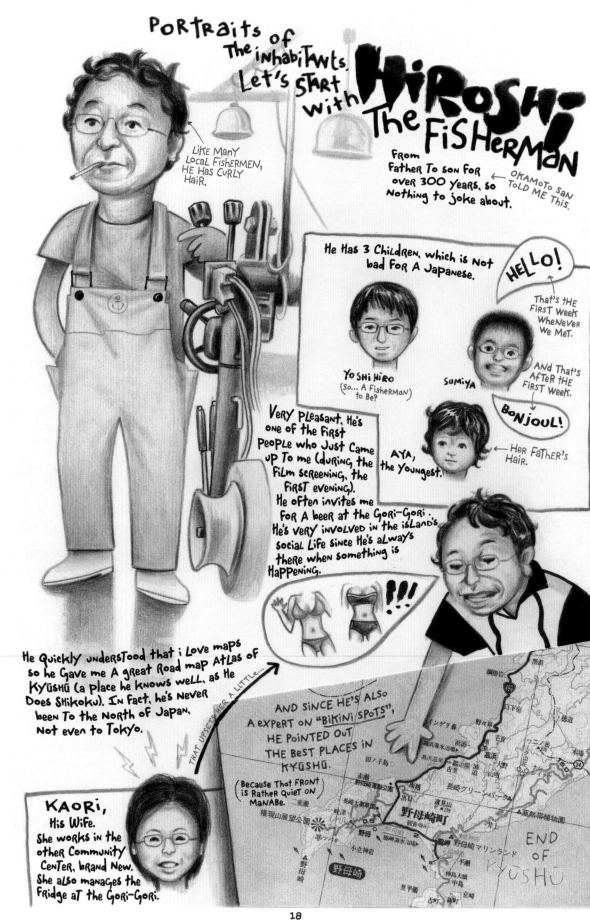

PORTRAITS of The inhabitants. Let's start with **HIROSHI, The FISHERMAN**

OKAMOTO SAN TOLD ME THIS.

FROM Father To son FOR over 300 years, so Nothing to joke about.

LIKE MANY LoCAL FISHERMEN, HE HAS CURLY HAIR.

He Has 3 ChildReN, which is not bad FOR A Japanese.

HELLO!

That's tHE FIRST Week WheNeVeR We MeT.

YOSHI HIRO (so... A FisheRMAN to Be?)

SUMIYA

AND That's AFTeR tHE FIRST Week.

BONJOUL!

AYA, the youngest.

Her FaThER's Hair.

VeRY PLeasant, He's one of the FIRST PeoPLe who Just Came up To me (duRING the FiLm screeNING, the FIRST eveNING). He often invites me FOR A beer at the GORI-GORI. He's veRY invoLved in the isLand's social Life siNce He's aLways there when something is HappeNING.

!!!

He Quickly undeRsTood that i Love maps so he Gave me A gReat Road map Atlas of KYūSHū (a place he kNows weLL, as He Does Shikoku). IN fact, he's NeveR been To the NoRth of Japan. Not even to Tokyo.

THAT UPSET HER A LITTLE...

AND SiNCE HE'S ALSO A eXPeRT ON "BiKiNi SPoTS", HE PoiNTeD OUT THE BEST PLACES IN KYūSHū. (Because That FRONT is Rather Quiet ON MaNABe.

KAORI, His Wife. She woRks in the other Community CeNTeR, bRand New. She also maNages the FRidge at the GORI-GORI.

END OF KYūSHū

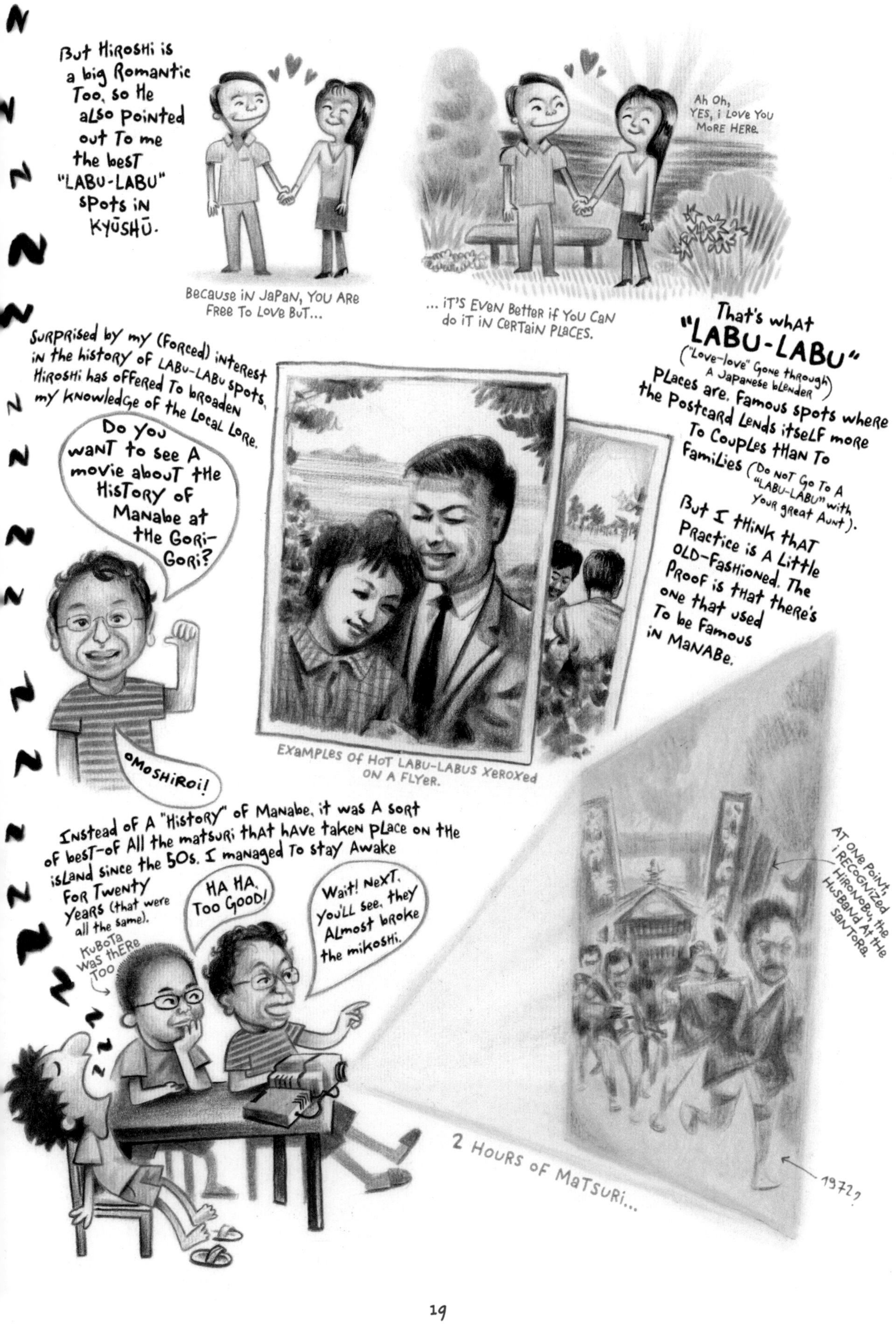

But Hiroshi is a big Romantic Too, so He also pointed out To me the best "LABU-LABU" spots in KYŪSHŪ.
Because in Japan, You Are Free To Love But...
Ah Oh, YES, i Love You More HERE.
... iT'S Even Better if You Can do iT in Certain Places.
That's what "LABU-LABU" ("Love-love" Gone through A Japanese blender) Places are. Famous spots where the Postcard Lends itself more To Couples than To Families (Do not Go To A "LABU-LABU" with Your great Aunt).
But I think that Practice is A Little OLD-Fashioned. The Proof is that there's one that used To be Famous in Manabe.
Surprised by my (Forced) interest in the history of LABU-LABU spots, Hiroshi has offered To broaden my knowledge of the Local Lore.
Do You want To see A movie about the History of Manabe at the Gori-Gori?
OMOSHIROi!
EXAMPLES OF HOT LABU-LABUS XEROXED ON A FLYER.
Instead of A "History" of Manabe, it was A sort of best-of All the matsuri that have taken place on the island since the 50s. I managed To stay Awake For Twenty Years (that were all the same).
HA HA. Too Good!
Wait! Next. You'll see, they Almost broke the mikoshi.
KuBoTa was thERe Too
AT ONE Point, i RECOGNiZED HiRONOBU, the HuSBaND AT the SaNTORa.
2 HOURS OF MaTSURi...
1972?

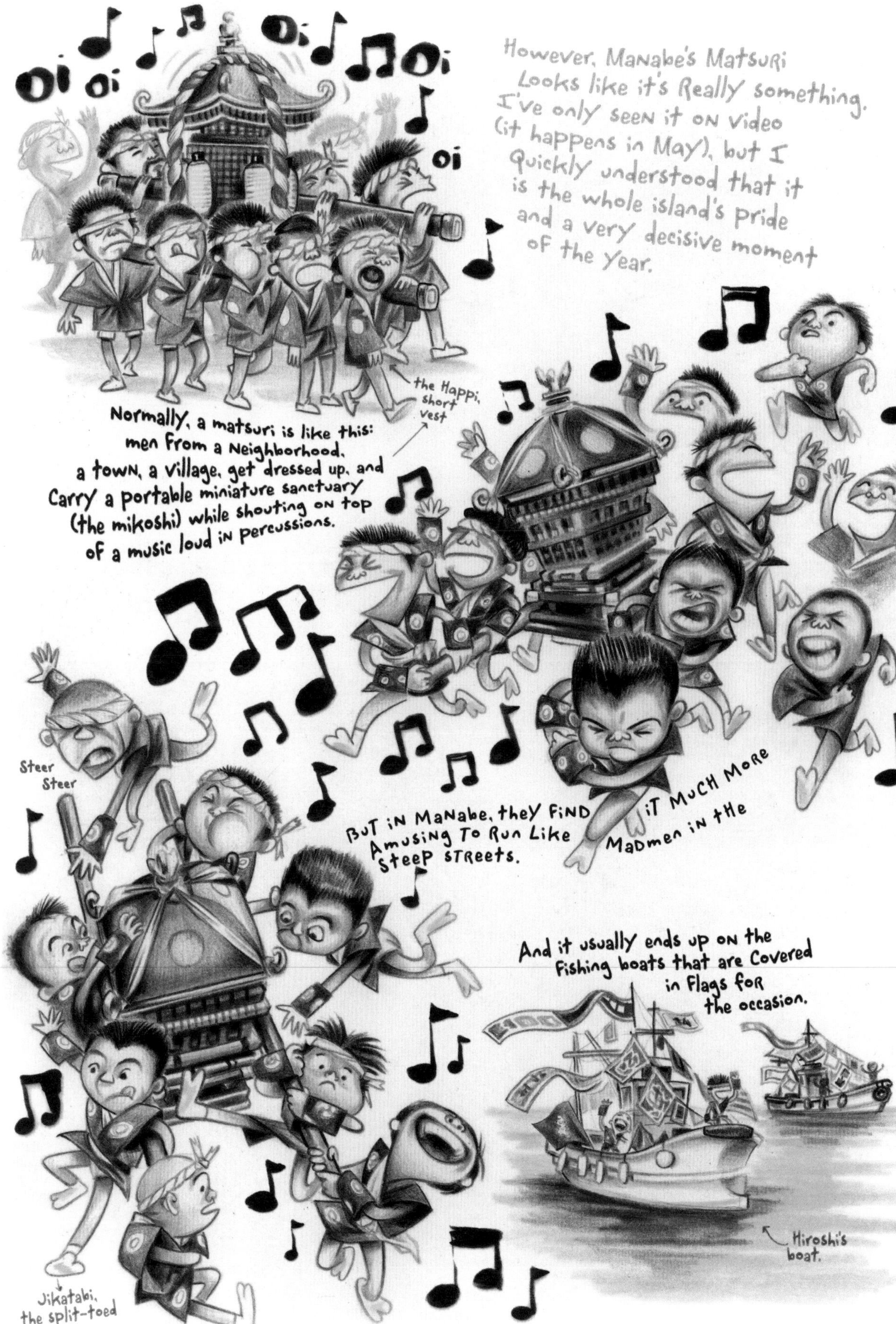
Oi Oi Oi Oi Oi
However, Manabe's Matsuri looks like it's really something. I've only seen it on video (it happens in May), but I quickly understood that it is the whole island's pride and a very decisive moment of the year.
Normally, a matsuri is like this: men from a neighborhood, a town, a village, get dressed up, and carry a portable miniature sanctuary (the mikoshi) while shouting on top of a music loud in percussions.
the Happi, short vest
Steer Steer
But in Manabe, they find it much more amusing to run like madmen in the steep streets.
And it usually ends up on the fishing boats that are covered in flags for the occasion.
Hiroshi's boat.
Jikatabi, the split-toed shoes.

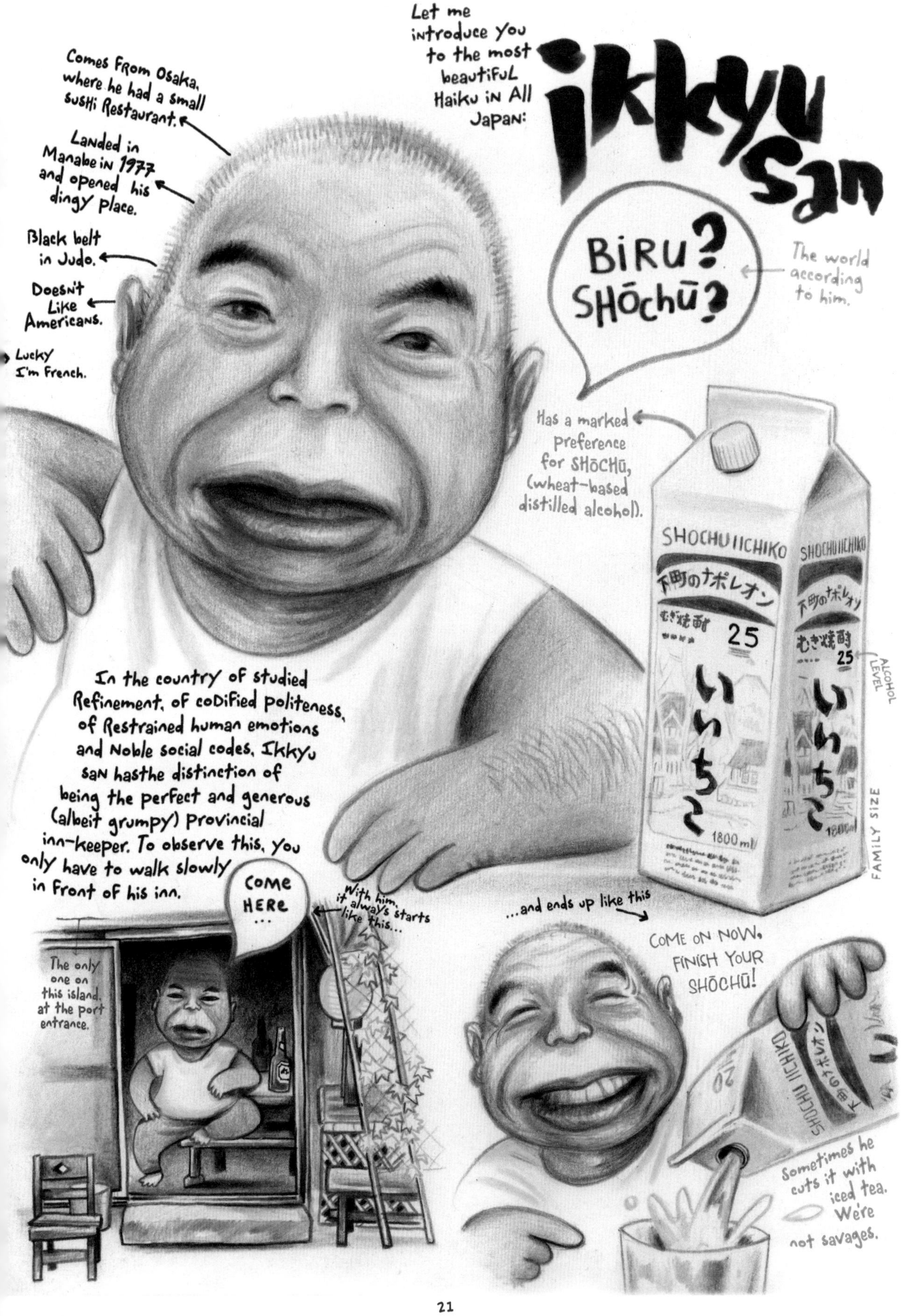
Let me introduce you to the most beautiful Haiku in All Japan:
Ikkyu San
Comes From Osaka, where he had a small sushi Restaurant.
Landed in Manabe in 1977 and opened his dingy place.
Black belt in Judo.
Doesn't Like Americans.
Lucky I'm French.
BIRU? SHŌCHŪ?
The world according to him.
Has a marked preference for SHŌCHŪ, (wheat-based distilled alcohol).
SHOCHU IICHIKO
下町のナポレオン
むぎ焼酎
25
いいちこ
1800ml
ALCOHOL LEVEL
FAMILY SIZE
In the country of studied Refinement, of codified politeness, of Restrained human emotions and Noble social codes, Ikkyu san has the distinction of being the perfect and generous (albeit grumpy) Provincial inn-keeper. To observe this, you only have to walk slowly in Front of his inn.
COME HERE...
With him, it always starts like this...
...and ends up like this
The only one on this island, at the port entrance.
COME ON NOW. FINISH YOUR SHŌCHŪ!
SHOCHU IICHIKO
Sometimes he cuts it with iced tea. We're not savages.

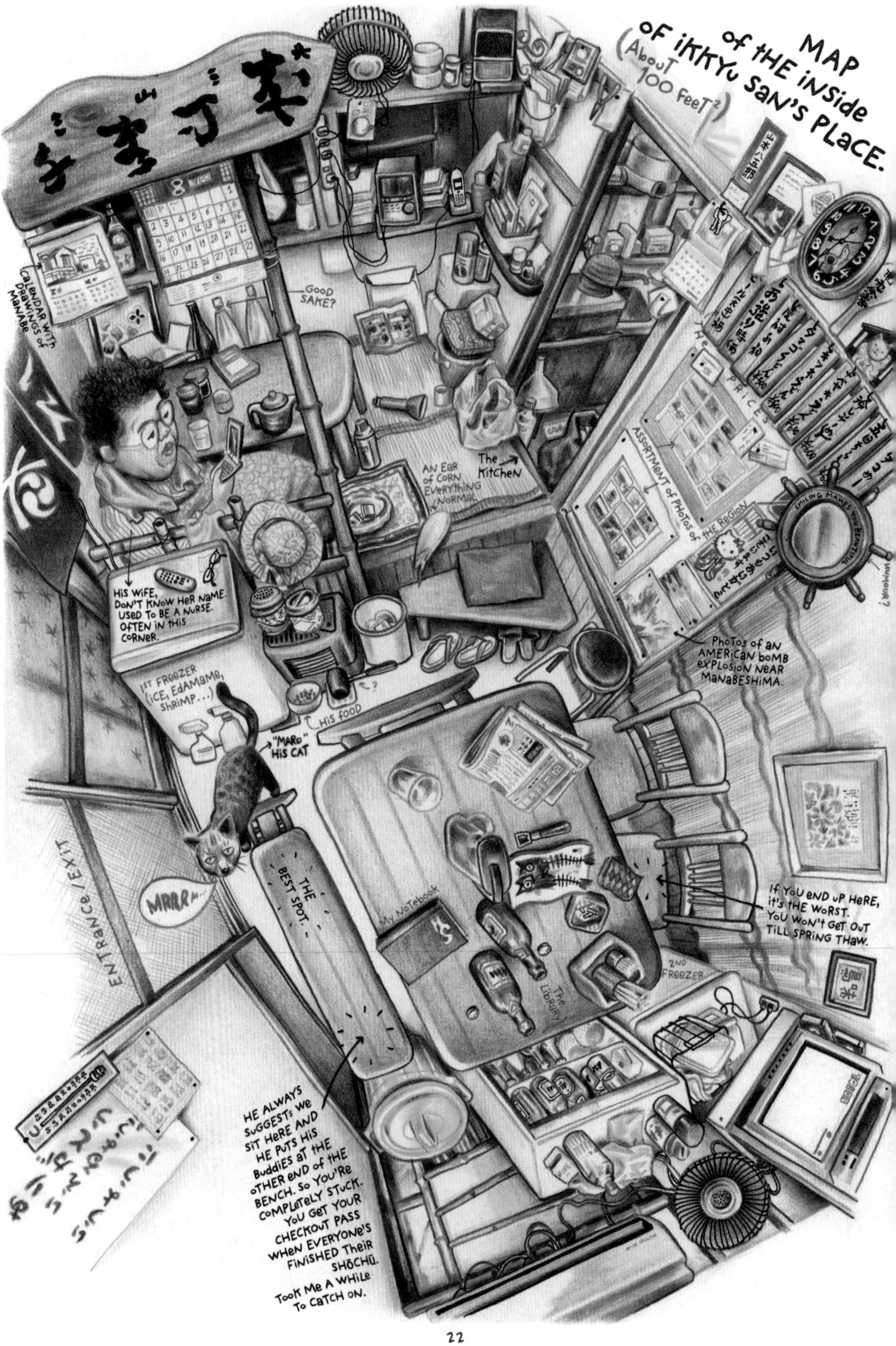

MAP of THE iNside of iKKYu SaN's PLaCE.
(AbouT 100 FeeT²)
CaLeNDaR WiTh DRaWiNGS of MaNaBe
GOOD SAKE?
AN EaR of CORN EVERYThiNG NORMAL
The KiTcheN
ASSORTMENT of PHOTOS of THE REGiON
THE PRICES
SMILING MAKES YOU BEAUTIFUL
humour?
HiS WiFE, DON'T KNOW HER NAME. USED TO BE A NURSE. OFTEN iN THiS CORNER.
1ST FREEZER (iCE, EDaMaMe, SHRiMP...)
His food
"MaRo" HiS CaT
PHOTOS of aN AMERiCaN boMB exPLOSioN NeaR MaNaBESHiMa.
MRRRM...
ENTRaNce/EXiT
THE BEST SPOT.
My NoTebook
The LibRaRy
2ND FREEZER
iF YOU END uP HeRE, iT's THE WoRST. YOU WON'T GeT OUT TiLL SPRiNG ThaW.
HE ALWAYS SuGGESTs WE SiT HeRE AND HE PuTS HiS Buddies aT THE oTHER eND of THE BENCH. So YOU'Re COMPLETeLY STuCK. YOU GET YOUR CHECKOUT PASS WHEN EVERYONe's FiNiSHED TheiR SHŌCHŪ. TooK Me A WHiLe To CaTCH ON.

The REGULAR MeMBeRs

DAILY MEMBER

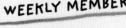

Day-GLo Cap Guy

He doesn't talk much, but He's ALways there. For him, CONversation is Like teLevision or A movie. He doesn't say A word and Nods From time To time (Counting Points?).

HA HA

He often Gets the Place in the back. It Looks as though he Likes being stuck there.

He aLways Has A sLight smile.

I think He is - or was - A FISHERMAN.

He has A small CaR, aLways PaRked in FRont of the joint.

WEEKLY MEMBER

Skinny Guy

He's often on the bench outside.

He's A kind of Gate-keeper.

Sometimes He Comes in to Check that everyone's drinking their shōchū.

Yup. veRy skinny.

He's Nice but i Don't ReaLLy Like him LeaFing through my dRawings. The FiRst time i saw Him, He FeLL off his stool and Hung oN To my Notebook.

MONTHLY MEMBER

GReasy-HaiRed Guy

As He's A FisheRman, He's theRe OccasionaLLy (meaning seveRal Times A week).

He has an "extended" FamiLy and im still Not sure who's the bRother-in-Law's Cousin's son's bRother.

As an OCCasional bonus, we get the buRping Grandma.

BuRRp

THE VERY GOOD SAUCE, MADE UP OF 12 MYSTERIOUS INGREDIENTS, OF WHICH I ONLY RECOGNIZE LEMON...

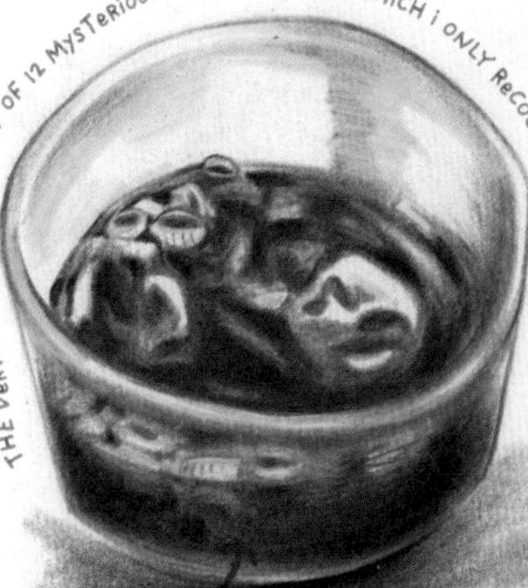

iKKYU SAN Does His CHemistry.

and there you are!

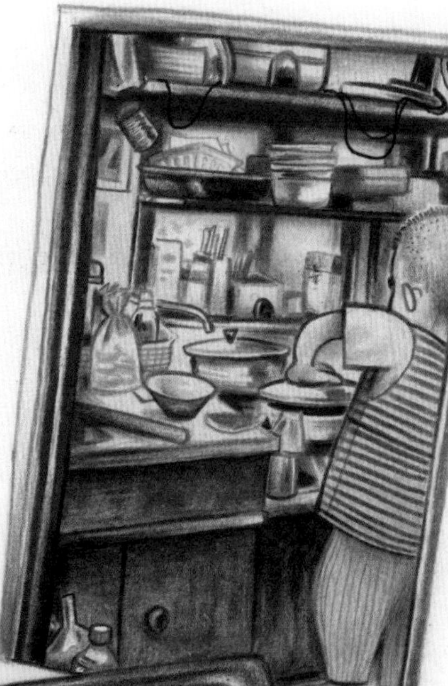

SECRET NOODLE LABORATORY.

DiP...

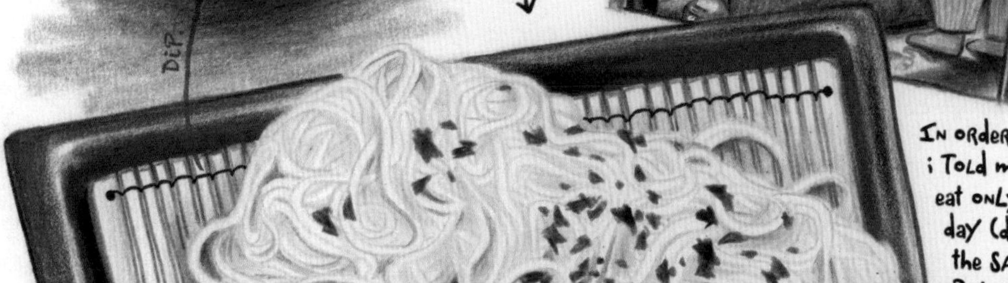

SHAVINGS OF DRIED NORI
MUCH THINNER THAN UDON

It's Not overdoing it to say that it's More Refreshing than A beer.

In order To save money, i Told myself i would eat only one meal A day (dinner At the SANTORA). But Ikkyu-san invites me For Lunch several Times and won't Let me pay (when None of his Fishermen Friends are around). The only way i've Found To pay without Him getting upset is To Hide Coins on the table while He's Cooking.

SŌMEN, a REAL SUMMER dish.

(Because SHŌCHŪ Can't provide ALL YOUR NUTRIENTS)

Like udon, these Noodles Are wheat-FLOUR based. And like udon, You can eat them Cold.

with ice Cubes Right on Top.

OR dipped in iced sauce.

FROM NOW ON, I CAN BE CONSIDERED To HAVE MY MEMBERSHIP CARD.

WEEKLY ONLY.

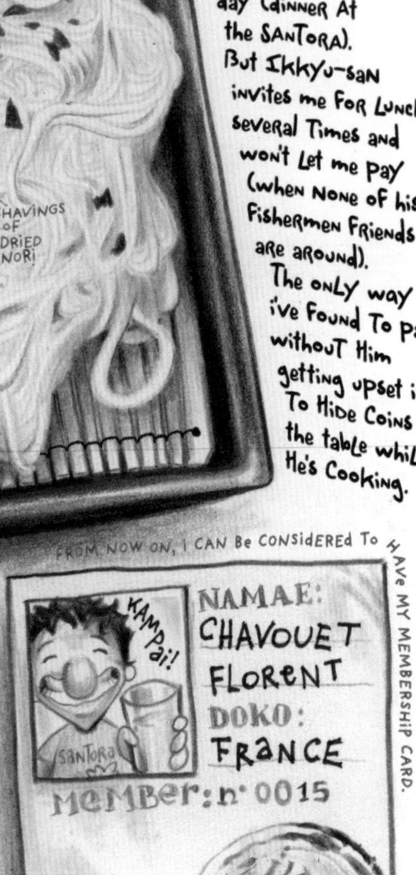

KAMPAi!
SANTORA
NAMAE: CHAVOUET FLORENT
DOKO: FRANCE
MEMBER: n° 0015

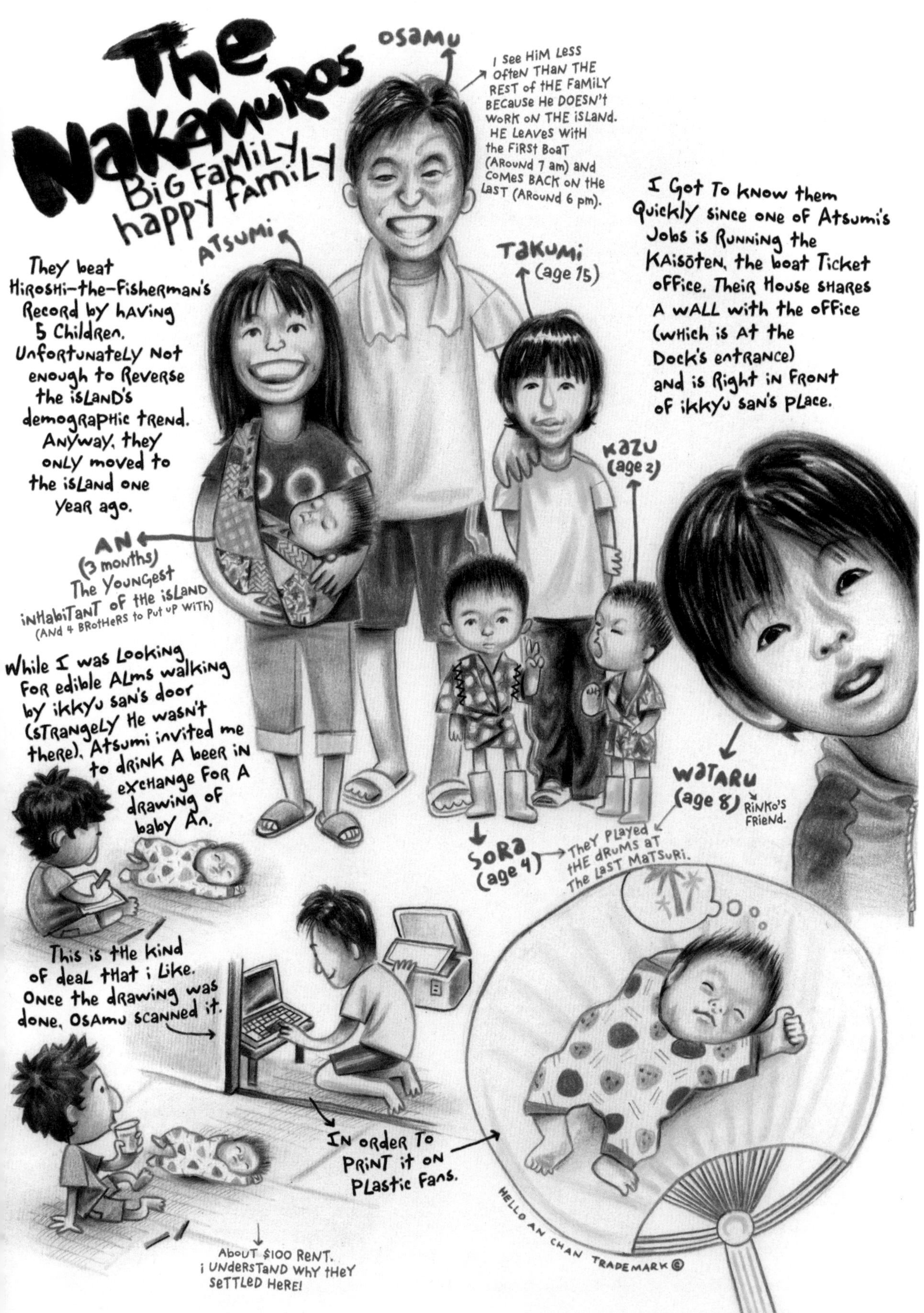

The Nakamuros
Big Family happy family
OSAMU
I see him less often than the rest of the family because he doesn't work on the island. He leaves with the first boat (around 7 am) and comes back on the last (around 6 pm).
ATSUMI
TAKUMI (age 15)
I got to know them quickly since one of Atsumi's jobs is running the Kaisōten, the boat ticket office. Their house shares a wall with the office (which is at the dock's entrance) and is right in front of Ikkyu San's place.
They beat Hiroshi-the-Fisherman's record by having 5 children. Unfortunately not enough to reverse the island's demographic trend. Anyway, they only moved to the island one year ago.
KAZU (age 2)
AN (3 months)
The youngest inhabitant of the island
(and 4 brothers to put up with)
While I was looking for edible alms walking by Ikkyu San's door (strangely he wasn't there), Atsumi invited me to drink a beer in exchange for a drawing of baby An.
WATARU (age 8)
Rinko's friend.
SORA (age 4)
They played the drums at the last Matsuri.
This is the kind of deal that I like. Once the drawing was done, Osamu scanned it.
In order to print it on plastic fans.
HELLO AN CHAN TRADEMARK ©
About $100 rent. I understand why they settled here!

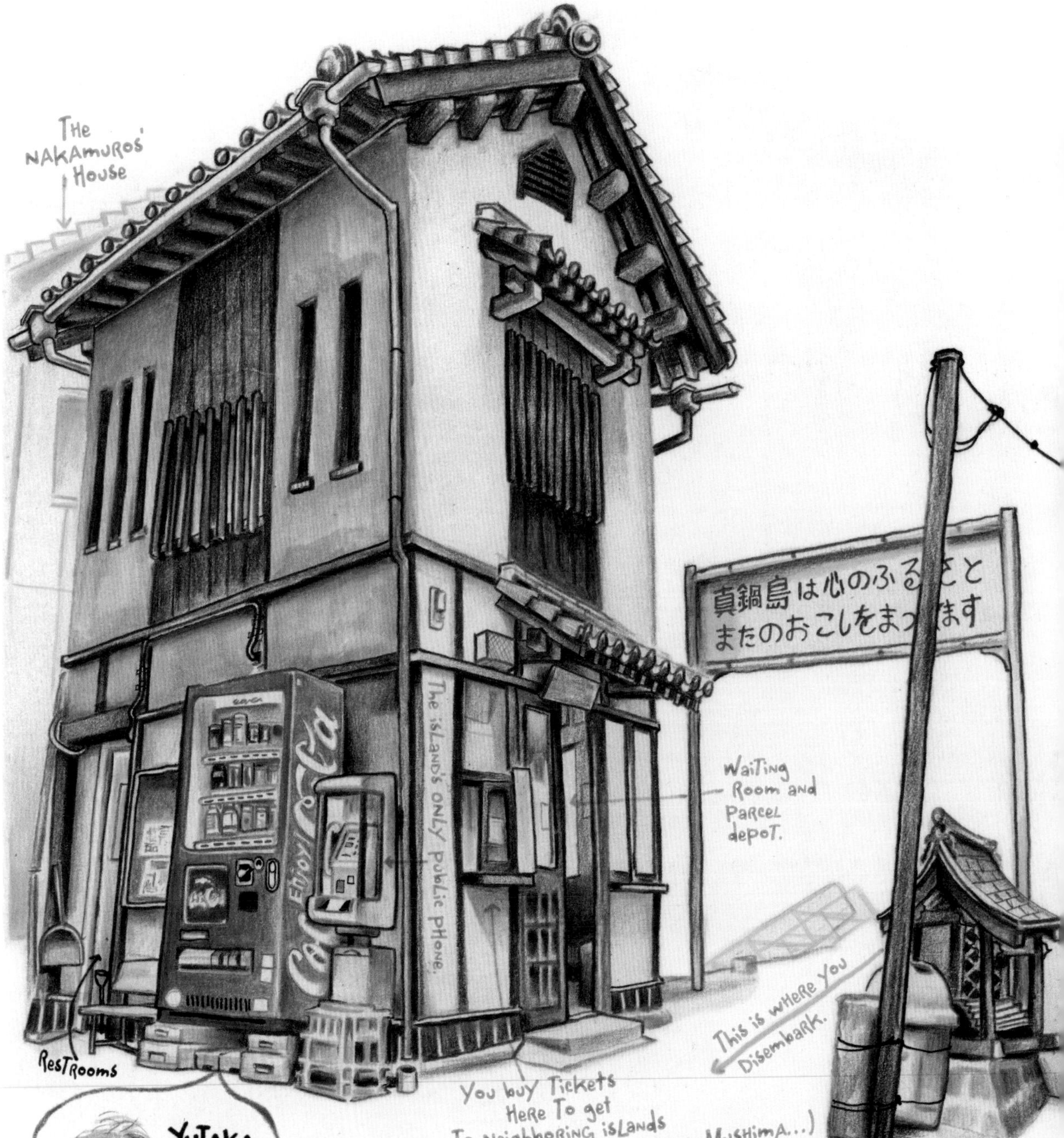

The NAKAMUROS' House
真鍋島は心のふる さと
またのおこしをまっ ます
The isLand's ONLY public pHone.
WaiTing Room and ParceL depoT.
This is where you Disembark.
ResTrooms
You buy Tickets Here To get To Neighboring isLands (ShiRaishishima, KiTagishima, Mushima...) or the "Continent" (Honshu).

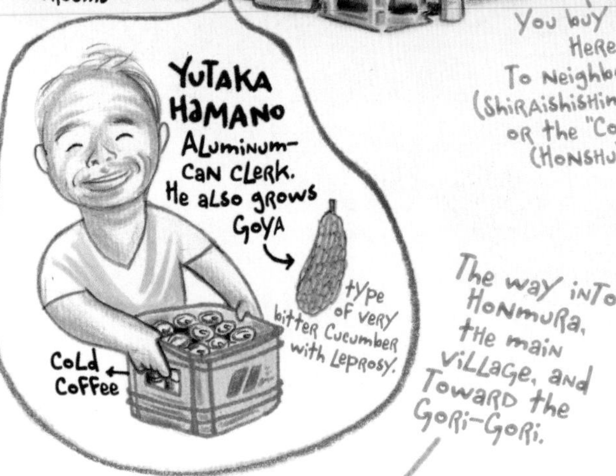

YUTAKA HAMANO
ALuminum-can cLerk.
He also grows Goya
type of very bitter Cucumber with Leprosy.
CoLd Coffee
The way inTo Honmura, the main viLLage, and Toward the Gori-Gori.

The Famous KaiSōten (回送店) (or Kaisouten)

This is one of The first drawings i did in public, and because I'd chosen The busiest place on The isLand, I became known To A lot of people in just one morning.

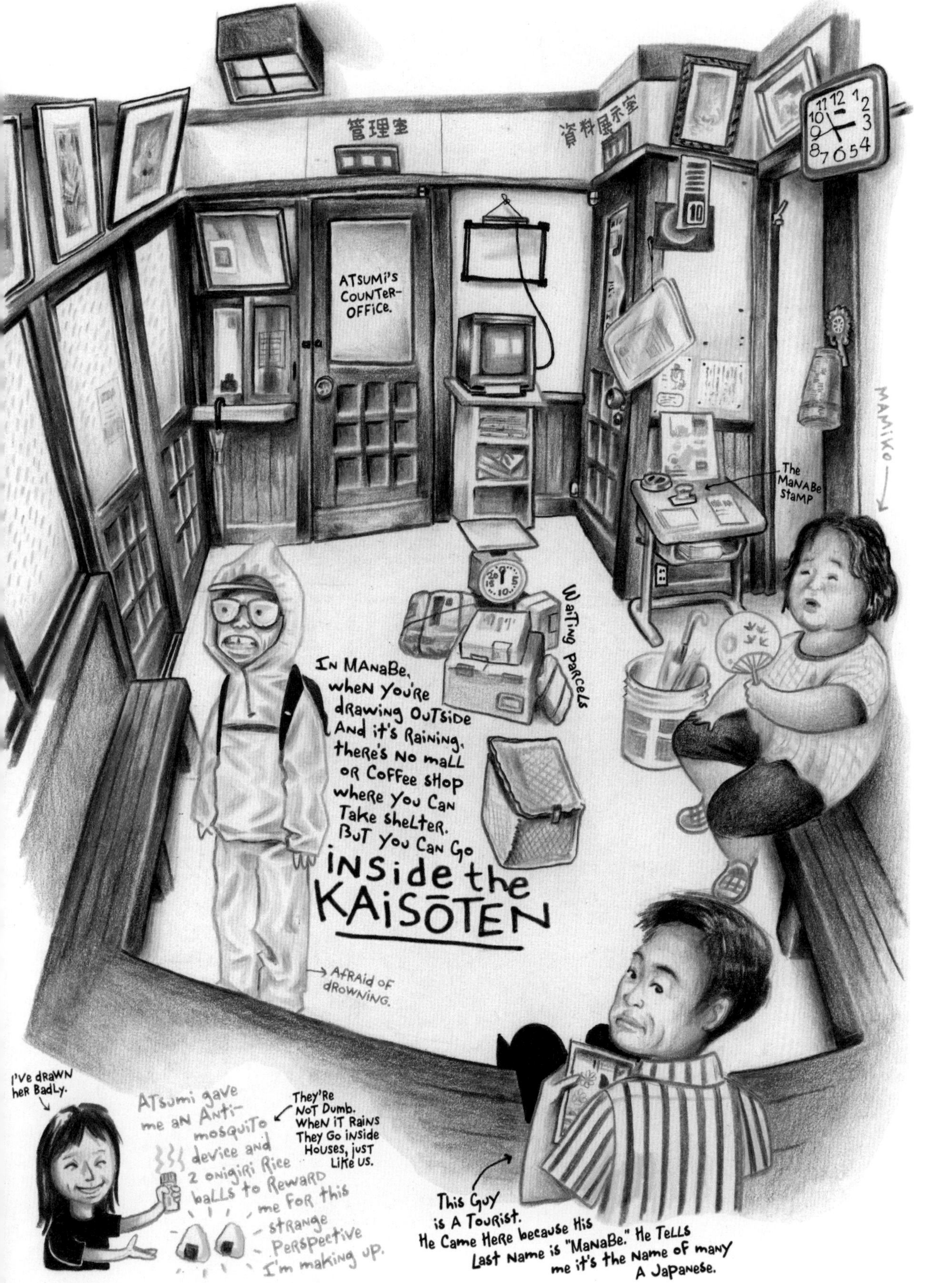

管理室
資料展示室
ATSUMi'S COUNTER-OFFICE.
MAMiKO
The MaNaBe STaMP
WaiTiNG ParceLs
IN MANaBe, when you're drawing OUTSIDE And it's Raining, there's No maLL OR Coffee sHop where you CaN Take sheLTeR. BuT you CaN Go
inside the KAISŌTEN
Afraid of dROWNiNG.
I've dRAWN heR BadLy.
ATsumi gave me aN Anti-mosquiTo device and 2 onigiRi Rice balls to Reward me FOR this strange Perspective I'm making up.
They're NOT Dumb. WheN iT RaiNs They Go iNside Houses, just Like us.
This Guy is A ToURist. He Came Here because His Last Name is "MaNaBe." He TeLLs me it's the Name of many A JaPaNese.

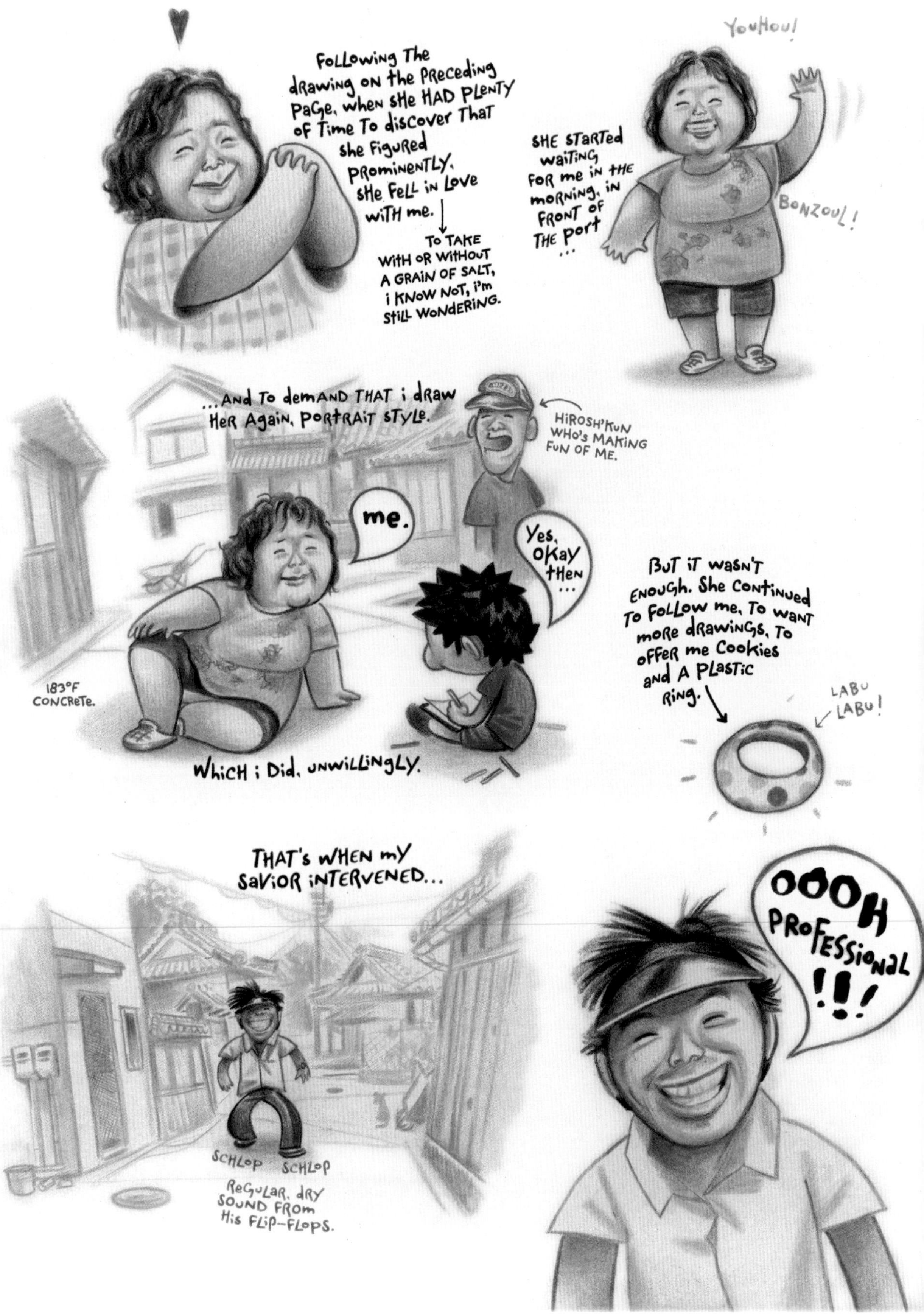
Following The drawing on the Preceding Page, when sHe HAD PLENTY of Time To discover That she figured prominently, sHe FeLL in Love with me.
To TAKE WITH OR WITHOUT A GRAIN OF SALT, i KNOW NOT, i'm STILL WONDERING.
YouHou!
SHE STARTED waiting for me in the morning, in front of the port ...
BONZOUL!
...AND To demAND THAT i draw Her Again, PORTRAIT STYLE.
HIROSH'KUN WHO'S MAKING FUN OF ME.
me.
Yes, okay then ...
183°F CONCRETE.
Which i Did, unwillingly.
BUT IT WASN'T ENOUGH. She continued To follow me, to want more drawings, to offer me Cookies and A PLASTIC RING.
LABU LABU!
THAT'S WHEN my SAVIOR INTERVENED...
SCHLOP SCHLOP
ReGuLAR, dry SOUND FROM His FLIP-FLOPS.
OOOH PROFESSIONAL !!!

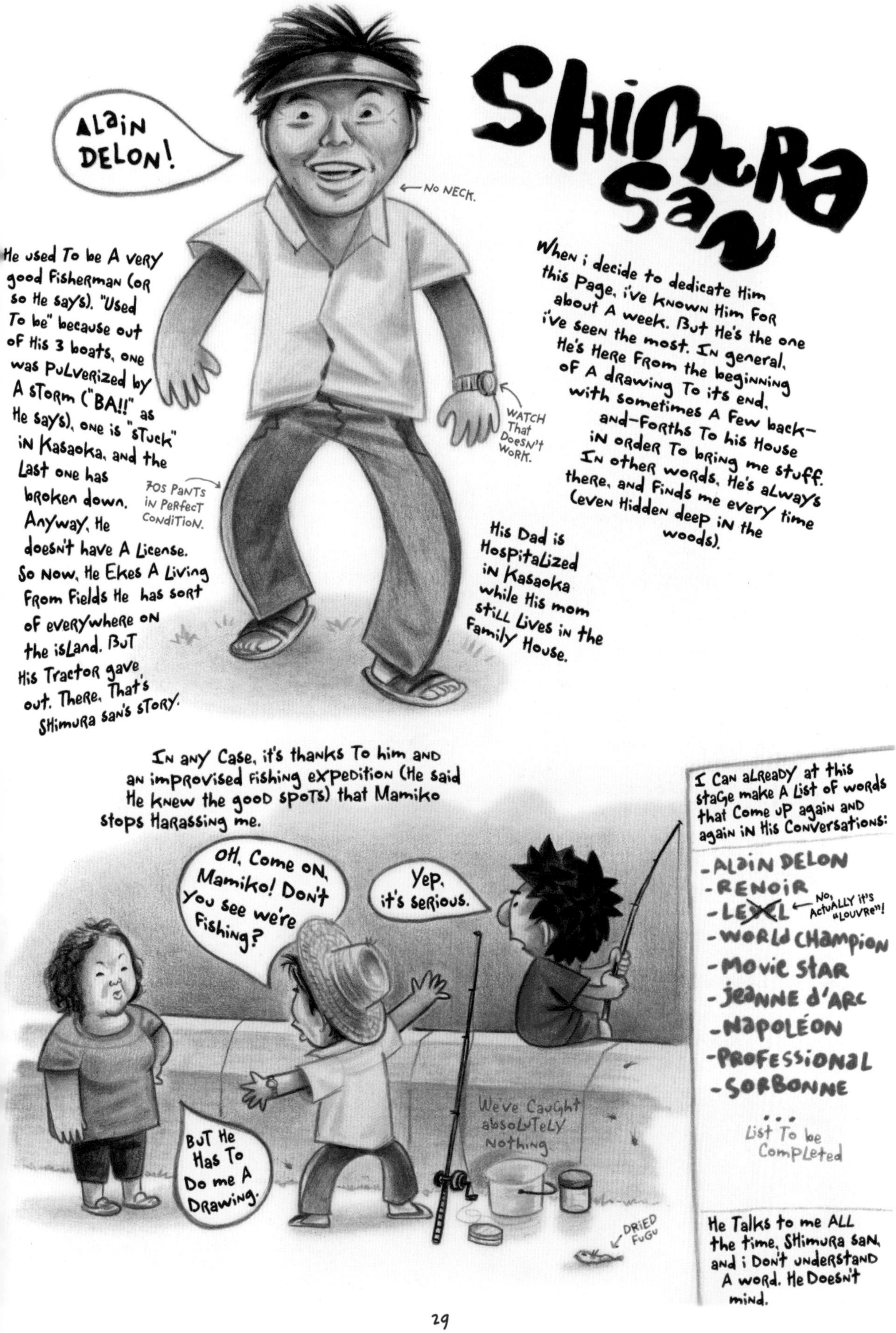
Shimura san
ALAIN DELON!
NO NECK.
He used To be A very good Fisherman (or so He says). "Used To be" because out of His 3 boats, one was Pulverized by A storm ("BA!!" as He says), one is "stuck" in Kasaoka, and the Last one has broken down. Anyway, He doesn't have A License. So now, He Ekes A Living From Fields He has sort of everywhere on the island. But His Tractor gave out. There. That's Shimura san's story.
70s PANTS IN PERFECT CONDITION.
WATCH That Doesn't WORK.
When i decide to dedicate Him this Page, i've known Him For about A week. But He's the one i've seen the most. In general, He's Here From the beginning of A drawing To its end, with sometimes A Few back-and-forths To his House in order To bring me stuff. In other words, He's always there, and Finds me every time (even Hidden deep in the woods).
His Dad is Hospitalized in Kasaoka while His mom still Lives in the Family House.
In any Case, it's thanks To him and an improvised fishing expedition (He said He knew the good spots) that Mamiko stops Harassing me.
I Can already at this stage make A List of words that Come up again and again in His Conversations:
-ALAIN DELON
-RENOIR
-LEXL
No, Actually it's "LOUVRE"!
-WORLD CHAMPION
-MOVIE STAR
-JEANNE D'ARC
-NAPOLÉON
-PROFESSIONAL
-SORBONNE
...
List To be Completed
OH, Come ON, Mamiko! Don't you see we're Fishing?
Yep, it's serious.
BUT He Has To Do me A Drawing.
We've Caught absolutely Nothing
DRIED FUGU
He Talks to me ALL the time, Shimura san, and i Don't understand A word. He Doesn't mind.

MORNING SCHEDULE

1A It's 9 am, the "boss", South Port's cat gang's chief, finds it a good reason to sleep.

1B The ship comes in and blows twice.

1C This is the signal for Atsumi who darts out of her house.

2A She barely manages the first turn, but takes it too sharply. The ship blew 12 seconds ago already.

2B Hirosh'kun and "Mister Gloomy*" are already hard at work, on the pontoon, ready to receive packages and travelers alike.

2C The "cool deckhand" comes to tie up the boat and prepare the merchandise.

2D The last 15 Yards for Atsumi

3A Loading mail for the mainland and unloading Manabe's. "Mister Gloomy" takes charge of the wheel-barrow and Atsumi checks the tickets.

3B Nature calls Ikkyu san and he runs to the public restrooms that he's completely colonized, in front of his house.

4 The little crowd ("Mister Gloomy", Hirosh'kun and Atsumi) bring back all the packages to the Kaisouten (in that order, from heavier to lighter).

5A Hironobu arrives by motor scooter while singing, to see whether there's anything for the Santora.

5B Dominique the Crab finds the day has begun well since he's managed to avoid the scooter.

6A The "cool deckhand" has 15 minutes in front of him before going back to Kasaoka. Plenty enough to empty an iced coffee can and to have a smoke.

6B During the 3 minutes and 41 seconds of this episode, the "boss" has journeyed 15 inches. A good reason for a nap.

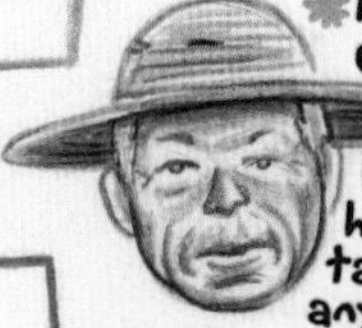

*Mister Gloomy because he never talks to anyone. A pure islander who has the peculiarity of having green eyes.

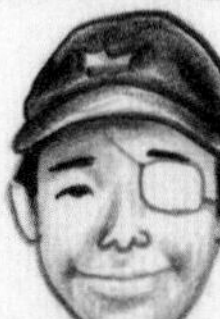
He often waves from his boat.

* This is the mooring for the taxi-boats that take you wherever you want, whenever you want. ⚠ Still, it's ¥10,000 each way.

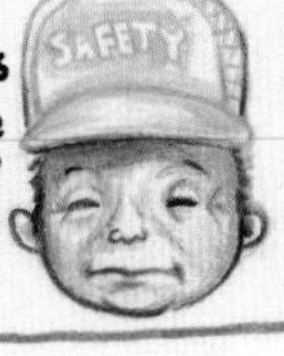
SAFETY

** What? Is he there already?

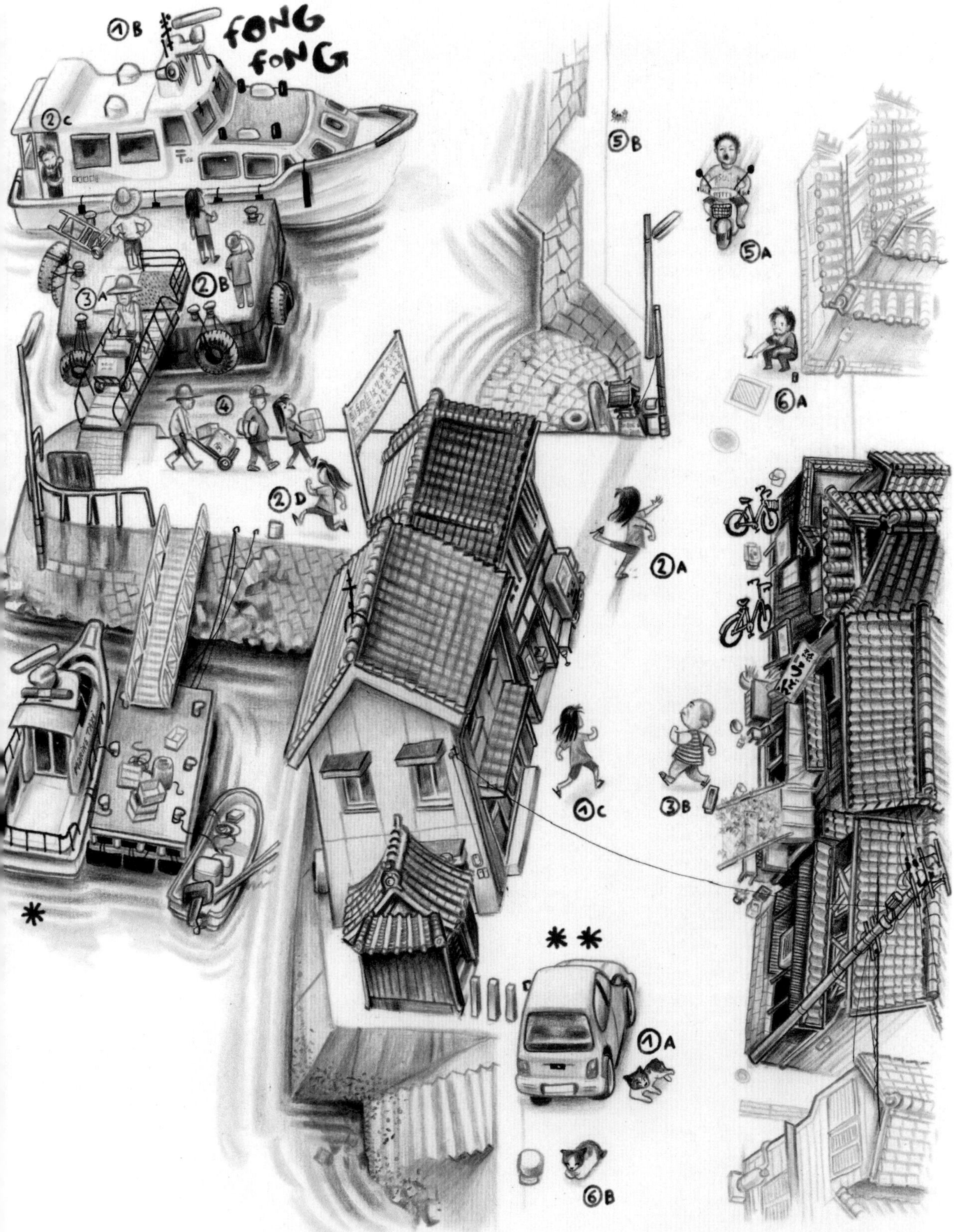
FONG
FONG
1B
2C
2B
3A
4
2D
5B
5A
6A
2A
1C
3B
*
**
1A
6B

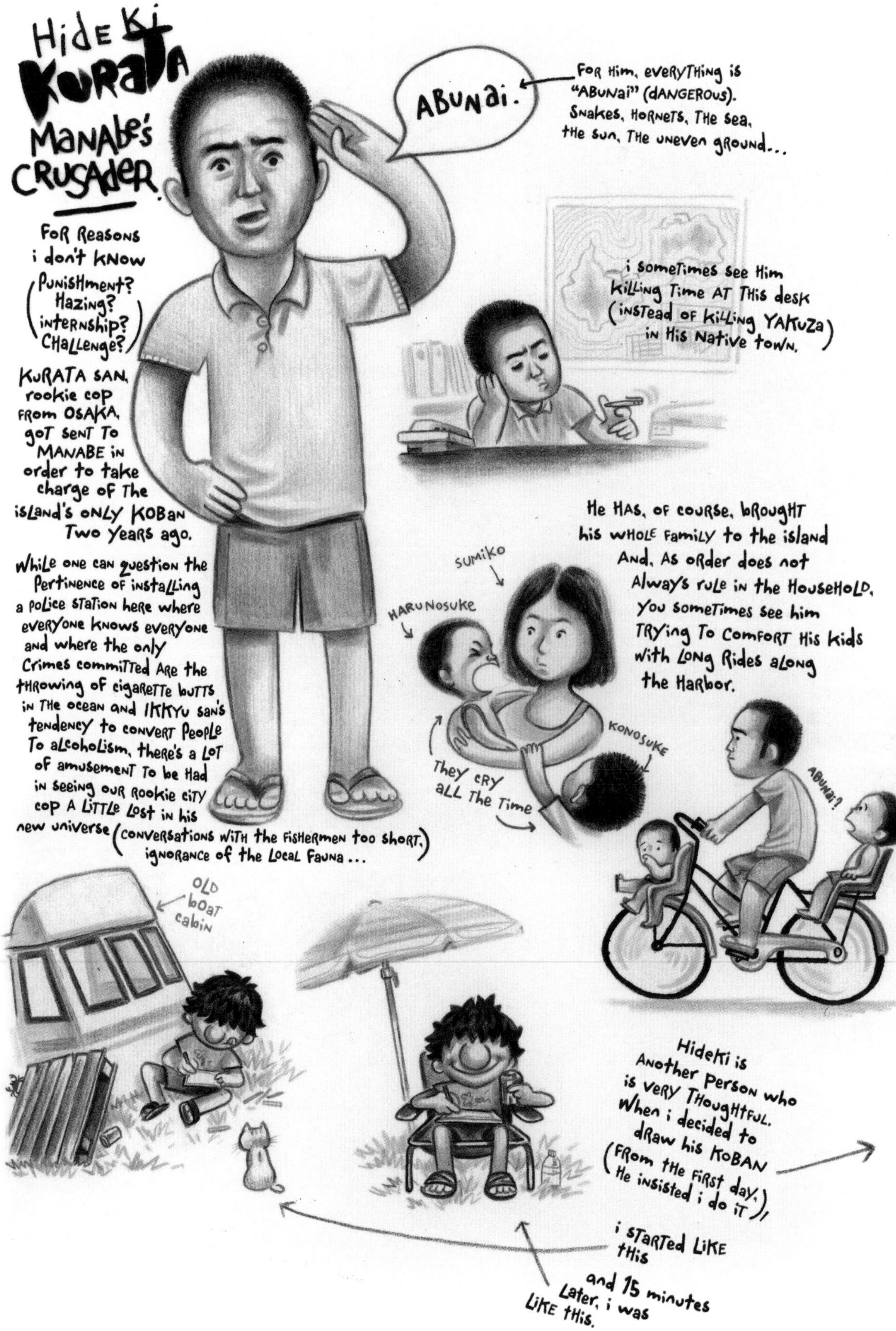
Hideki Kurata
Manabe's Crusader.
ABUNai.
For Him, everything is "ABUNai" (dangerous). Snakes, hornets, The sea, the sun, The uneven ground...
For Reasons i don't know (Punishment? Hazing? internship? Challenge?)
KURATA SAN, rookie cop from OSAKA, got sent to MANABE in order to take charge of The island's only KOBan Two years ago.
While one can question the Pertinence of installing a police station here where everyone knows everyone and where the only Crimes committed Are the throwing of cigarette butts in The ocean and IKKYU san's tendency to convert People To alcoholism, there's a lot of amusement To be Had in seeing our rookie city cop A little lost in his new universe (conversations with the fishermen too short, ignorance of the Local Fauna...
i sometimes see Him killing Time AT This desk (instead of killing YAKUZA) in His Native town.
He HAS, of course, brought his whole family to the island And, As order does not Always rule in the Household, You sometimes see him Trying To comfort His kids with Long Rides along the Harbor.
SUMIKO
HARUNOSUKE
KONOSUKE
They cry all The Time
ABUNai?
OLD boat cabin
Hideki is Another Person who is very Thoughtful. When i decided to draw his KOBAN (From the first day, He insisted i do it),
i started like this
and 15 minutes Later, i was like this.

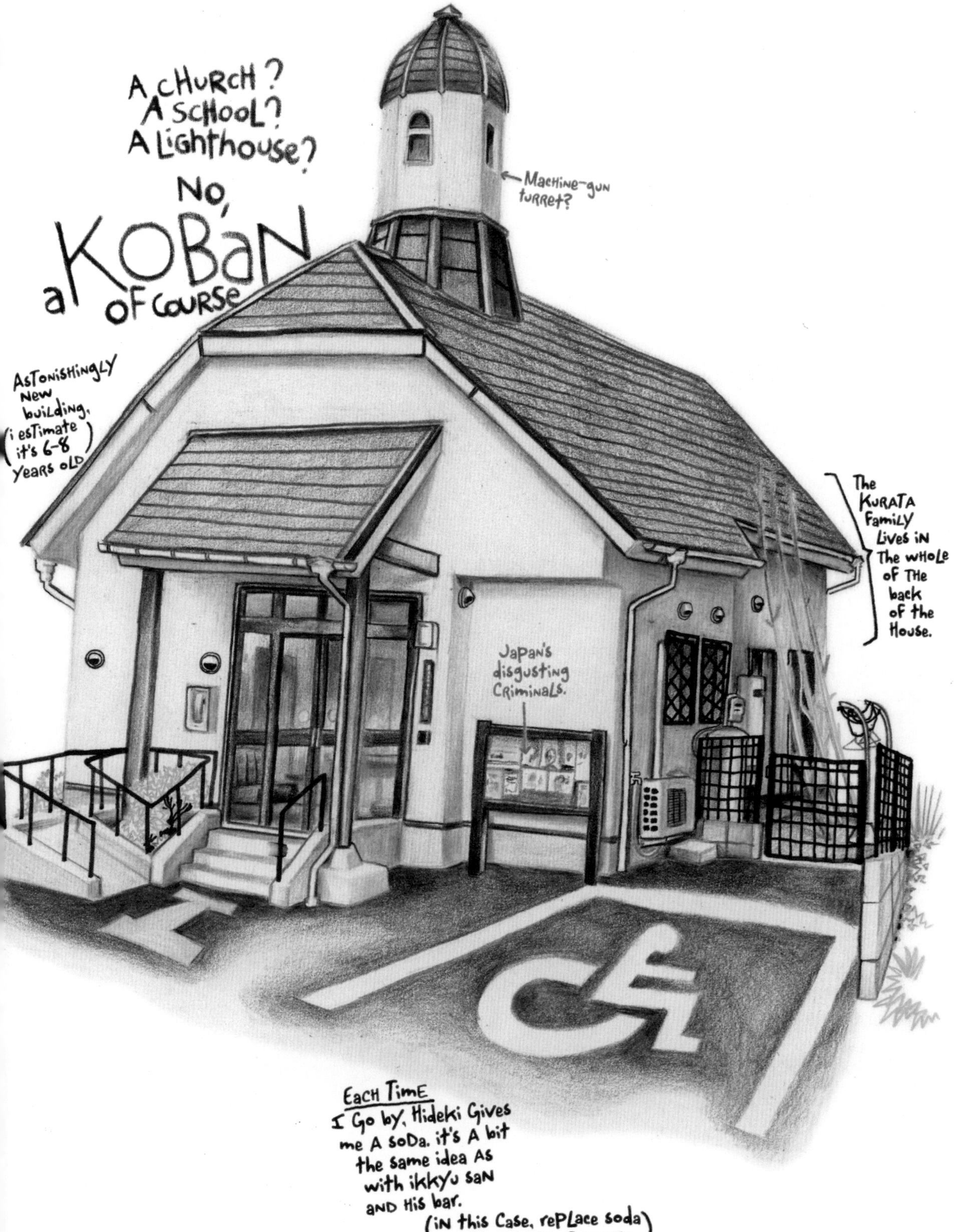

A CHURCH?
A SCHOOL?
A Lighthouse?
NO,
a KOBAN
OF COURSE
← Machine-gun turret?
Astonishingly New building, (i estimate it's 6-8 years old)
The Kurata Family Lives in The whole of The back of the House.
Japan's disgusting Criminals.
Each Time I Go by, Hideki Gives me A soda. it's A bit the same idea As with ikkyu san and his bar.
(in this Case, replace soda with shōchū of course.)

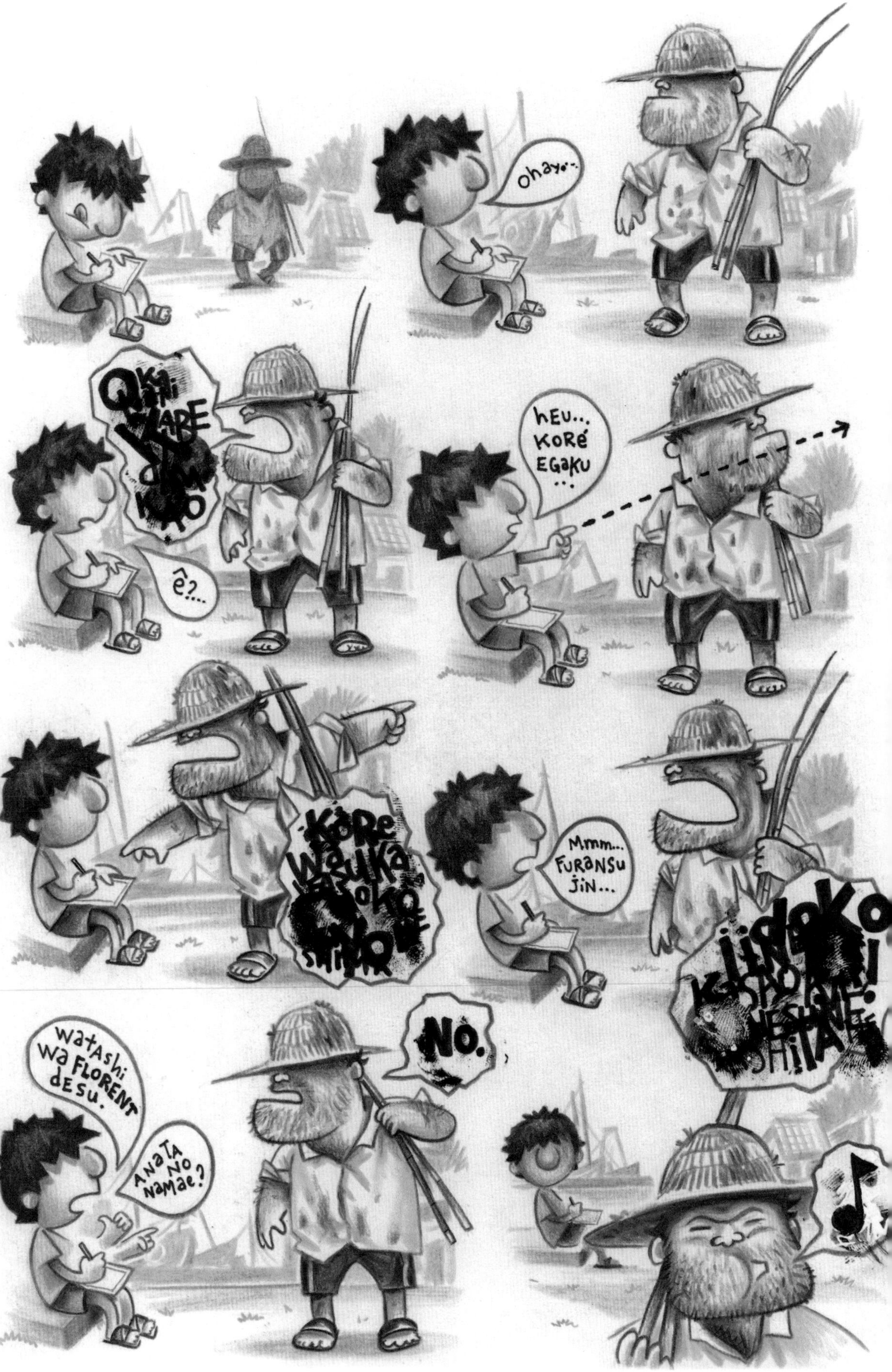
ohayo...
ê?...
heu... koré egaku ...
Mmm... Furansu jin...
watashi wa FLORENT desu.
ANATA NO NAMAE?
NO.

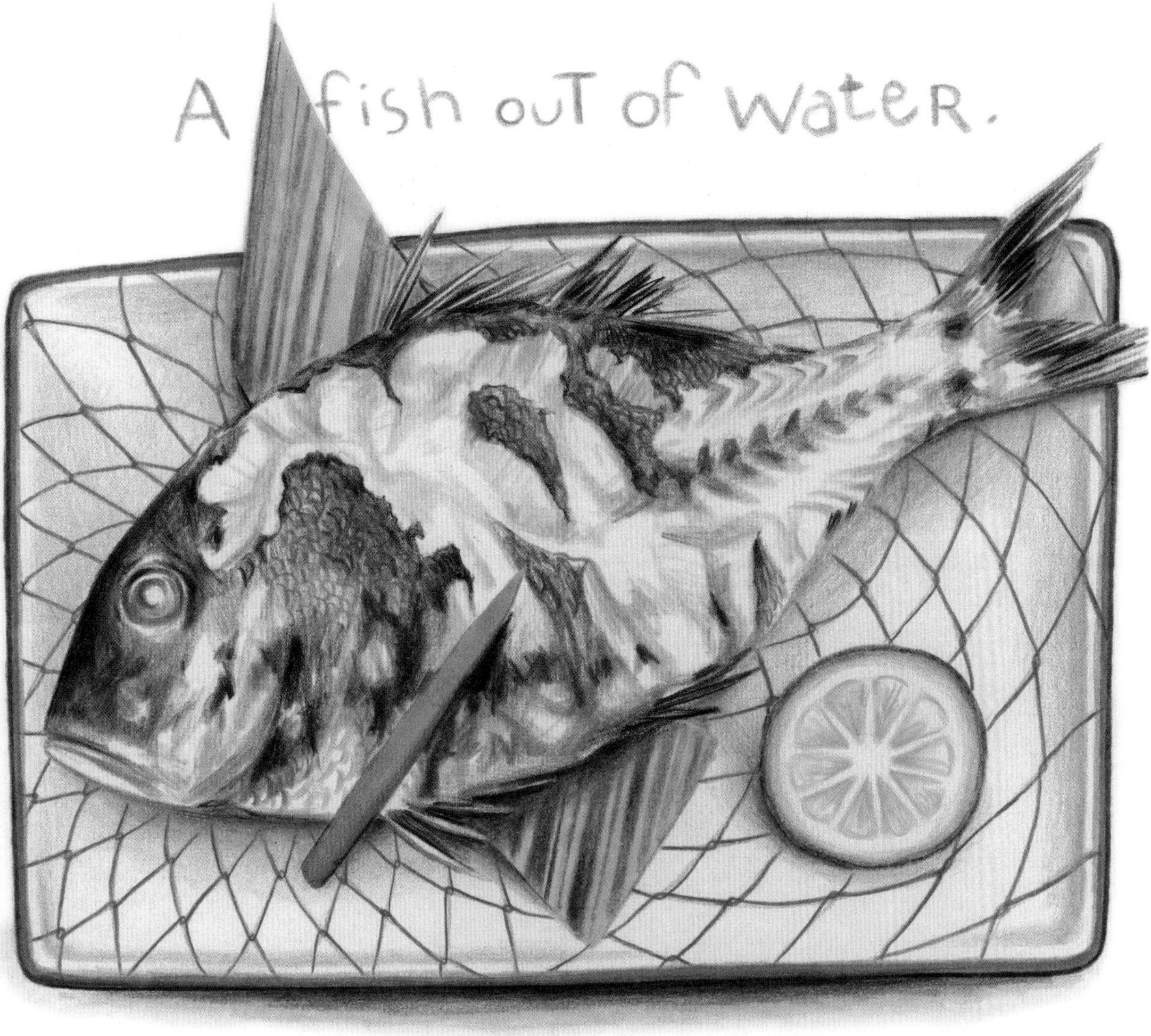
A fish out of water.

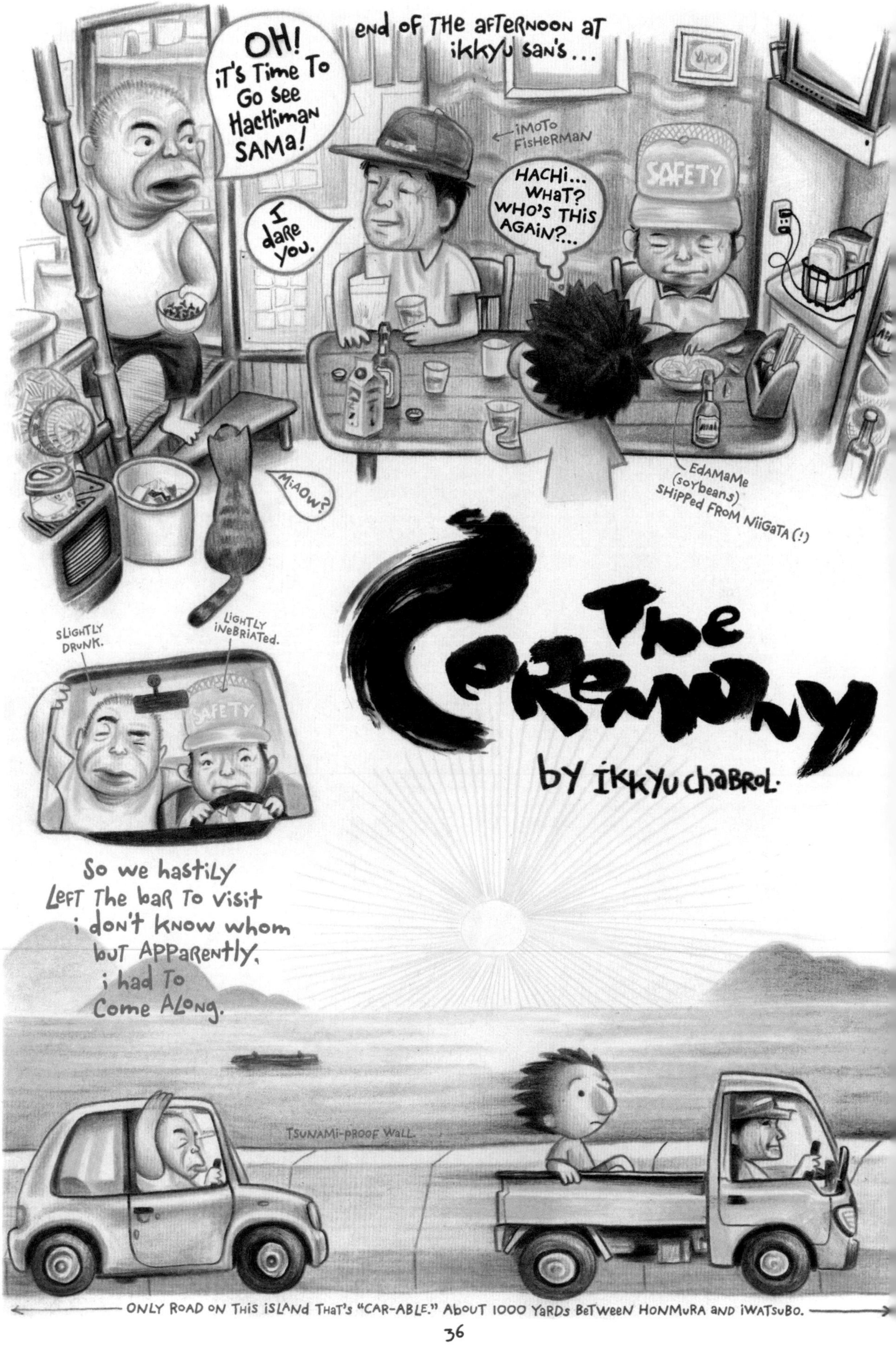
end of THe afTeRNOON aT ikkyu san's...
OH! iT's Time To Go see Hachiman SAMa!
I dare you.
←iMoTo FisHeRMAN
HACHi... WHAT? WHO'S THIS AGAiN?...
SAFETY
MiAOW?
EdAMaMe (soybeans) SHiPPed FROM NiiGaTA (!)
SLiGHTLY DRUNK.
LiGHTLY iNeBRIATed.
SAFETY
So we hastiLy LeFT The bar To visit i don't know whom buT APPaRently, i had To Come ALong.
TSUNAMi-PROOF WALL
ONLY ROAD ON THIS iSLANd THAT's "CAR-ABLE." AbouT 1000 YARDS BeTWeeN HONMuRA AND iWATSuBo.

The Ceremony

by Ikkyu Chabrol.

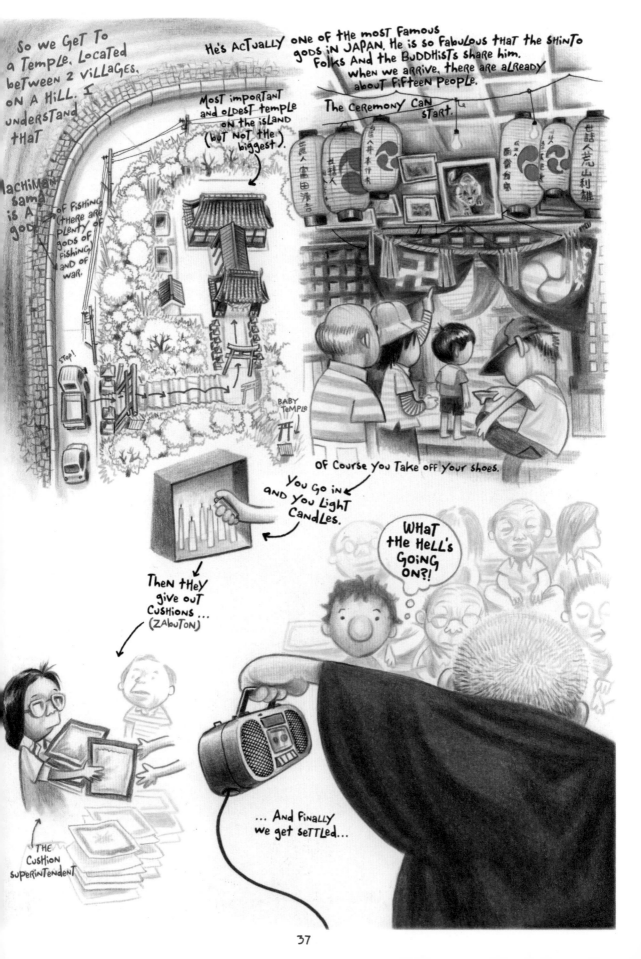

So we get to a temple, located between 2 villages, on a hill. I understand that

Hachiman-sama is a god... of fishing (there are plenty of gods of fishing, and of war.

He's actually one of the most famous gods in Japan. He is so fabulous that the Shinto folks and the Buddhists share him. When we arrive, there are already about fifteen people.

The ceremony can start.

Most important and oldest temple on the island (but not the biggest).

STOP!

BABY TEMPLE

Of course you take off your shoes.

You go in and you light candles.

Then they give out cushions... (ZABUTON)

THE CUSHION SUPERINTENDENT

WHAT THE HELL'S GOING ON?!

... And finally we get settled...

37

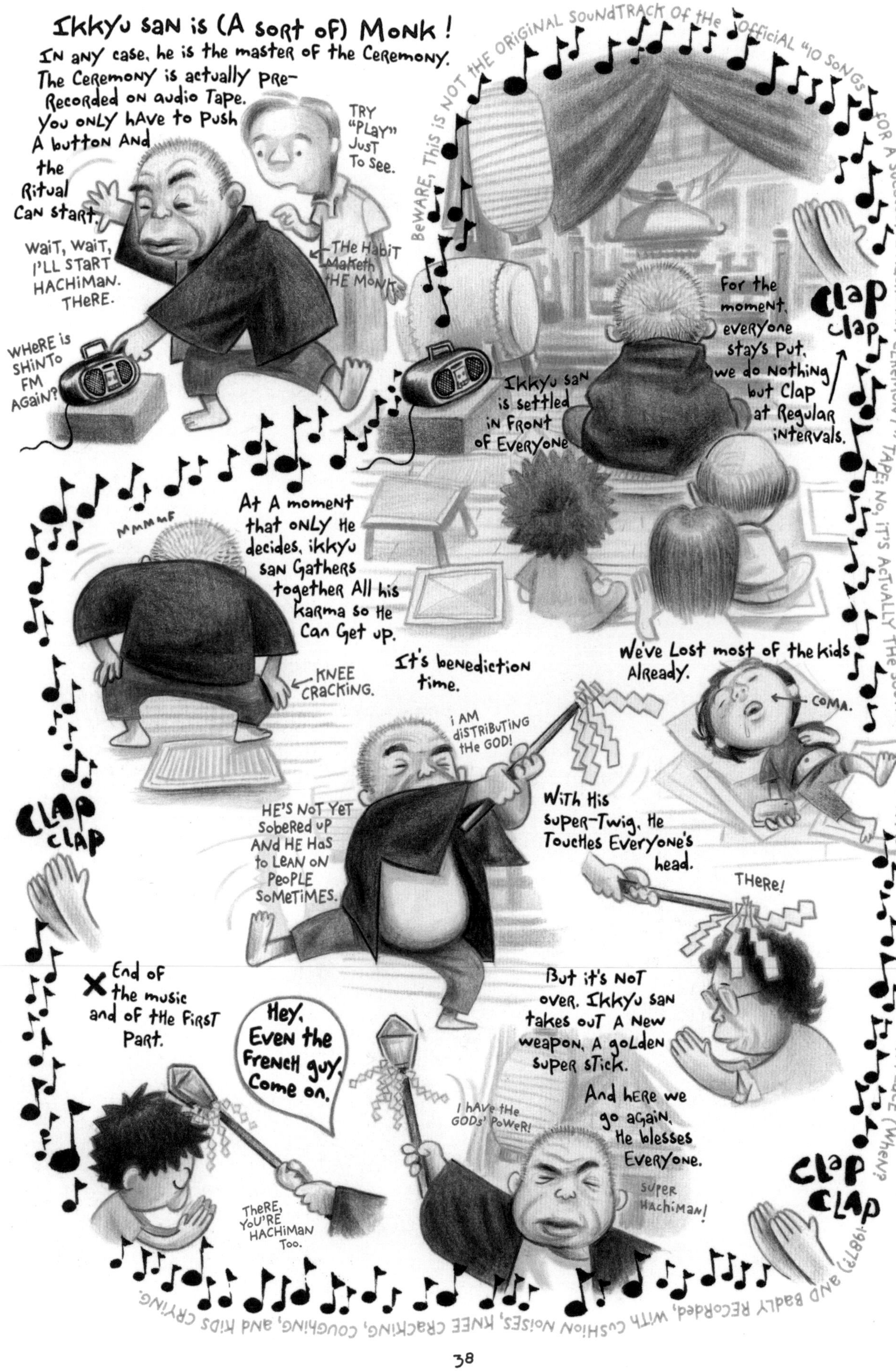
Ikkyu san is (A sort of) Monk!
In any case, he is the master of the Ceremony.
The Ceremony is actually pre-Recorded on audio Tape.
You only have to Push A button And the Ritual Can start.
TRY "PLAY" JUST To See.
THe HabiT Maketh THE MONK
WaiT, WaiT, I'LL START HACHiMAN. THeRE.
WHeRE is SHINTo FM AGAIN?
BeWARE, This is NOT the ORIGINAL SOUNDTRACK OF the OFFICIAL "10 SONGS FOR A SUCCESSFUL HACHIMAN CEREMONY" TAPE; NO, IT'S ACTUALLY THE SOUNDTRACK OF A MEETING THAT ALREADY TOOK PLACE (WHEN? 1987?) AND BADLY RECORDED, WITH CUSHION NOISES, KNEE CRACKING, COUGHING, AND KIDS CRYING.
For the moment, everyone stays Put, we do Nothing but Clap at Regular intervals.
Clap clap
Ikkyu san is settled in Front of Everyone
MMMMF
At A moment that ONLY He decides, ikkyu san Gathers together All his karma so He Can Get up.
KNEE CRACKING.
It's benediction time.
We've Lost most of the kids Already.
COMA.
i AM diSTRIBUTING tHe GOD!
Clap clap
HE'S NOT YET Sobered up AND HE HaS to LEAN ON PEOPLE SoMeTiMES.
With His super-Twig, He Touches Everyone's head.
THeRe!
End of the music and of tHe First Part.
Hey, Even the French guy, Come on.
But it's NoT over. Ikkyu san takes out A New weapon, A golden super sTick.
I hAve tHe GODs' PoweR!
And here we go again. He blesses Everyone.
THeRE, YoU'RE HACHiMAN Too.
SuPER HAchiMAN!
Clap Clap

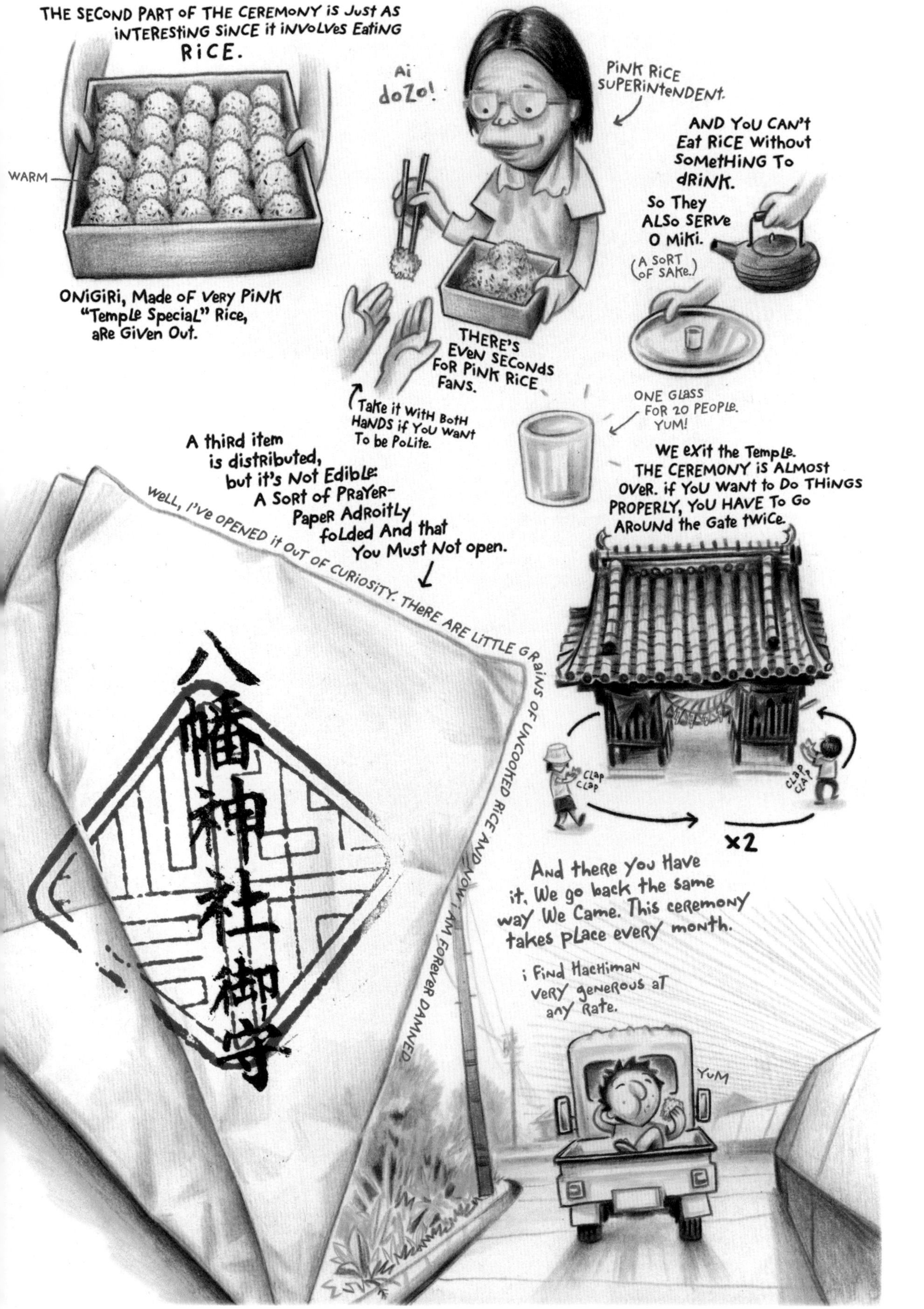
THE SECOND PART OF THE CEREMONY is Just AS INTERESTING SINCE it involves Eating RICE.
WARM
ONIGIRI, Made of Very PINK "Temple Special" Rice, are Given Out.
Ai doZo!
PINK RICE SUPERINTENDENT.
THERE'S EVEN SECONDS FOR PINK RICE FANS.
Take it With Both HANDS if You Want To be Polite.
AND You CAN'T Eat RICE Without SOMETHING To dRINK.
So They ALSo SERVE O MIKI.
(A SORT OF SAKE.)
ONE GLASS FOR 20 PEOPLE. YUM!
A third item is distributed, but it's Not Edible: A Sort of PRAYER-Paper Adroitly folded And that You Must Not open.
WELL, I'VE OPENED it OUT OF CURIOSITY. THERE ARE LITTLE GRAINS OF UNCOOKED RICE AND NOW I AM FOREVER DAMNED.
八幡神社御守
WE exit the Temple. THE CEREMONY IS ALMOST OVER. if YOU WANT to Do THINGS PROPERLY, YOU HAVE To Go AROUND the Gate twice.
Clap Clap
Clap Clap
x2
And there You Have it. We go back the same way We Came. This ceremony takes place every month.
i Find Hachiman very generous at any Rate.
YUM

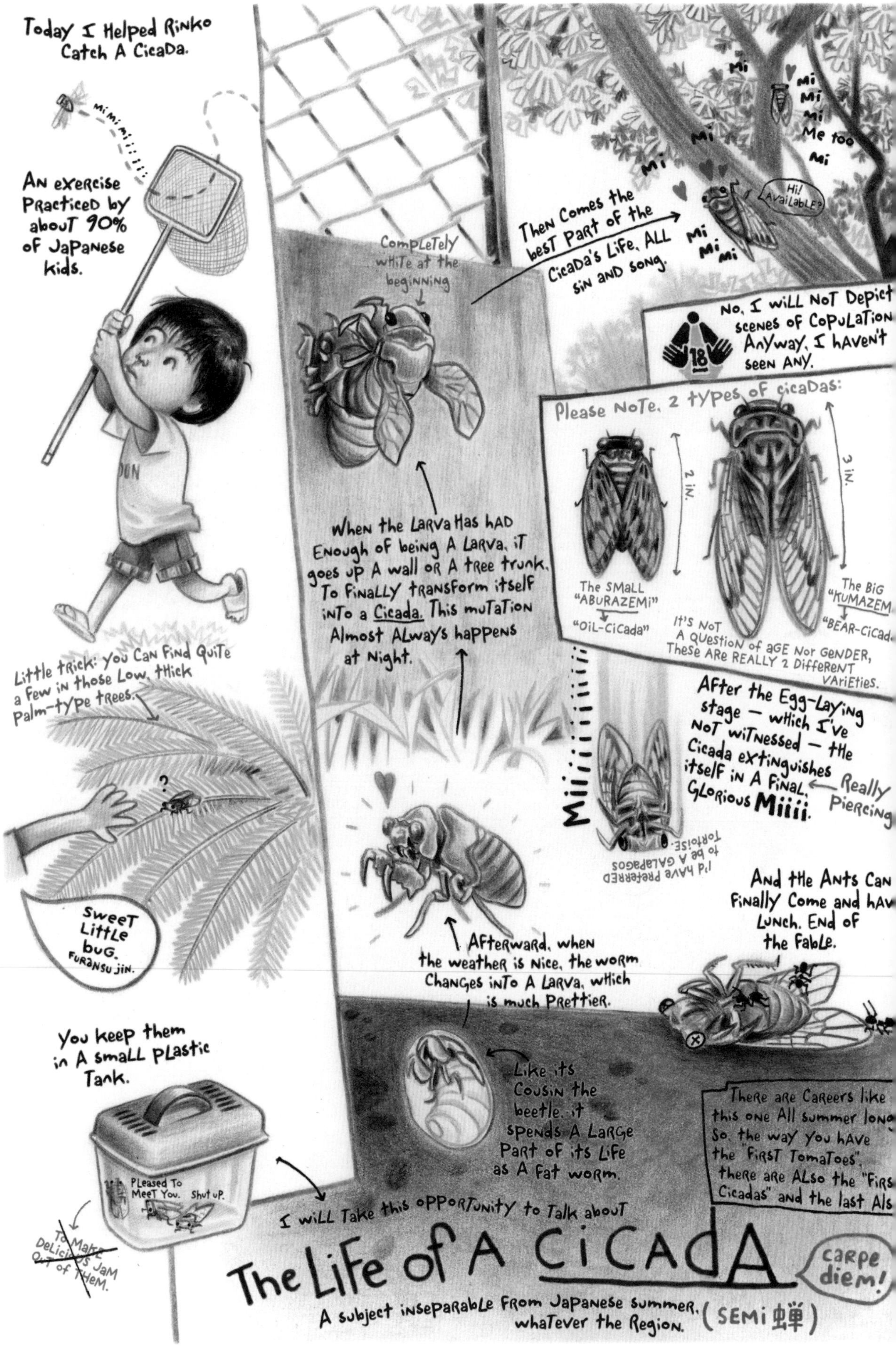
Today I Helped Rinko Catch A Cicada.
Mi Mi Mi i i i i
An exercise Practiced by about 90% of Japanese kids.
Little trick: you can find quite a few in those low, thick palm-type trees.
?
Sweet little bug.
Furansu jin.
You keep them in a small plastic tank.
Pleased To Meet You.
Shut up.
~~To Make Delicious Jam Out of Them.~~
I will take this opportunity to talk about
The Life of A Cicada
carpe diem!
A subject inseparable from Japanese summer, whatever the Region.
(SEMI 蟬)
Like its cousin the beetle, it spends a large part of its life as a fat worm.
Afterward, when the weather is nice, the worm changes into a larva, which is much prettier.
When the larva has had enough of being a larva, it goes up a wall or a tree trunk, to finally transform itself into a Cicada. This mutation almost always happens at night.
Completely white at the beginning
Then comes the best part of the Cicada's life. All sin and song.
Mi
Mi
Mi
Mi
Me too
Mi
Mi
Mi
Mi
Mi
Hi! Available?
No, I will not depict scenes of copulation. Anyway, I haven't seen any.
18
Please Note, 2 types of cicadas:
2 in.
3 in.
The small "ABURAZEMi"
"Oil-Cicada"
The big "KUMAZEM
"BEAR-Cicad
It's not a question of age nor gender, these are really 2 different varieties.
Miiiiiiiiiiiiii
After the egg-laying stage — which I've not witnessed — the Cicada extinguishes itself in a final, glorious Miiii.
Really piercing
I'd have preferred to be a Galapagos tortoise.
And the ants can finally come and hav lunch. End of the fable.
There are careers like this one all summer long. So, the way you have the "first tomatoes", there are also the "firs Cicadas" and the last als

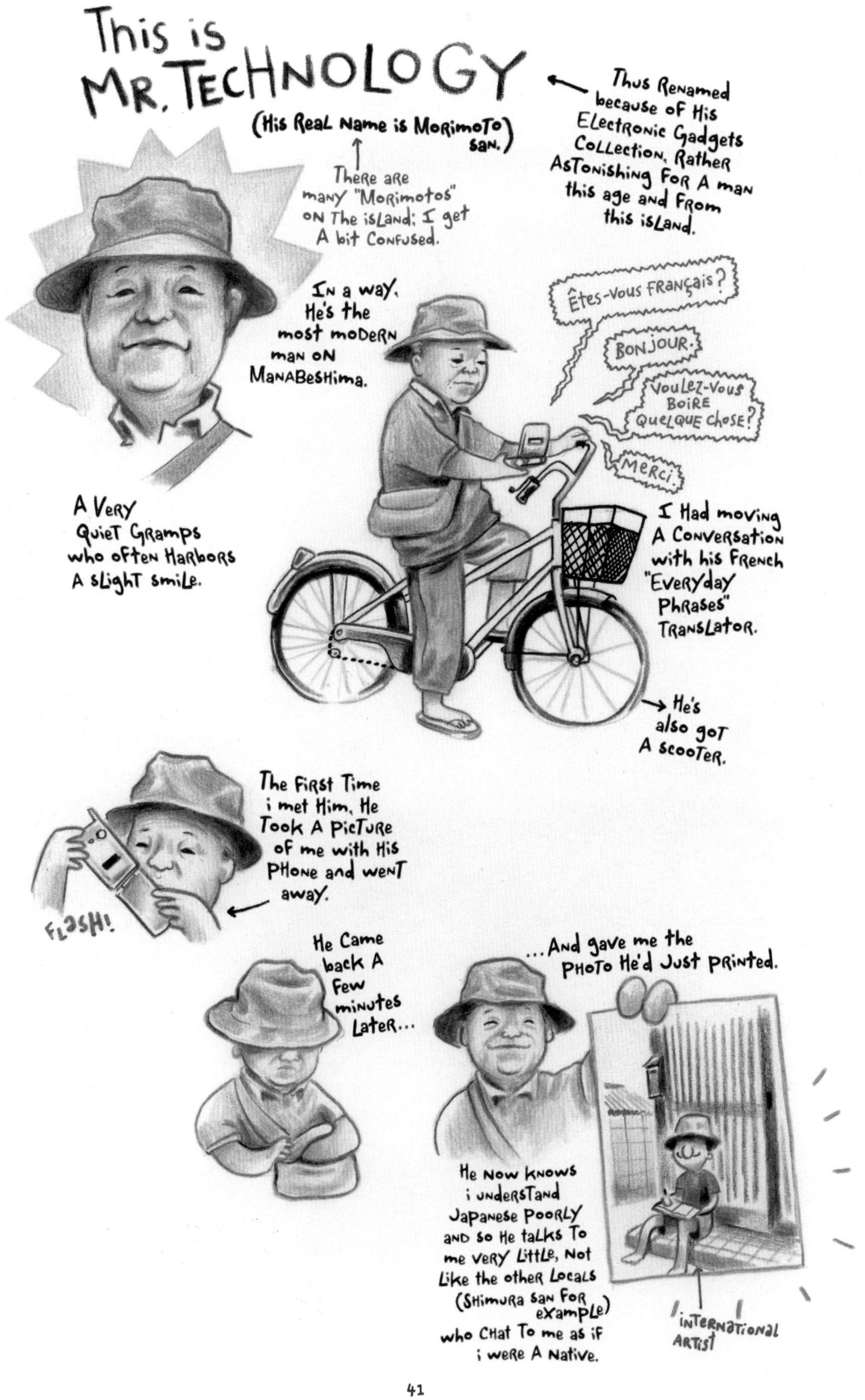
This is MR. TECHNOLOGY
Thus Renamed because of His Electronic Gadgets Collection, Rather Astonishing for A man this age and from this island.
(His Real Name is Morimoto san.)
There are many "Morimotos" on the island; I get A bit Confused.
In a way, He's the most modern man on Manabeshima.
Êtes-vous Français?
Bonjour.
Voulez-vous boire quelque chose?
Merci.
A Very Quiet Gramps who often Harbors A slight smile.
I Had moving A Conversation with his French "Everyday Phrases" Translator.
He's also got A scooter.
The First Time i met Him, He Took A Picture of me with His Phone and went away.
FLASH!
He Came back A Few minutes Later...
...And gave me the Photo He'd Just Printed.
He Now knows i understand Japanese Poorly and so He talks To me very Little, Not Like the other Locals (Shimura san for example) who Chat To me as if i were A Native.
International Artist

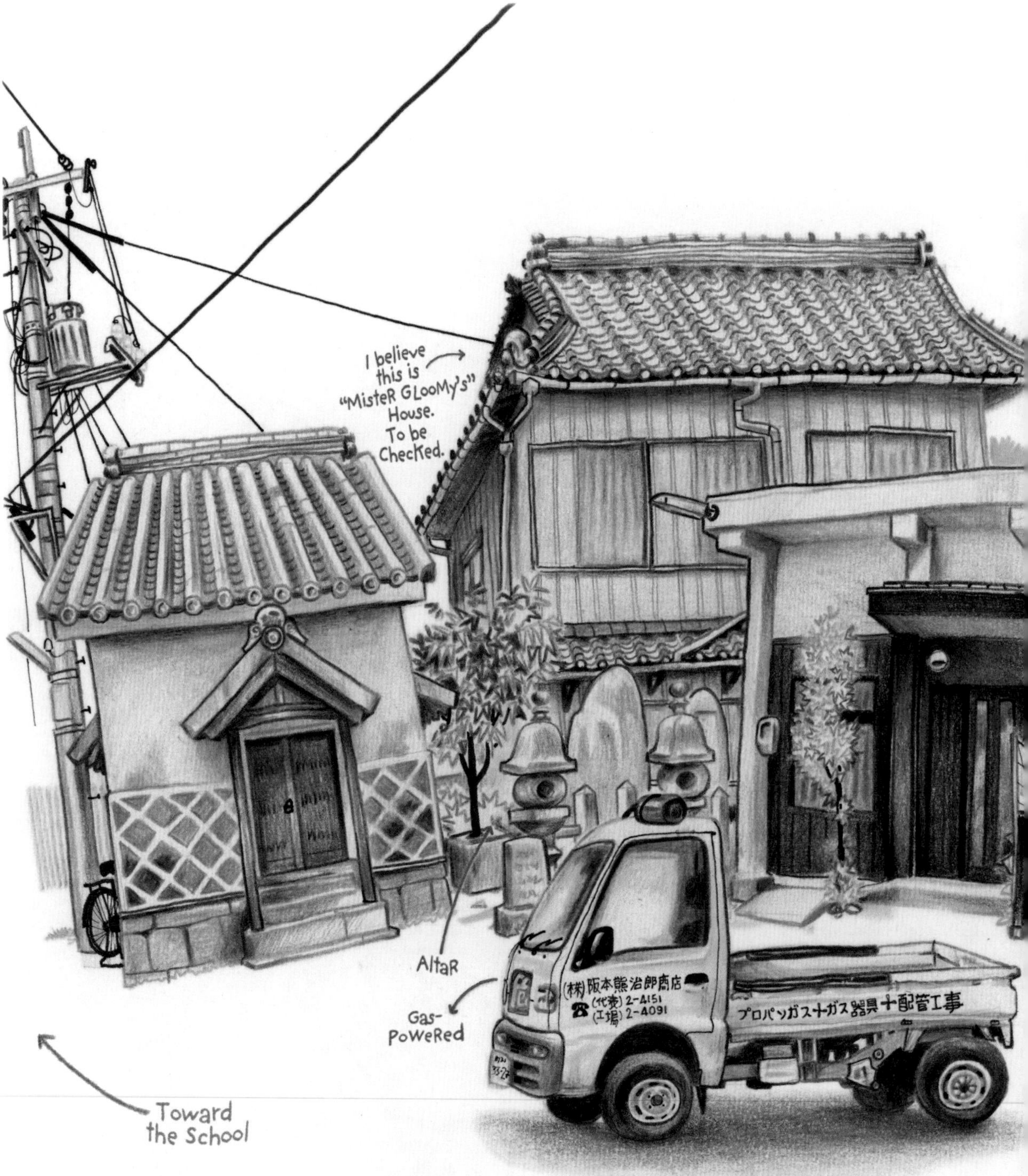
I believe this is "Mister Gloomy's" House. To be Checked.
Altar
Gas-Powered
(株)阪本熊治郎商店
(代表) 2-4151
(工場) 2-4091
プロパンガス+ガス器具+配管工事
Toward the School

The GORI-

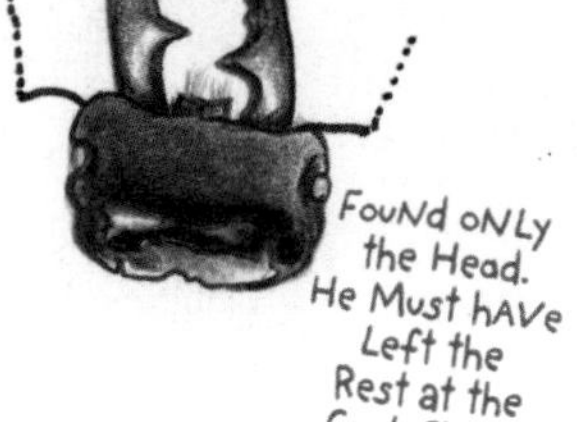
Found only the Head. He Must have Left the Rest at the Coat-Check.

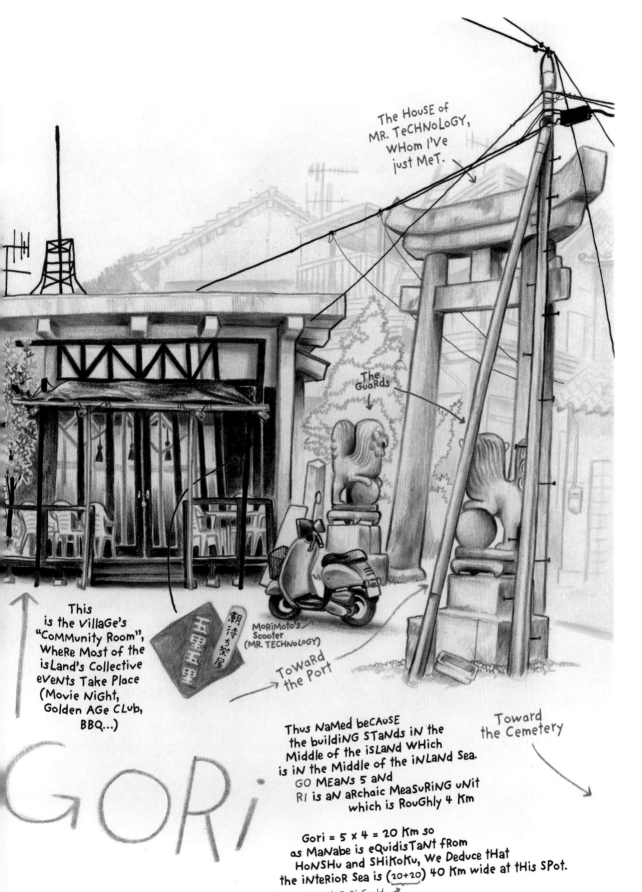

The HoUSE of MR. TeCHNoLoGY, WHom I'Ve just MeT.

The GuaRds

This is the VillaGe's "CoMMunity RooM", WheRe Most of the isLand's Collective eVents Take Place (Movie NiGht, Golden AGe CLub, BBQ...)

MoRiMoto's Scooter (MR. TECHNoLoGY)

TowaRd the Port

GoRi

Toward the Cemetery

Thus NaMed beCAuSE the buildiNG STAnds iN the Middle of the isLAnd WHich is iN the Middle of the iNLAnd Sea. GO MEANs 5 aNd RI is aN aRchaic MeaSuRiNG uNit which is RouGhly 4 Km

Gori = 5 x 4 = 20 Km so as MaNabe is eQuidisTaNt fRom HoNSHu and SHiKoKu, We Deduce tHat the iNteRioR Sea is (20+20) 40 Km wide at tHis SPot.

In the End, GoRi-GoRi Could be TRaNsLated As 20Km-20Km.

43

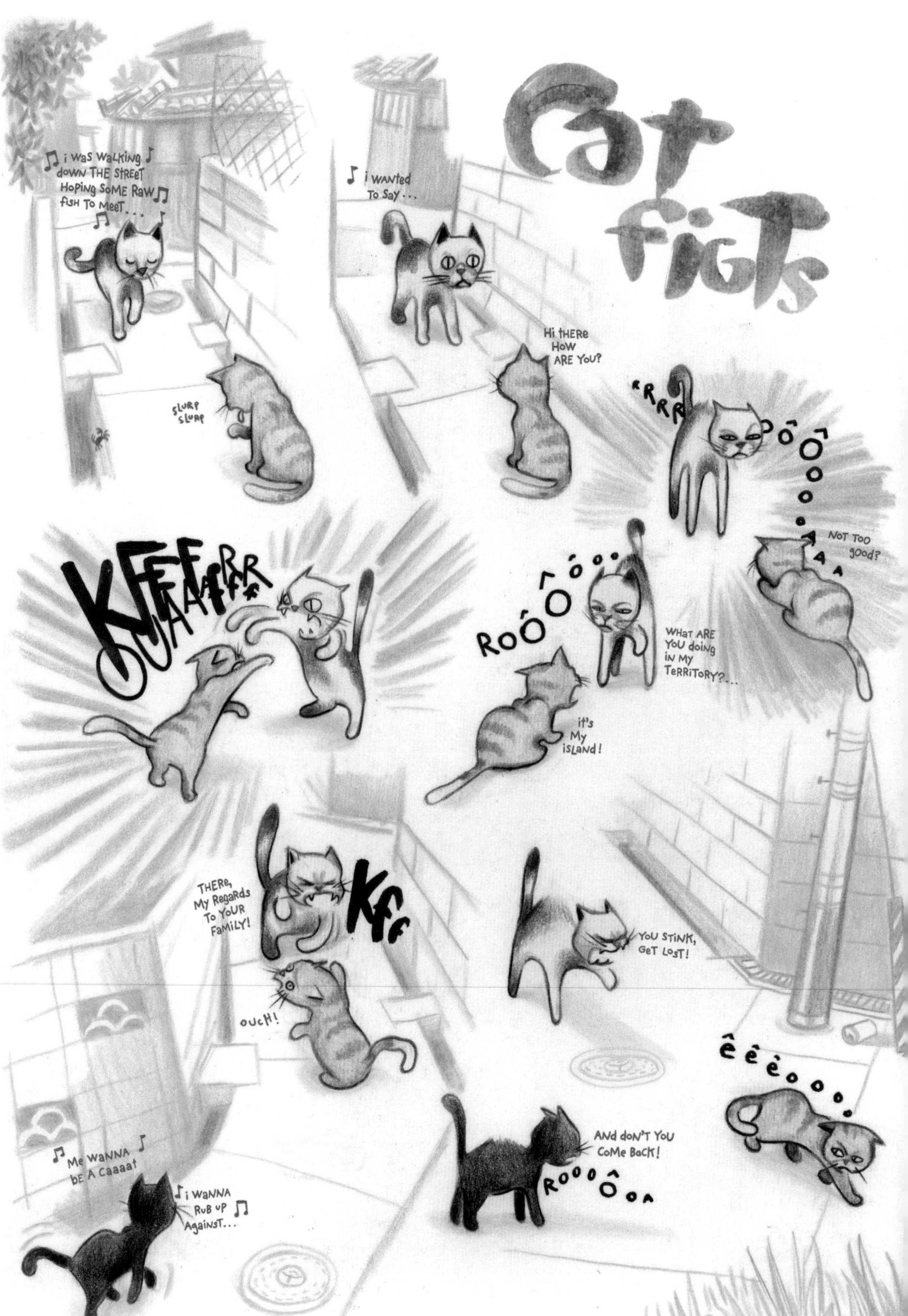
Cat Figts
♫ i was walking ♪ down THE STREET Hoping SOME RAW ♫ fish To MeeT... ♫
slurp slurp
♪ i wanted To Say...
Hi THERE HOW ARE YOU?
RRRR
ÔÔOOOOAA
NOT TOO good?
ROÓÔOOO
WHAT ARE YOU doing in MY TERRITORY?...
it's My isLand!
KFFFUAAAFRRR
THERE, My Regards To YOUR FaMILY!
KFF
ouCH!
YOU STINK, GET LOST!
ÊÊÈOOO
AND don'T YOU COMe BACK!
ROOOÔOA
♫ Me WANNA ♪ be A Caaaat
♪ i WANNA RUB UP ♫ AgainsT...

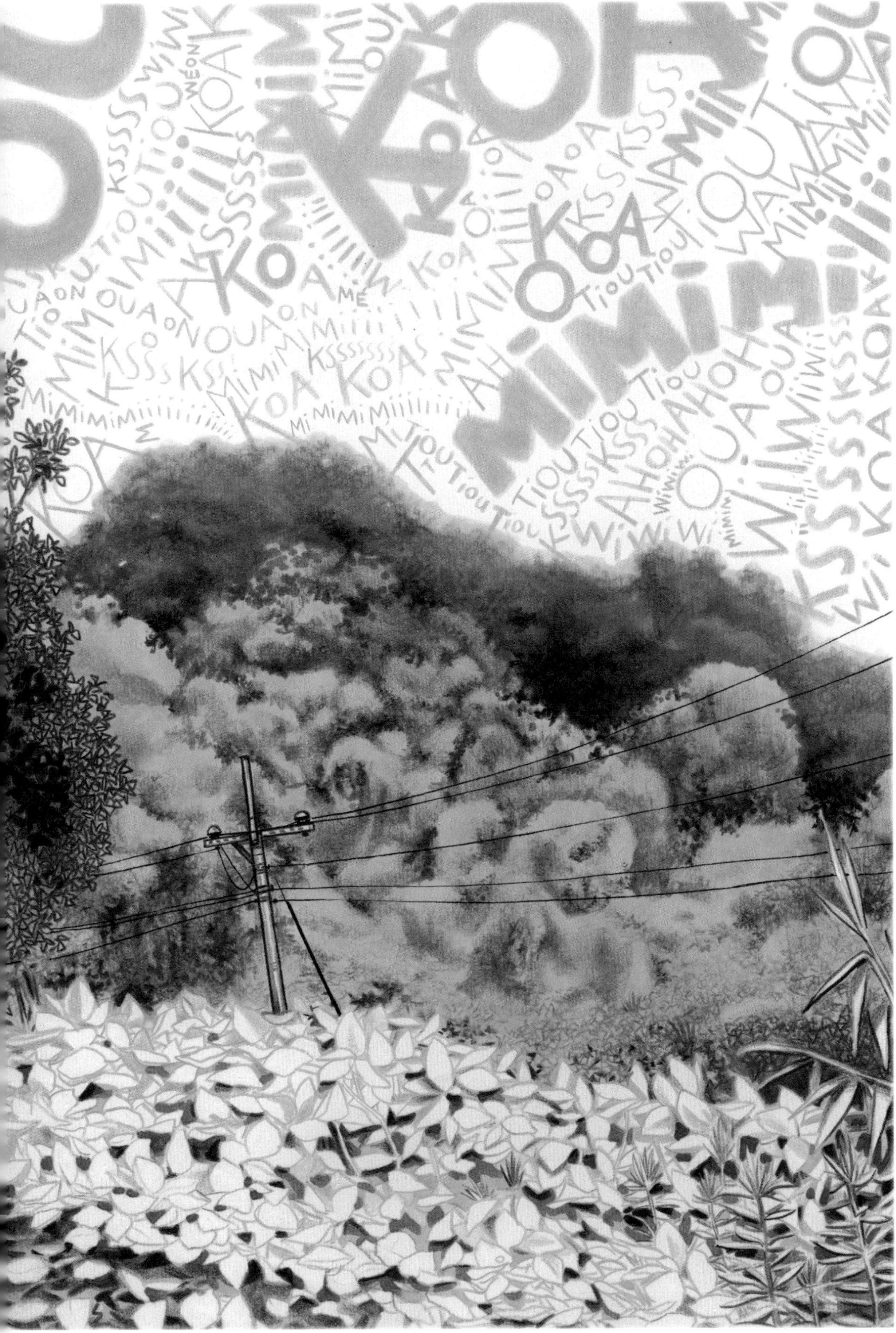

KOA
KOA
KOA KOAS
MiMiMi
MiMiMiMi
KSSSS
TiOU TiOU
NOUA
AHOH
WiWiWi

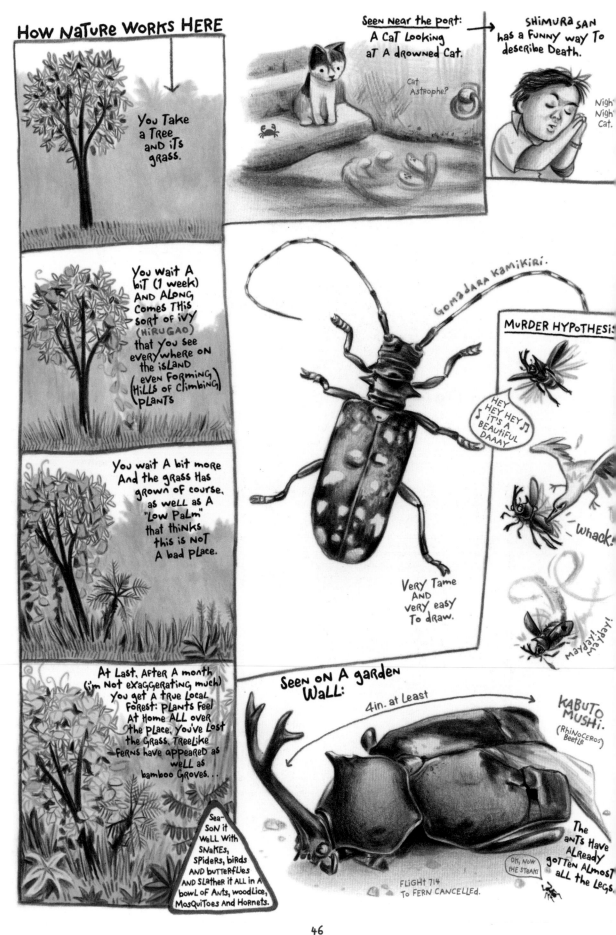

HOW NATURE WORKS HERE

You take a tree and its grass.

You wait a bit (1 week) and along comes this sort of ivy (HIRUGAO) that you see everywhere on the island even forming (hills of climbing) plants

You wait a bit more and the grass has grown of course. as well as a "Low Palm" that thinks this is not a bad place.

At last. After a month (i'm not exaggerating much) you get a true local forest: plants feel at home all over the place. You've lost the grass. Treelike ferns have appeared as well as bamboo groves...

Season it well with snakes, spiders, birds and butterflies and slather it all in a bowl of ants, woodlice, mosquitoes and hornets.

Seen near the port: A cat looking at a drowned cat.

Cat Astrophe?

Shimura san has a funny way to describe Death.

Nigh Nigh Cat.

Gomadara kamikiri.

Very tame and very easy to draw.

MURDER HYPOTHESIS

♪ HEY HEY HEY IT'S A BEAUTIFUL DAAAY

...whack.

mayday! mayday!

Seen on a garden wall:

4 in. at least

KABUTO MUSHI. (Rhinoceros Beetle)

OK, NOW THE STEAK!

The ants have already gotten almost all the legs.

FLIGHT 714 TO FERN CANCELLED.

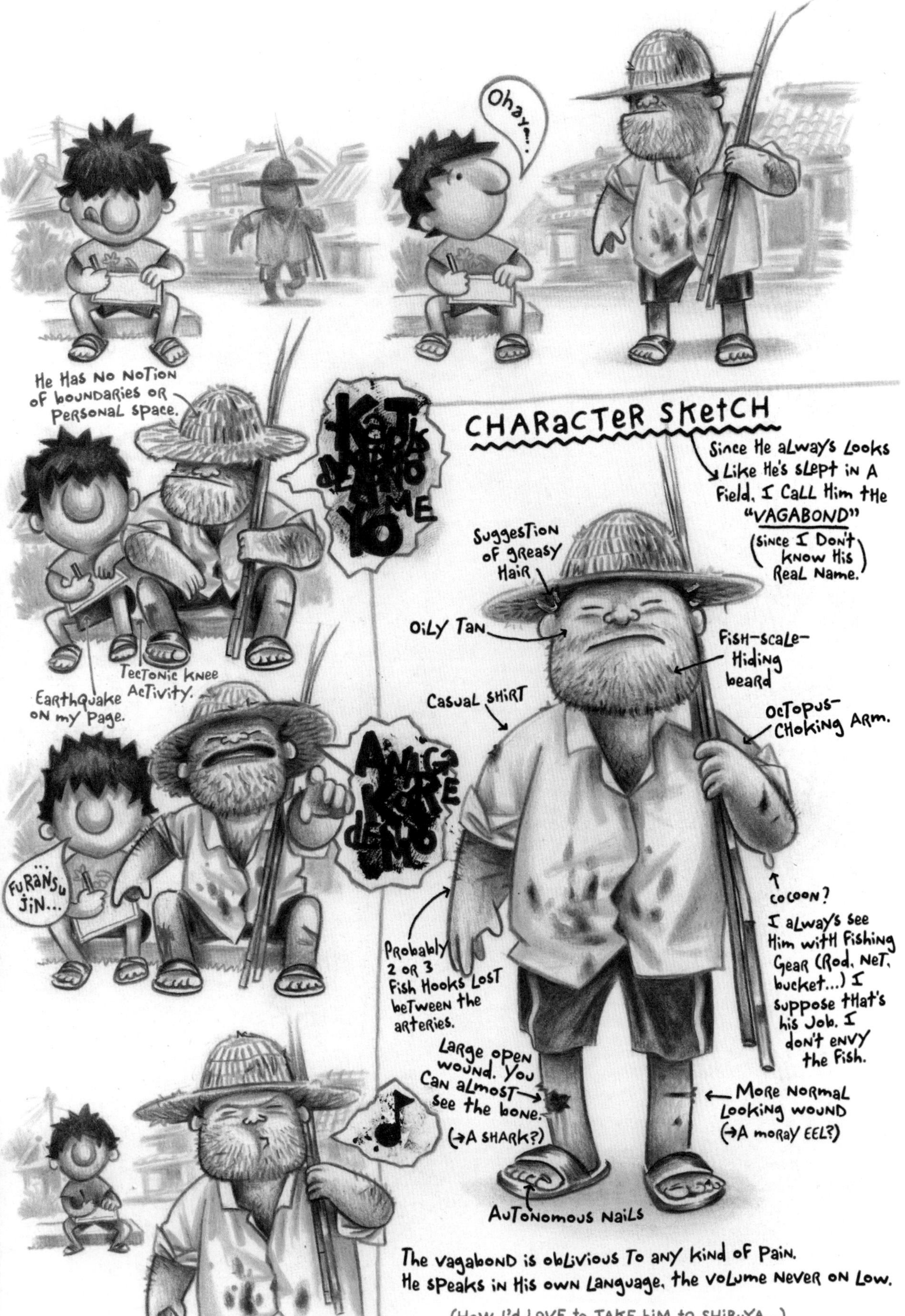
Ohayo!..
He Has no notion of boundaries or personal space.
Tectonic knee activity.
Earthquake on my page.
... Furansu jin...
CHARACTER SKETCH
Since He always looks like He's slept in a field, I call Him the "VAGABOND"
(Since I Don't know His Real Name.)
Suggestion of greasy Hair
Oily Tan
Fish-scale-Hiding beard
Casual shirt
Octopus-choking arm.
cocoon?
I always see Him with fishing gear (Rod, Net, bucket...) I suppose that's his Job. I don't envy the fish.
Probably 2 or 3 fish hooks lost between the arteries.
Large open wound. You can almost see the bone.
(→A shark?)
More normal looking wound
(→A moray eel?)
Autonomous nails
The vagabond is oblivious to any kind of pain.
He speaks in His own language, the volume never on low.
(How I'd love to take him to Shibuya...)

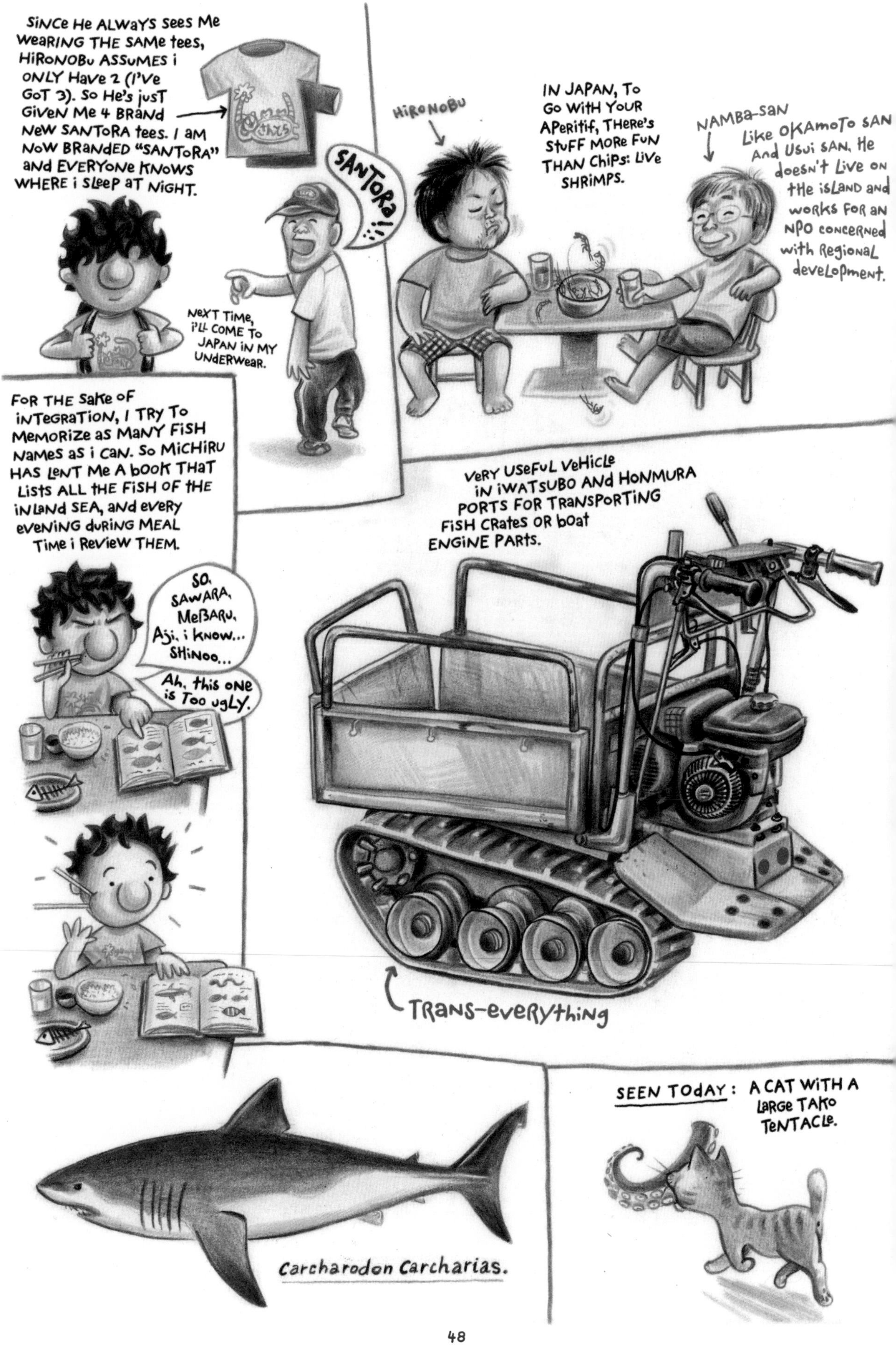
SINCE HE ALWAYS SEES ME WEARING THE SAME TEES, HIRONOBU ASSUMES I ONLY HAVE 2 (I'VE GOT 3). SO HE'S JUST GIVEN ME 4 BRAND NEW SANTORA TEES. I AM NOW BRANDED "SANTORA" AND EVERYONE KNOWS WHERE I SLEEP AT NIGHT.
SANTORA
NEXT TIME, I'LL COME TO JAPAN IN MY UNDERWEAR.
HIRONOBU
IN JAPAN, TO GO WITH YOUR APERITIF, THERE'S STUFF MORE FUN THAN CHIPS: LIVE SHRIMPS.
NAMBA-SAN
LIKE OKAMOTO SAN AND USUI SAN, HE DOESN'T LIVE ON THE ISLAND AND WORKS FOR AN NPO CONCERNED WITH REGIONAL DEVELOPMENT.
FOR THE SAKE OF INTEGRATION, I TRY TO MEMORIZE AS MANY FISH NAMES AS I CAN. SO MICHIRU HAS LENT ME A BOOK THAT LISTS ALL THE FISH OF THE INLAND SEA, AND EVERY EVENING DURING MEAL TIME I REVIEW THEM.
SO, SAWARA, MEBARU, AJI, I KNOW... SHINOO...
AH, THIS ONE IS TOO UGLY.
VERY USEFUL VEHICLE IN IWATSUBO AND HONMURA PORTS FOR TRANSPORTING FISH CRATES OR BOAT ENGINE PARTS.
TRANS-EVERYTHING
Carcharodon Carcharias.
SEEN TODAY: A CAT WITH A LARGE TAKO TENTACLE.

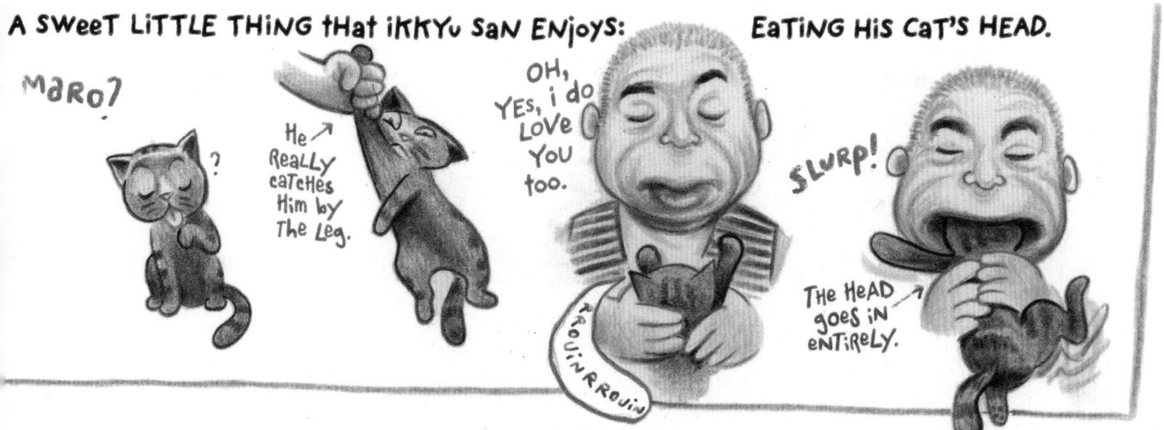
A SWEET LITTLE THING THAT IKKYU SAN ENJOYS: EATING HIS CAT'S HEAD.
MARO?
?
He Really catches Him by The Leg.
OH, YES, I do LOVE YOU too.
RROUINRROUIN
SLURP!
The HEAD goes in entirely.

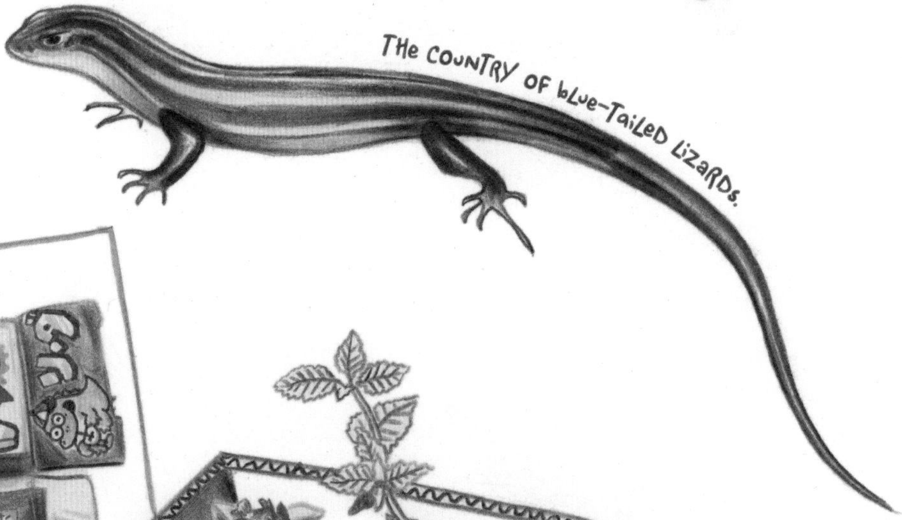
The COUNTRY OF blue-Tailed Lizards.

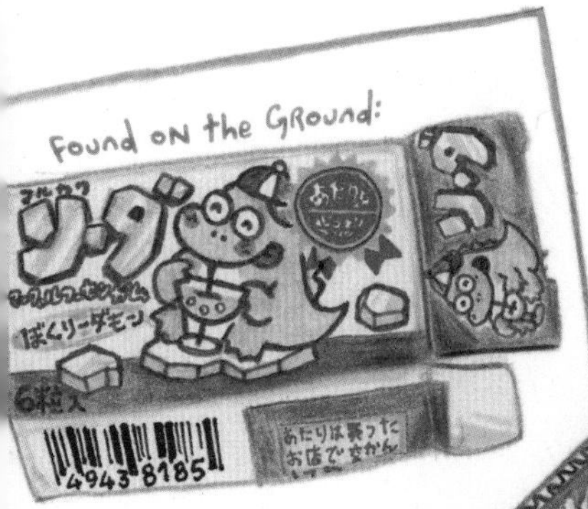
Found on the Ground:
4943 8185

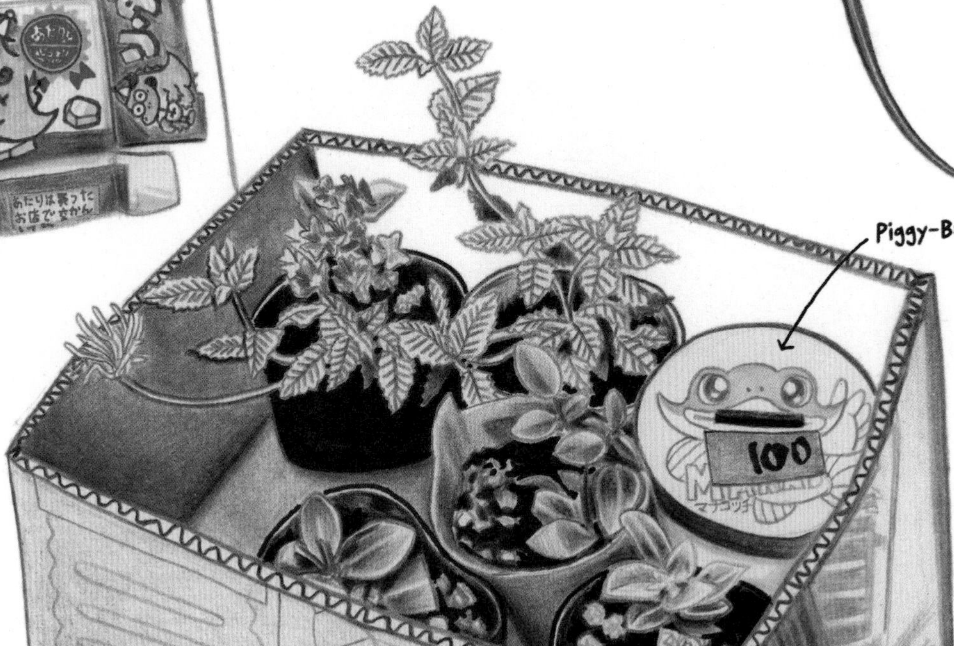
Piggy-BANK
100
DAKARA
SMALL CARDBOARD box You Find Regularly at The ENTRANCE TO THE PORT, WHERE PLANTS, FLOWERS, FRUITS, and Vegetables ARE OFFERED ACCORDING TO THE HARVEST.

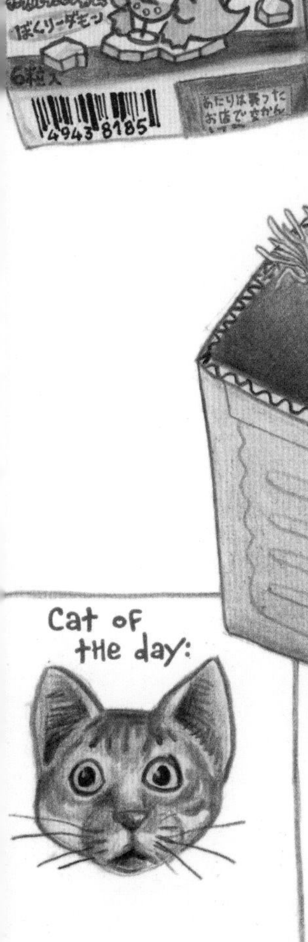
Cat of the day:

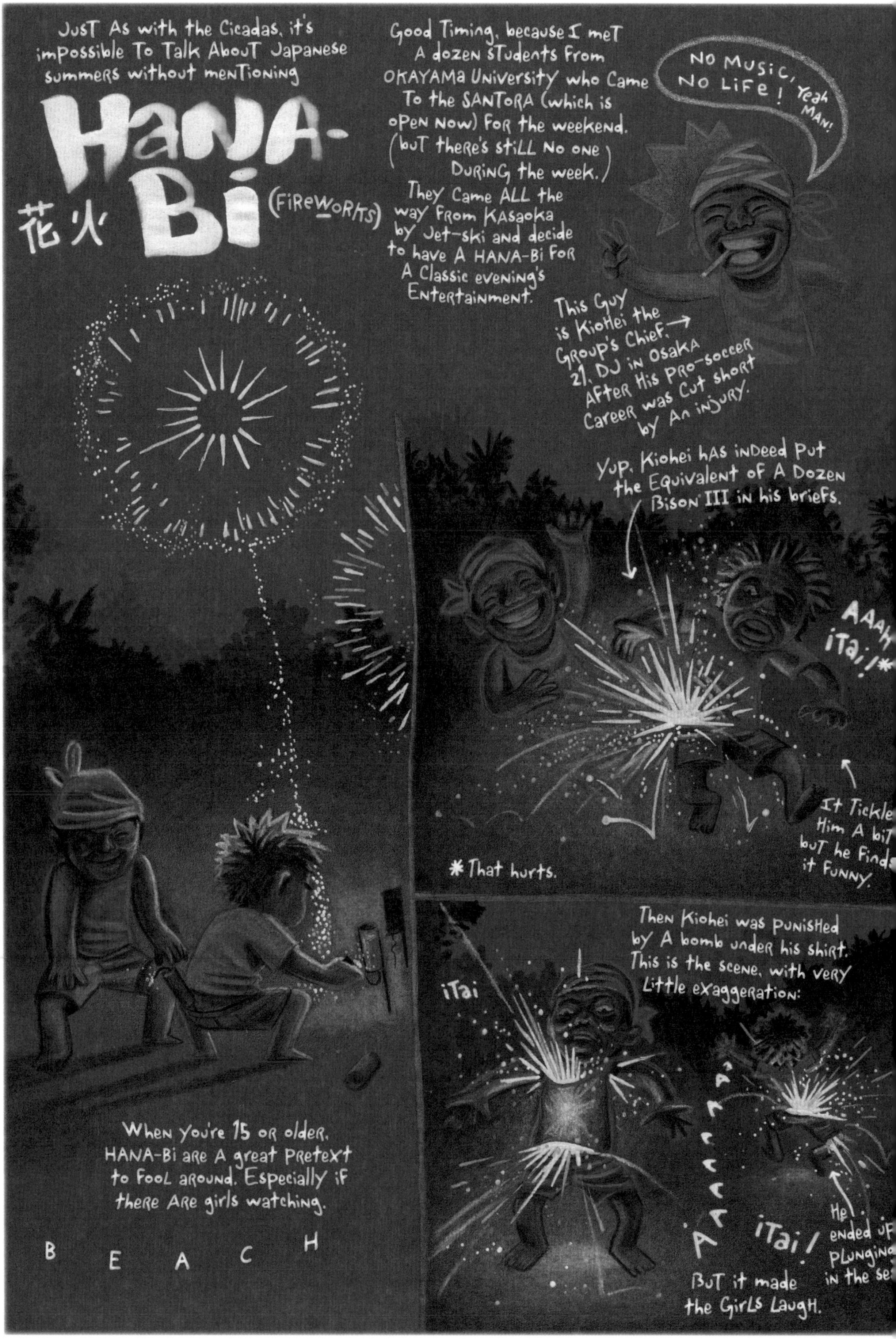
JUST As with the Cicadas, it's impossible To Talk AbouT Japanese summers without menTioning
HANA-Bi 花火 (FIREWORKS)
Good Timing, because I meT A dozen STudents from OKAYAMA University who Came To the SANTORA (which is open Now) For the weekend. (buT there's stiLL No one DuRing the week.)
They Came ALL the way From KAsaoka by Jet-ski and decide to have A HANA-Bi FOR A Classic evening's EnTertainment.
No Music, No Life! Yeah MAN!
This Guy is Kiohei the Group's Chief.→ 21, DJ in Osaka After His Pro-soccer Career was Cut short by An injury.
When you're 15 or older, HANA-Bi are A great PreTexT to fooL around. Especially if there Are girls watching.
B E A C H
Yup, Kiohei hAS inDeed Put the Equivalent of A Dozen Bison III in his briefs.
AAAK iTai!*
It Tickle Him A bit buT he Finds it FUNNY.
*That hurts.
Then Kiohei was PuNisHed by A bomb under his shirt. This is the scene, with very Little exaggeration:
iTai
AAAAAAA
iTai!
BuT it made the GirLs Laugh.
He ended up PLunging in the se

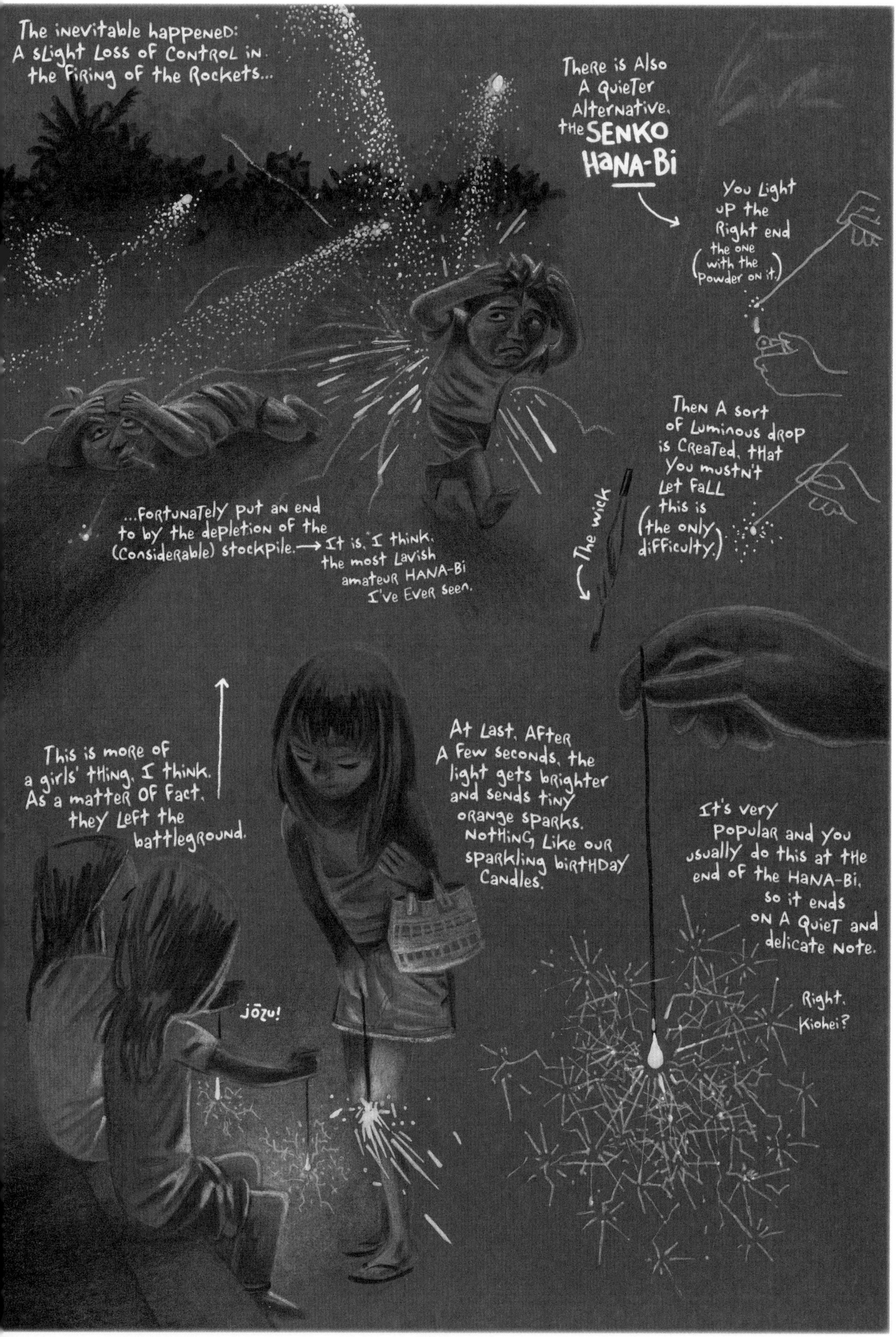

The inevitable happened: A slight Loss of Control in the Firing of the Rockets...
...Fortunately put an end to by the depletion of the (Considerable) stockpile. → It is, I think, the most Lavish amateur HANA-BI I've Ever seen.
There is Also A Quieter Alternative, the SENKO HANA-BI
You Light up the Right end (the one with the Powder on it.)
Then A sort of Luminous drop is Created, that you mustn't let fall (this is the only difficulty.)
The wick
This is more of a girls' thing, I think. As a matter of fact, they left the battleground.
At Last, After A Few seconds, the light gets brighter and sends tiny orange sparks. Nothing Like our sparkling birthday Candles.
It's very Popular and you usually do this at the end of the HANA-Bi, so it ends on A Quiet and delicate note.
jōzu!
Right, Kiohei?

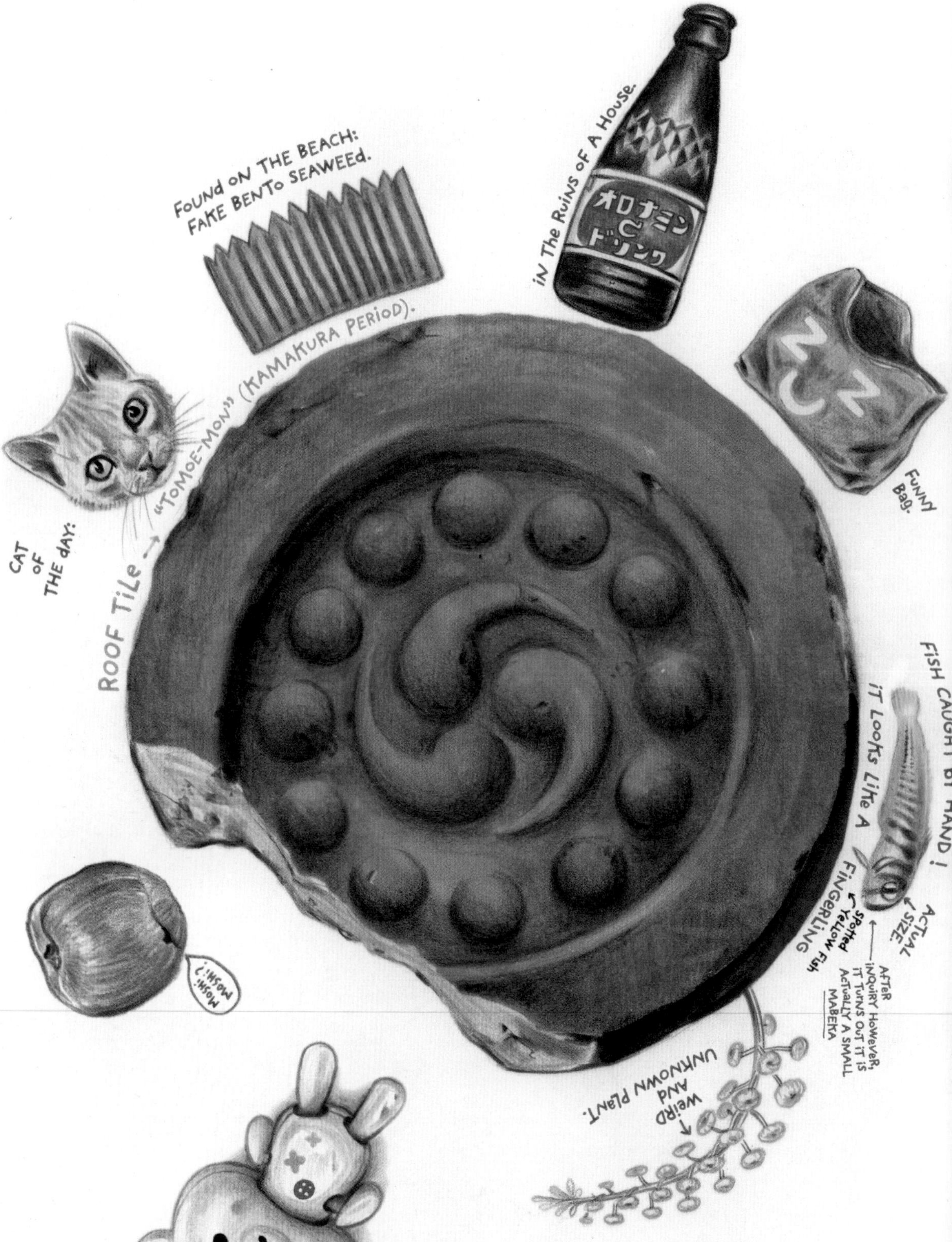
FOUND ON THE BEACH:
FAKE BENTO SEAWEED.
IN THE RUINS OF A HOUSE.
オロナミン C ドリンク
FUNNY BAG.
CAT OF THE DAY:
ROOF TILE → "TOMOE-MON" (KAMAKURA PERIOD).
FISH CAUGHT BY HAND!
IT LOOKS LIKE A FINGERLING
SPOTTED YELLOW FISH
ACTUAL SIZE
AFTER INQUIRY HOWEVER, IT TURNS OUT IT IS ACTUALLY A SMALL MABEKA
WEIRD AND UNKNOWN PLANT.
MOSHI MOSHI?

Reizo San

Manabeshima's Hard Drive

It's very simple: at Reizo san's, the newest thing is his house, built at the beginning of the Meiji era (end of the 19th century). Like him, it's in a very good shape.

Well, here, for page-layout reasons, I have him walking upon the roof of his house, but Reizo san is actually a very sensible person.

It's a real unofficial museum, always open. You can go in the little garden reception area at any time, any way you want.
↓

Tree from Portugal, over 200 years old.
↑

entrance →

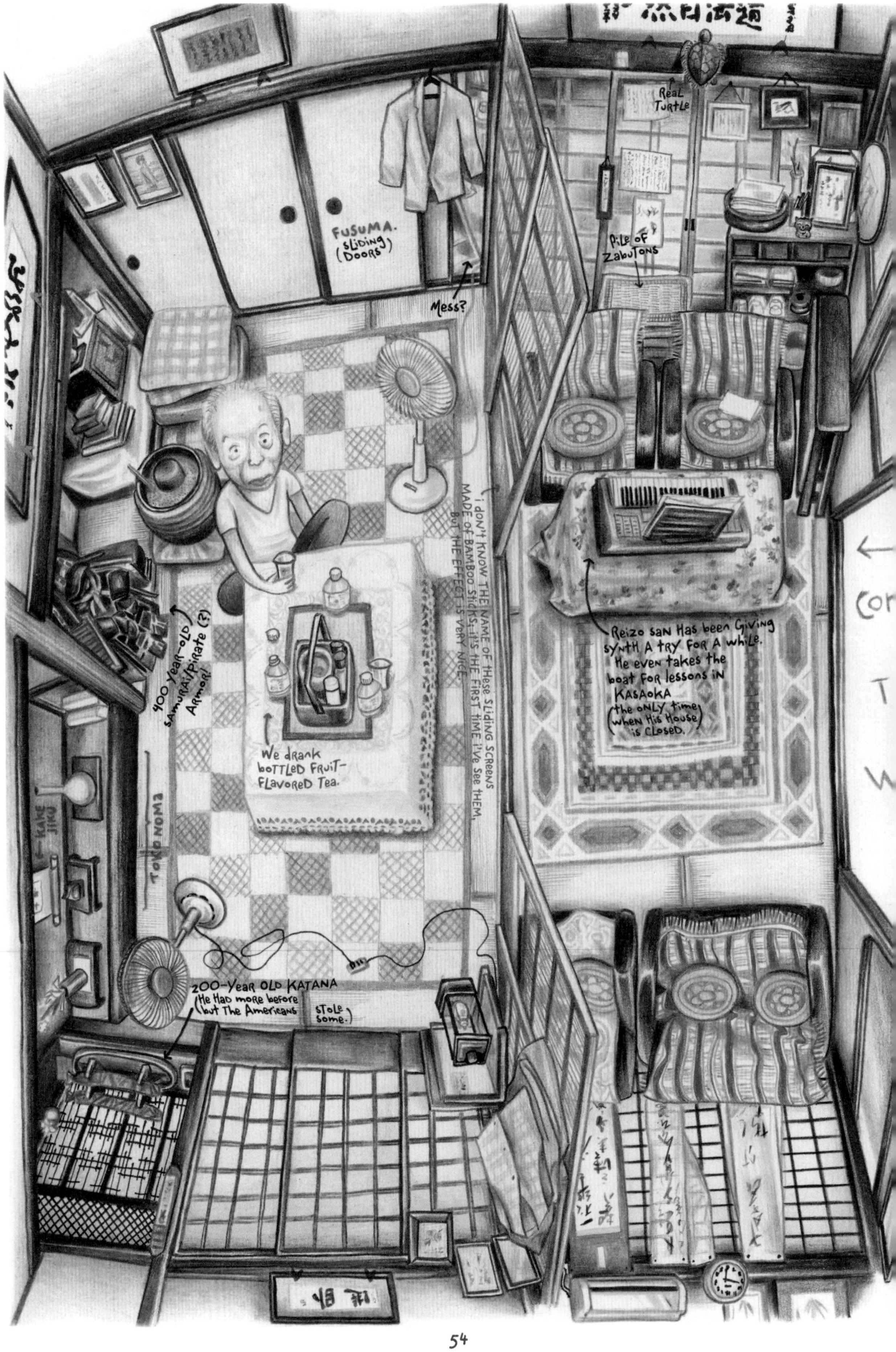

Real Turtle
FUSUMA. Sliding (Doors)
Pile of Zabutons
Mess?
i don't know the name of these sliding screens made of Bamboo sticks, it's the first time i've see them. But the effect is very nice.
Reizo san has been giving synth a try for a while. He even takes the boat for lessons in Kasaoka (the only time when his house is closed.)
400 Year-old samurai/pirate (?) Armor!
We drank bottled fruit-flavored Tea.
Tokonoma
← Kake jiku
200-Year old Katana (He had more before but the Americans stole some.)

AT REIZO SAN'S.

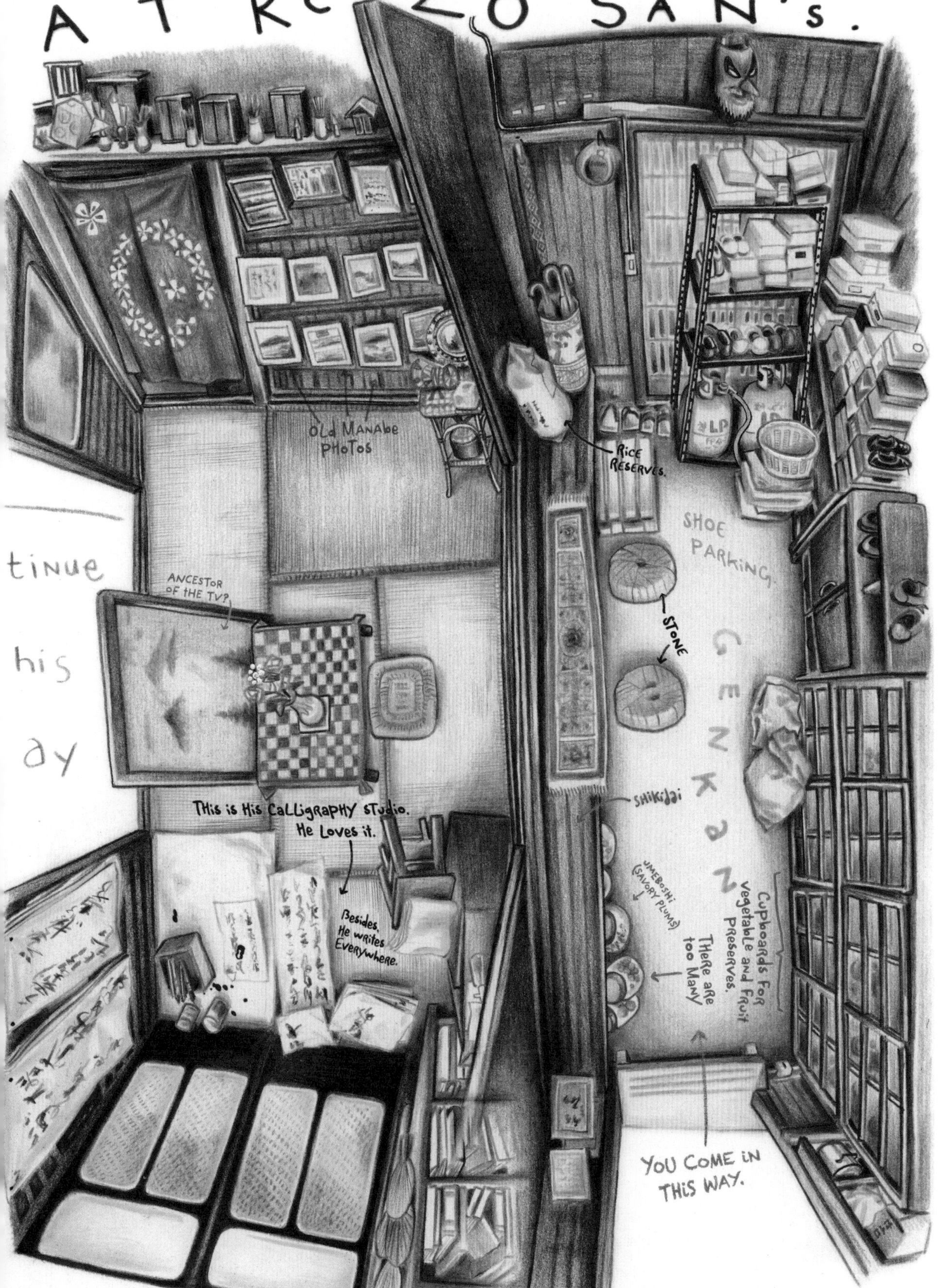

OLD MANABE PHOTOS
RICE RESERVES.
SHOE PARKING
STONE
GENKAN
ANCESTOR OF THE TV?
This is His Calligraphy studio. He Loves it.
Besides, He writes Everywhere.
SHIKIDAI
UMEBOSHI (SAVORY PLUMS)
Cupboards for vegetable and fruit preserves.
There are too Many
YOU COME IN THIS WAY.
tinue
his
ay

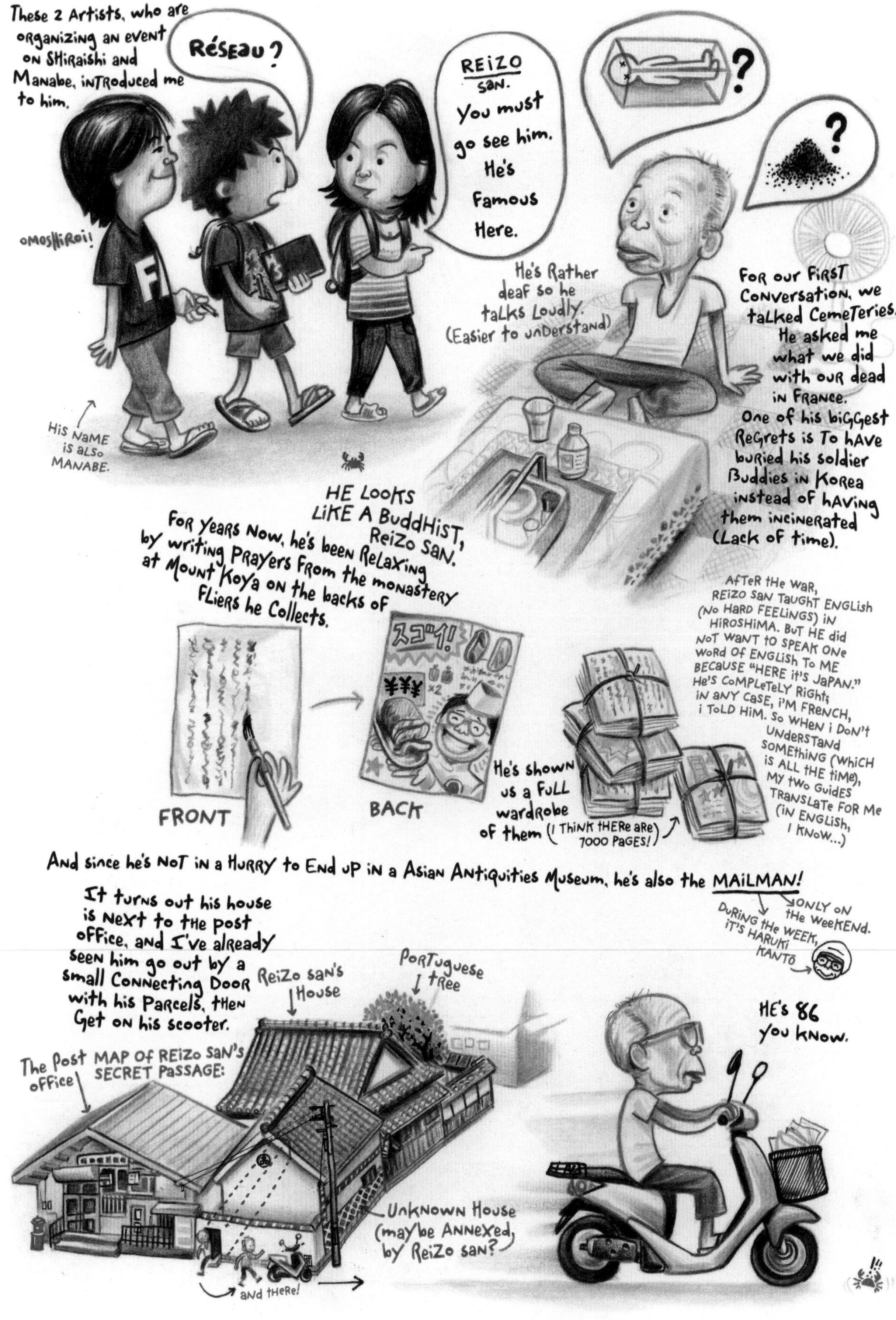
These 2 Artists, who are organizing an event on Shiraishi and Manabe, introduced me to him.
Réseau?
Reizo san. You must go see him. He's Famous Here.
omoshiroi!
His name is also Manabe.
He's Rather deaf so he talks Loudly. (Easier to understand)
For our First Conversation, we talked Cemeteries. He asked me what we did with our dead in France. One of his biggest Regrets is To have buried his soldier Buddies in Korea instead of having them incinerated (Lack of time).
HE LOOKS LIKE A BuddHist, Reizo san.
For years Now, he's been Relaxing by writing Prayers from the monastery at Mount Koya on the backs of Fliers he Collects.
FRONT
スゴイ!
BACK
He's shown us a Full wardrobe of them (I think there are 7000 pages!)
After the war, Reizo san taught English (No hard feelings) in Hiroshima. But he did not want to speak one word of English to me because "Here it's Japan." He's completely right; in any case, I'm French, I told him. So when I don't understand something (which is all the time), my two guides translate for me (in English, I know...)
And since he's NOT in a Hurry to End up in a Asian Antiquities Museum, he's also the MAILMAN!
Only on the weekend.
During the week, it's Haruki Kantō
It turns out his house is Next to the post office, and I've already seen him go out by a small Connecting Door with his Parcels, then Get on his scooter.
Reizo san's House
Portuguese tree
The Post office
MAP OF REIZO SAN'S SECRET PASSAGE:
Unknown House (maybe Annexed by Reizo san?
and there!
HE's 86 you know.
!!

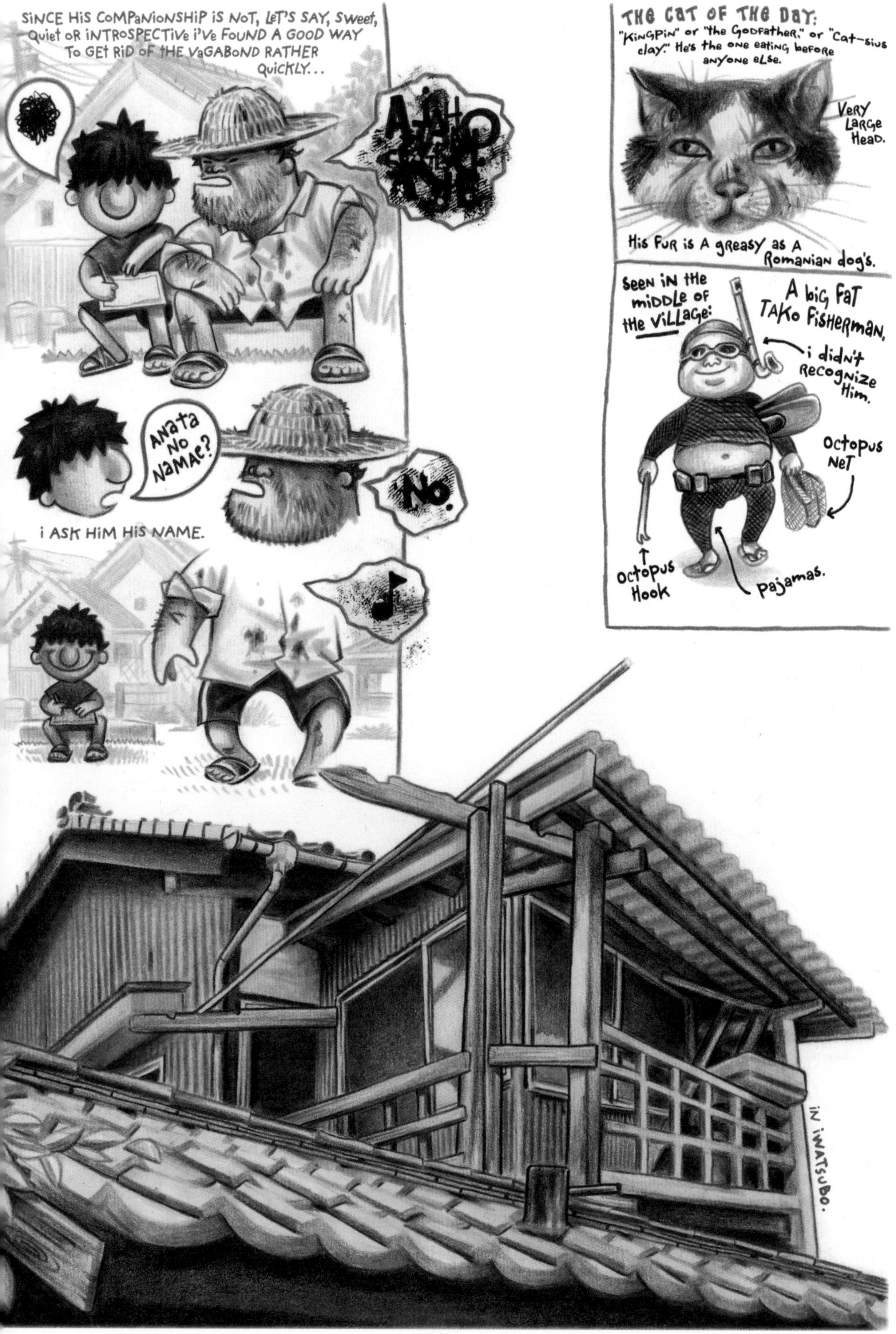
SINCE HIS COMPANIONSHIP IS NOT, LET'S SAY, SWEET, QUIET OR INTROSPECTIVE I'VE FOUND A GOOD WAY TO GET RID OF THE VAGABOND RATHER QUICKLY...
ANATA NO NAMAE?
NO.
I ASK HIM HIS NAME.
THE CAT OF THE DAY:
"KINGPIN" or "the GODFATHER," or "Cat-sius clay." He's the one eating before anyone else.
VERY LARGE HEAD.
His FUR is A greasy as A Romanian dog's.
Seen in the middle of the village:
A big Fat TAKO Fisherman,
i didn't Recognize Him.
Octopus Net
Octopus Hook
Pajamas.
in iwatsubo.

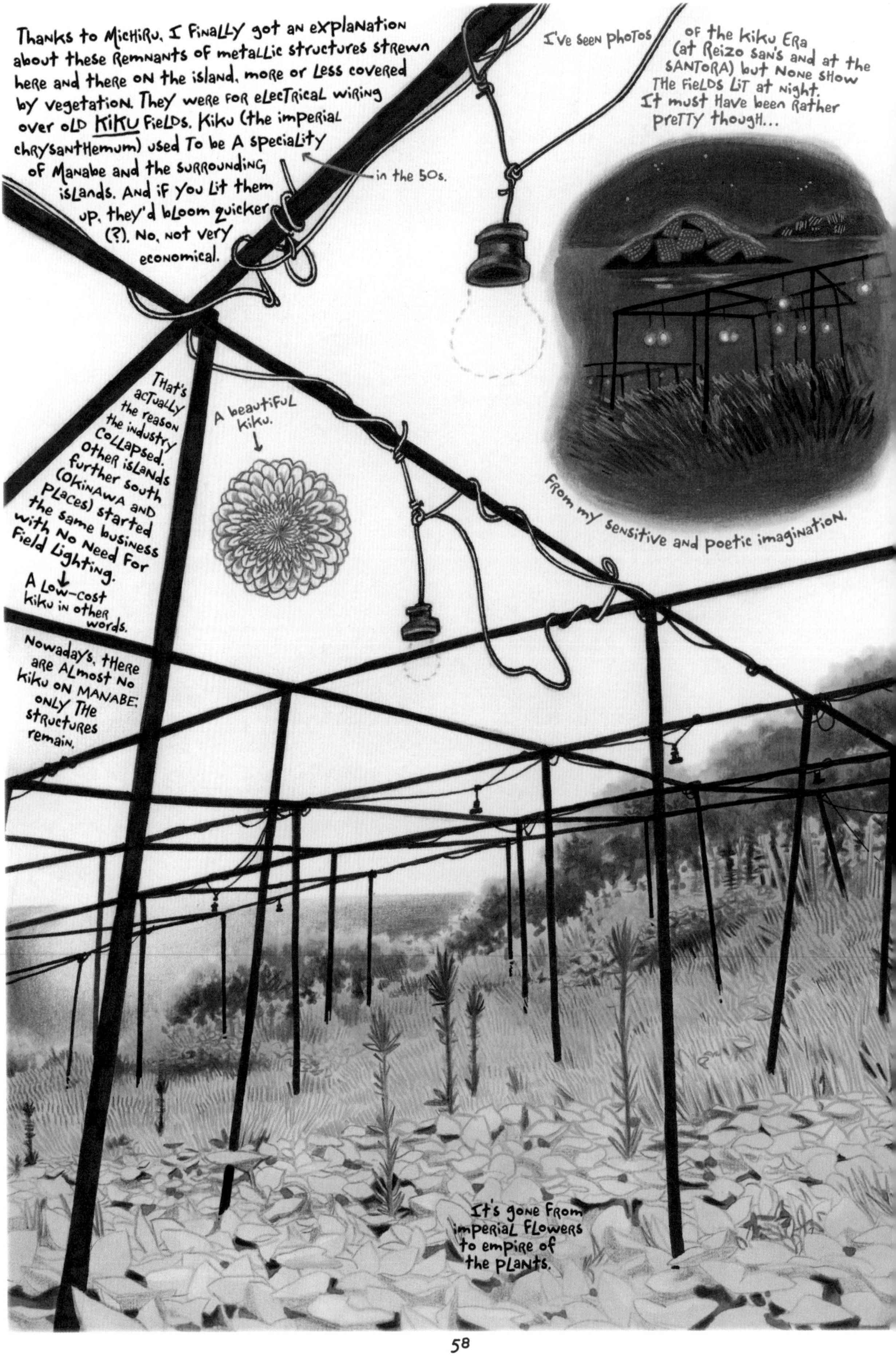

Thanks to Michiru, I finally got an explanation about these remnants of metallic structures strewn here and there on the island, more or less covered by vegetation. They were for electrical wiring over old KIKU fields. Kiku (the imperial chrysanthemum) used to be a speciality of Manabe and the surrounding islands. And if you lit them up, they'd bloom quicker (?). No, not very economical.
in the 50s.
I've seen photos of the kiku era (at Reizo san's and at the SANTORA) but none show the fields lit at night. It must have been rather pretty though...
From my sensitive and poetic imagination.
That's actually the reason the industry collapsed. Other islands further south (Okinawa and places) started the same business with no need for field lighting.
A low-cost kiku in other words.
A beautiful kiku.
Nowadays, there are almost no kiku on Manabe; only the structures remain.
It's gone from imperial flowers to empire of the plants.

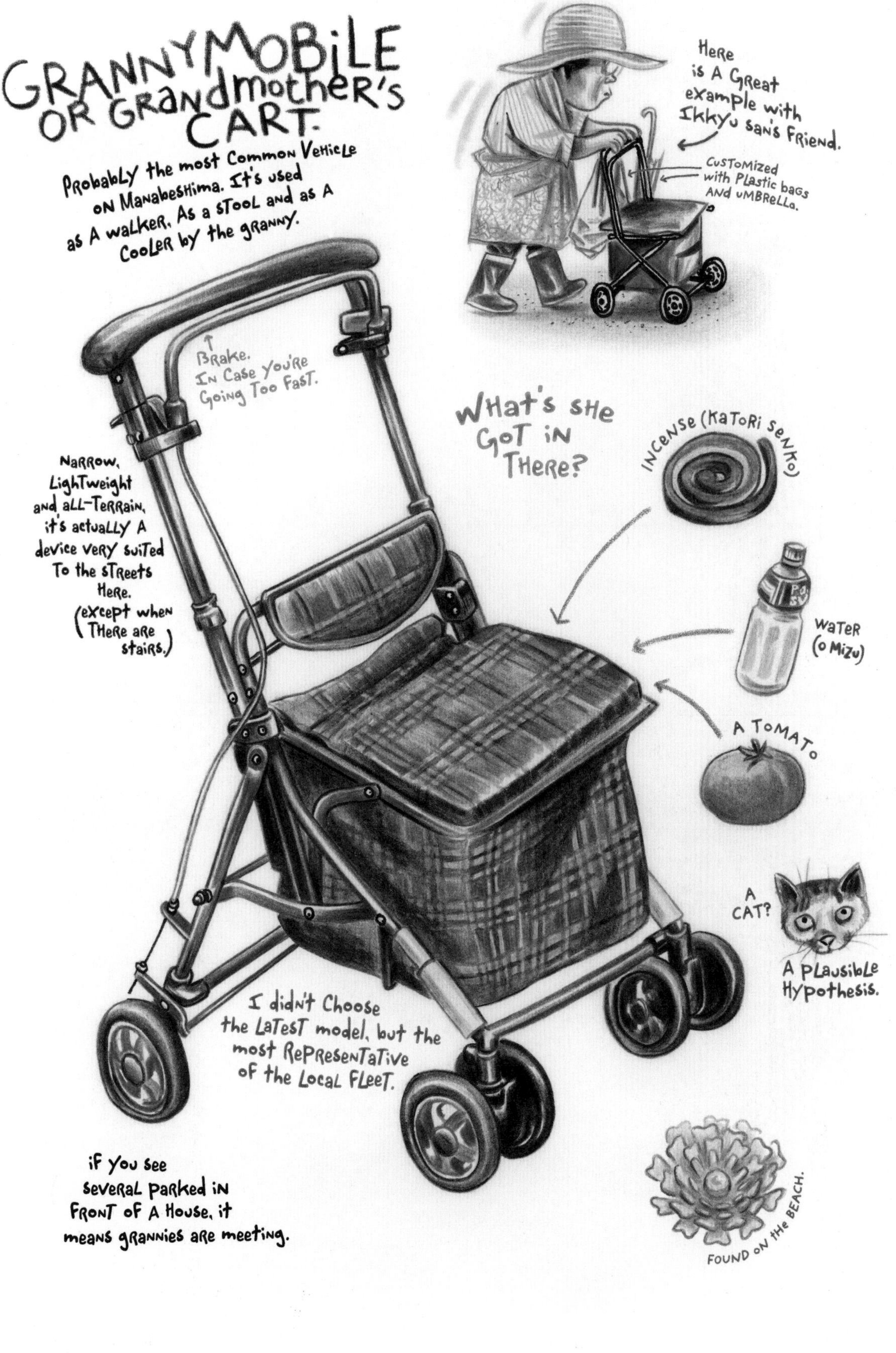
GRANNYMOBILE OR Grandmother's CART.
Probably the most Common Vehicle on Manabeshima. It's used as A walker, As a stool and as A Cooler by the granny.
Here is A Great example with Ikkyu san's Friend.
Customized with Plastic bags And umbrella.
Brake. In Case You're Going Too Fast.
What's she Got in There?
Incense (Katori Senko)
Narrow, Lightweight and all-Terrain, it's actually A device very suited To the streets Here. (except when There are stairs.)
Water (o Mizu)
A Tomato
A CAT?
A Plausible Hypothesis.
I didn't Choose the Latest model, but the most Representative of the Local Fleet.
if You see several parked in Front of A House, it means grannies are meeting.
Found on the beach.

AND FOR GRANNIES
iN MORE oF a HURRY, THeRe's
The MiNi-Car!
THe MISSING LiNK BeTWEEN THe
LAWN MoweR aND
THe AuToMobiLe.

I'd ALReady spotted it
once withouT having The
time To draw it. ShimuRa
saN helped me Track it
down. It belongs To
HISAKo ARAYAMA,
a gRaNNy who Lives at
The NoRth end of
iwatsubo PoRt.

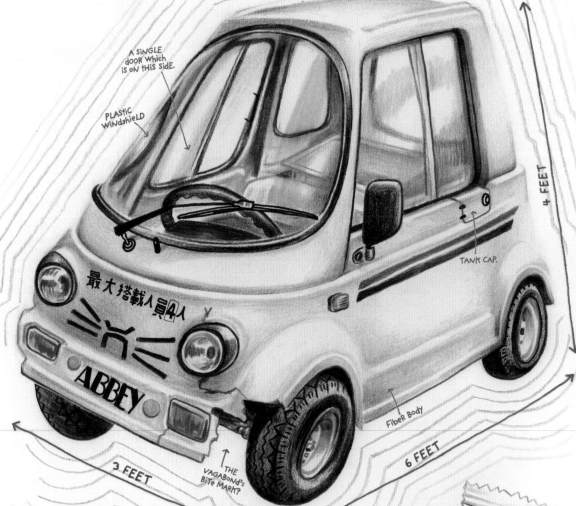

A SiNGLE
dooR Which
IS oN THIS SiDe.

PLAStiC
WiNdshieLD

TANK CAP.

4 FEET

最大搭載人員4人

FibeR Body

ABBEY

THE
VAGABoND's
BiTe MARK?

3 FEET

6 FEET

A gift FRoM SHimuRa:
Cookies FiLLed with Anko
(Red beaN paste, wHich
makes up 90% of
Japanese desseRts.)

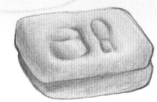

華

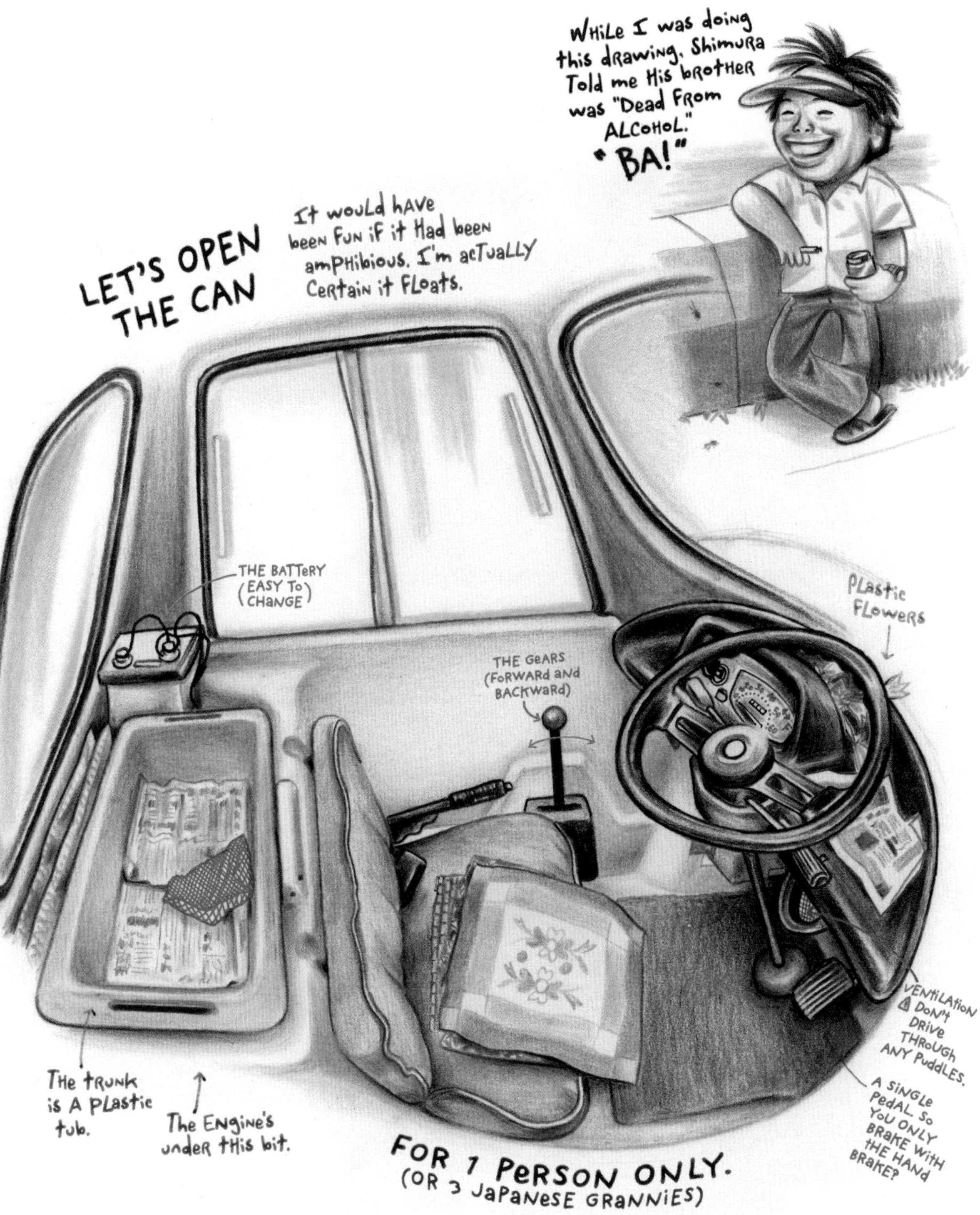
WHiLe I was doing this drawing, Shimura Told me His brother was "Dead From ALCOHoL."
"BA!"
LET'S OPEN THE CAN
It would have been Fun if it Had been amphibious. I'm actually Certain it Floats.
THE BATTery (EASY To CHANGE)
THE GeARS (FoRWARd aNd BACKWARd)
Plastic Flowers
VENtiLAtion ⚠ Don't DRive THROUGH ANY Puddles.
A SiNGLe PedAL. So You ONLY BRAKE WITH tHE HAND BRAKE?
The trunk is A PLastic tub.
The Engine's under this bit.
FOR 1 PeRSON ONLY.
(OR 3 JaPaNeSE GRANNiES)

This drawing was difficult to Produce since it was done while standing up To peer in From the side window (and while Resting my Pencils oN the Roof).
I would Have Liked SHimura san to be my easel, but I HAD No idea How To say easel.

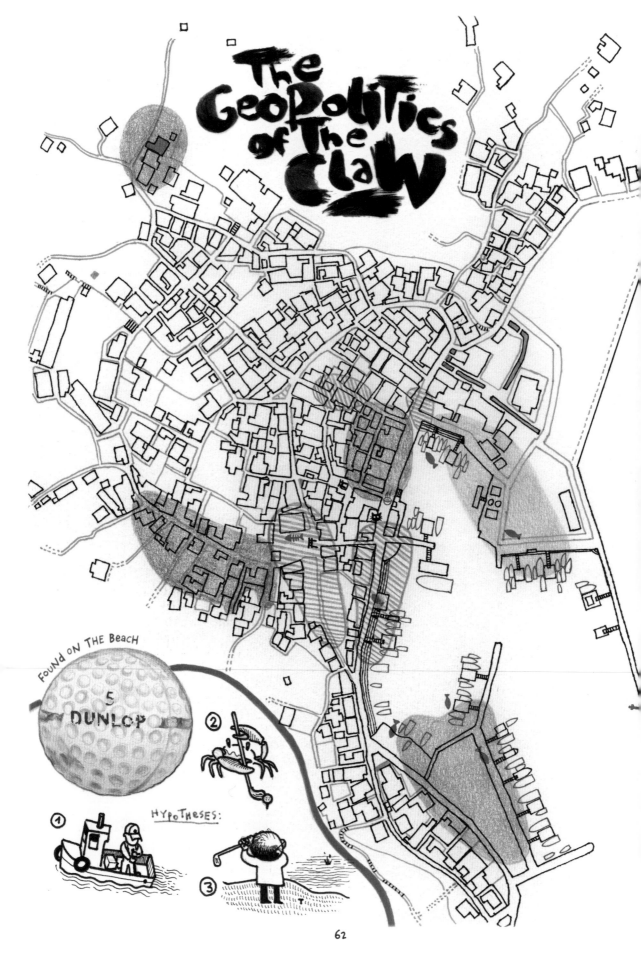

The GeoPolitics of The Claw

FOUND ON THE BEACH

5 DUNLOP

HYPOTHESES:

① ② ③

CAT GANGS

Black book of whiskered small-time delinquents.

KINGPIN'S GANG.

THE BACKUP

6 or 8 Members, all adults and submissive to the super boss, the "Kingpin", the island's Toughest Cat. It's also in this gang that you find "Fleabag", the island's weakest.

THE A-DOCKS GANG.

5-8 Members. Kittens, Couples. Weakened by the recent loss of a member (by drowning).

THE TOWN GANG.

VERY YELLOW

How many Members? They don't know themselves. Hang out in the Vegetable Patch in front of the house with the Tree (Page 93) and in a nearby alley. All very lazy. They all know my drawings.

THE B-DOCKS GANG.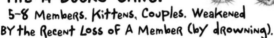

Between 5 and 10 Members. Hard to say. But several kittens. New blood in other words. but Rather disorganized. To Each His Fish. Sleep regularly Aboard the boats.

THE Hippies

Between 12 and 15 Members, more or less from the same family. Have questionable sexual and social morals (incest, They all squat at the house of a granny that lives on the outskirts of the village, (Pedophilia, swinging ...) up a hill. Slightly marginalized gang.

CONFLICT ZONES

And no un peacekeeping force in operation

 MARO, Ikkyu san's Cat. Only Cat to have a legit owner. Manages to have good relationships with the A-Docks Cats while keeping his own small Territory. (The bar's hallway, the Kaisōten...).

SOURCES of food.

LEFTOVERS FROM the OCCASIONAL BARBECUES AT the GORI-GORI.

BOWL of UDON Provided every day by the Granny next door to ikkyu san (on the right). Exclusively Reserved for Kingpin's gang.

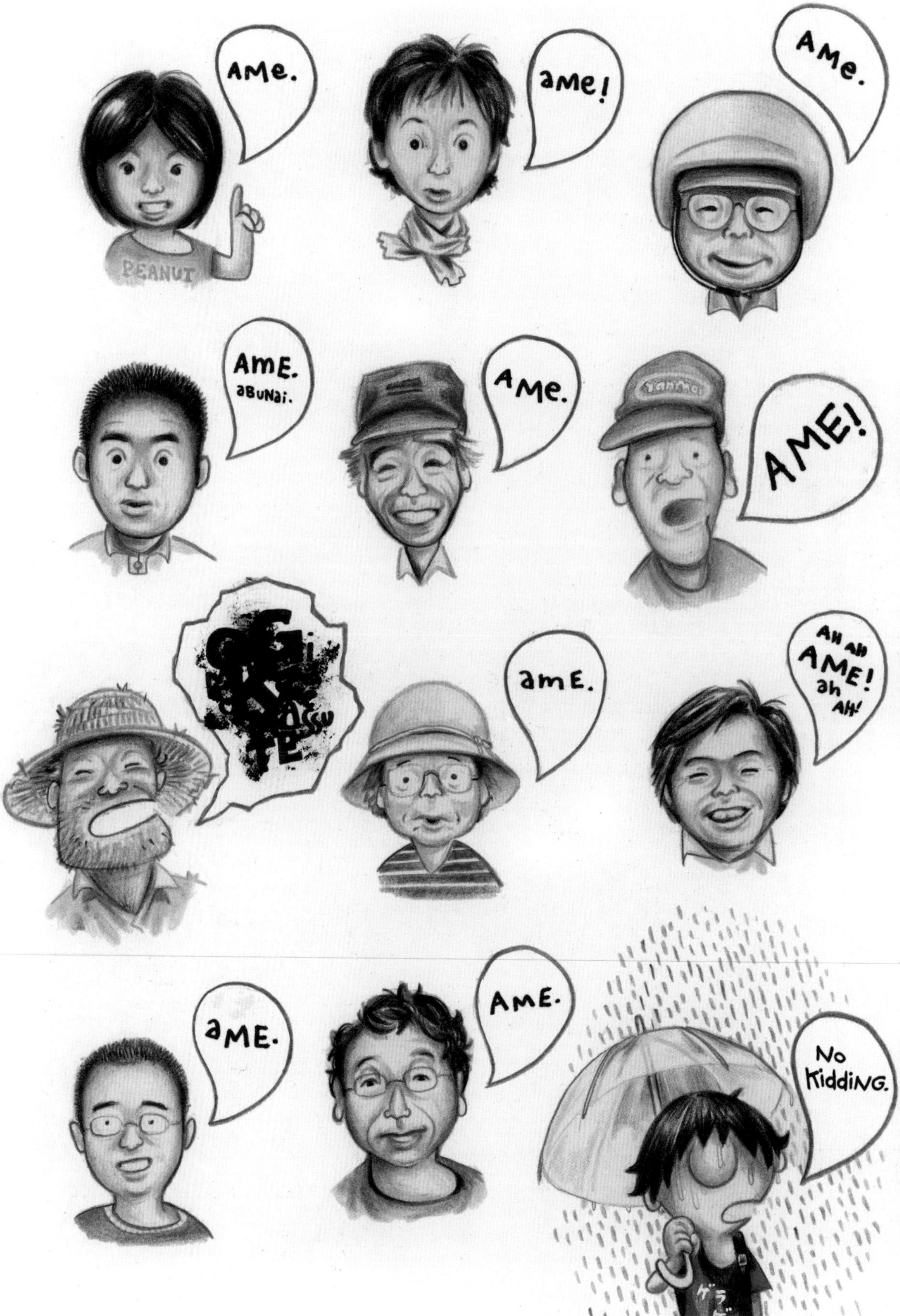
AMe.
PEANUT
ame!
AMe.
AME.
aBuNai.
AMe.
AME!
amE.
AH AH
AME!
ah
AH!
aME.
AME.
No
KiddiNG.
ゲラゲラ

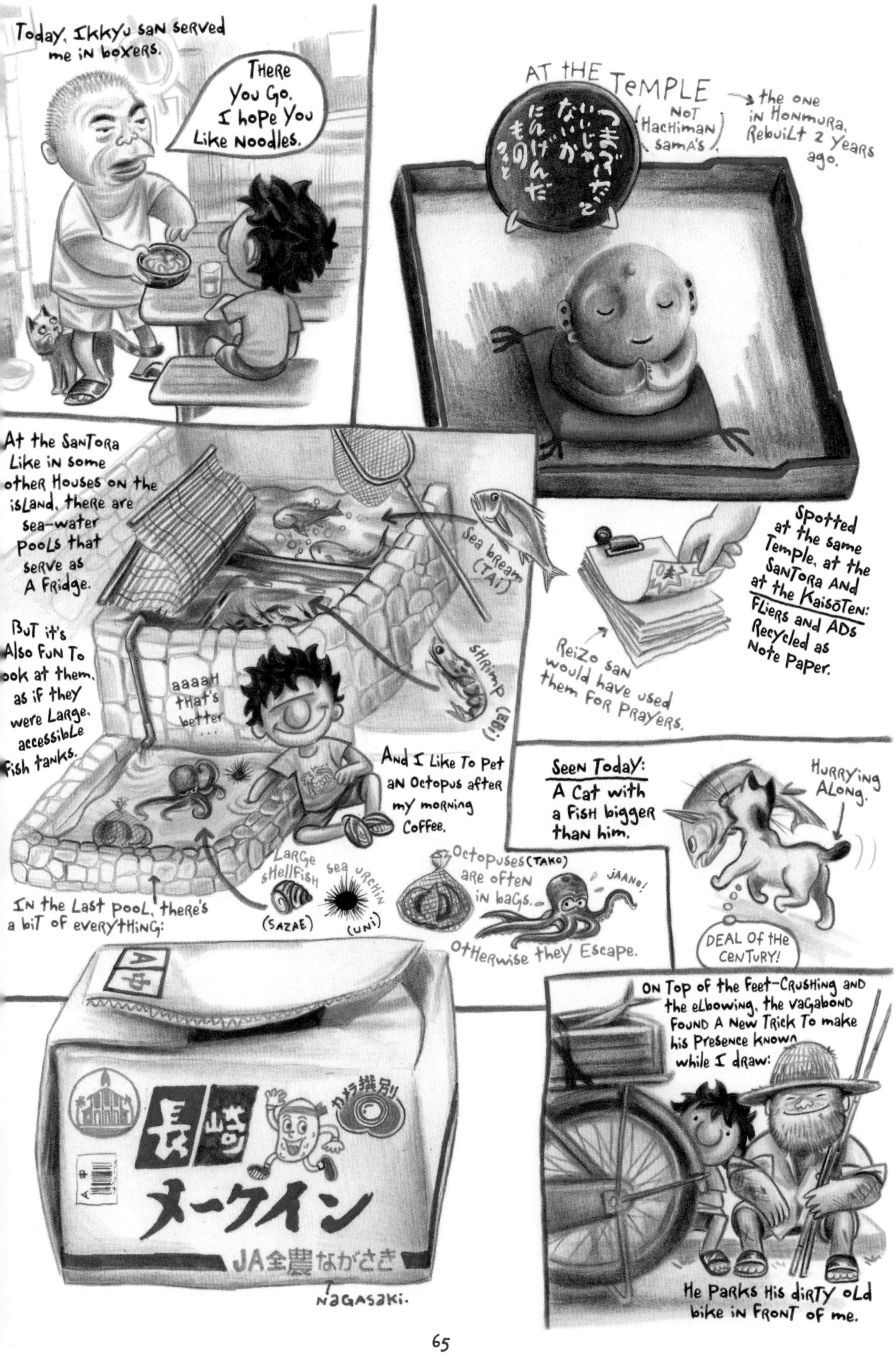

Today, Ikkyu san served me in boxers.
There you go. I hope you like noodles.
AT THE TEMPLE
(NOT HACHIMAN SAMA'S)
→ the one in Honmura, rebuilt 2 years ago.
つまづいたって
いいじゃないか
にんげんだ
もの
At the SanTora like in some other houses on the island, there are sea-water pools that serve as a fridge.
But it's also fun to look at them, as if they were large, accessible fish tanks.
Sea bream (TAI)
SHRIMP (EBI)
aaaaH that's better...
And I like to pet an octopus after my morning coffee.
In the last pool, there's a bit of everything:
Large shellfish (SAZAE)
sea urchin (uni)
Octopuses (TAKO) are often in bags...
JAANE!
Otherwise they escape.
Spotted at the same temple, at the SanTora and at the Kaisōten: Fliers and ADs recycled as note paper.
ReiZo san would have used them for prayers.
Seen Today: A cat with a fish bigger than him.
Hurrying along.
DEAL OF THE CENTURY!
長崎
カメラ撰別
メークイン
JA全農ながさき
Nagasaki.
On top of the feet-crushing and the elbowing, the vagabond found a new trick to make his presence known while I draw:
He parks his dirty old bike in front of me.

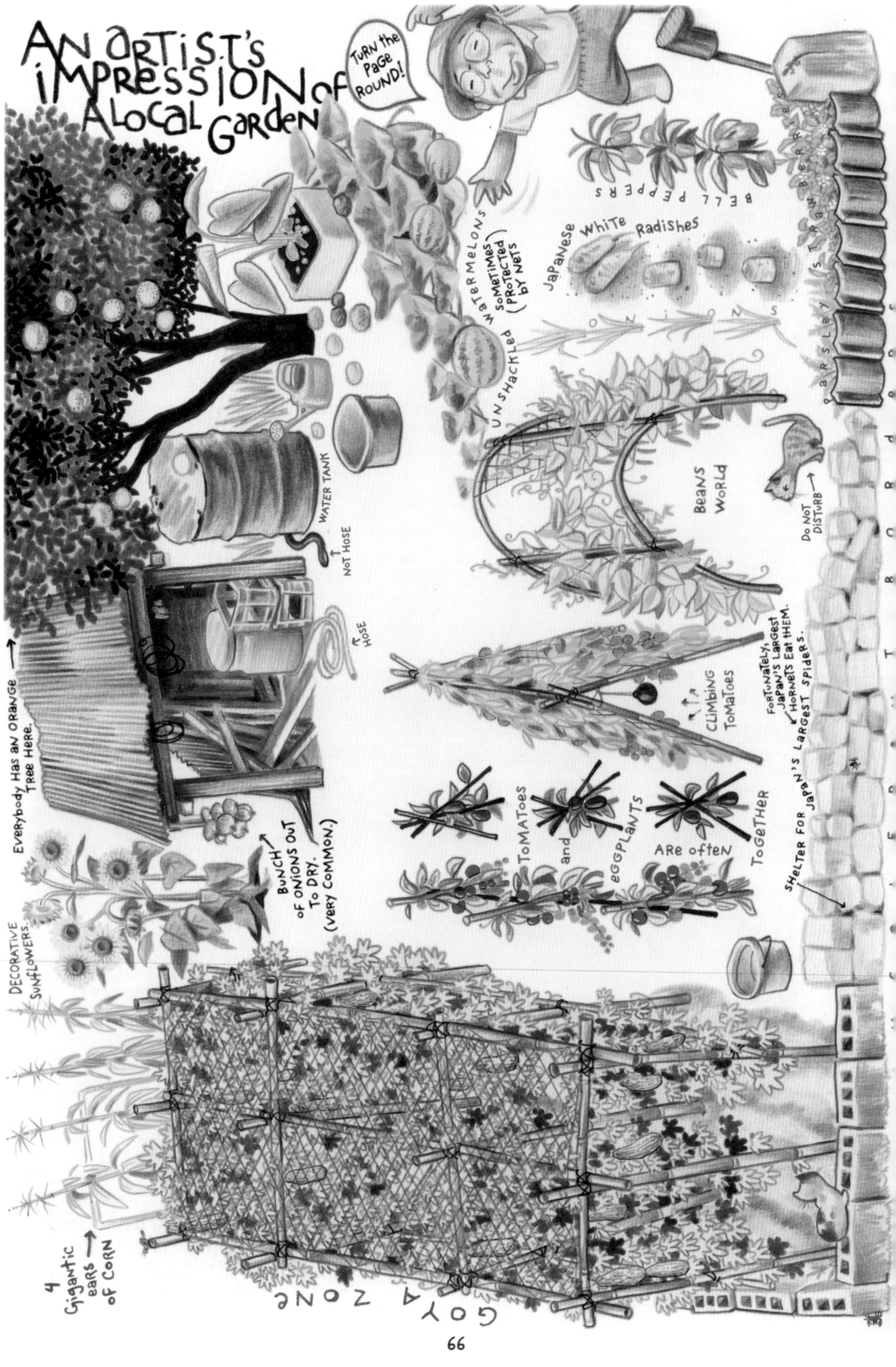

AN ARTIST'S IMPRESSION OF A LOCAL GARDEN
TURN the PaGe ROUND!
Everybody Has an ORANGE Tree Here.
WATER TANK
NOT HOSE
HOSE
UNSHACKLED WATERMELONS SOMETIMES (PROTECTED BY NETS)
JAPANESE WHITE RADISHES
BELL PEPPERS
ONIONS
PARSLEY
STRAWBERRIES
BEANS WORLD
DO NOT DISTURB
CLIMBING TOMATOES
FORTUNATELY, JAPAN'S LARGEST HORNETS EAT THEM.
SHELTER FOR JAPAN'S LARGEST SPIDERS.
TOMATOES and EGGPLANTS ARE often TOGETHER
BUNCH OF ONIONS OUT TO DRY. (VERY COMMON.)
DECORATIVE SUNFLOWERS.
4 Gigantic ears of CORN
GOYA ZONE

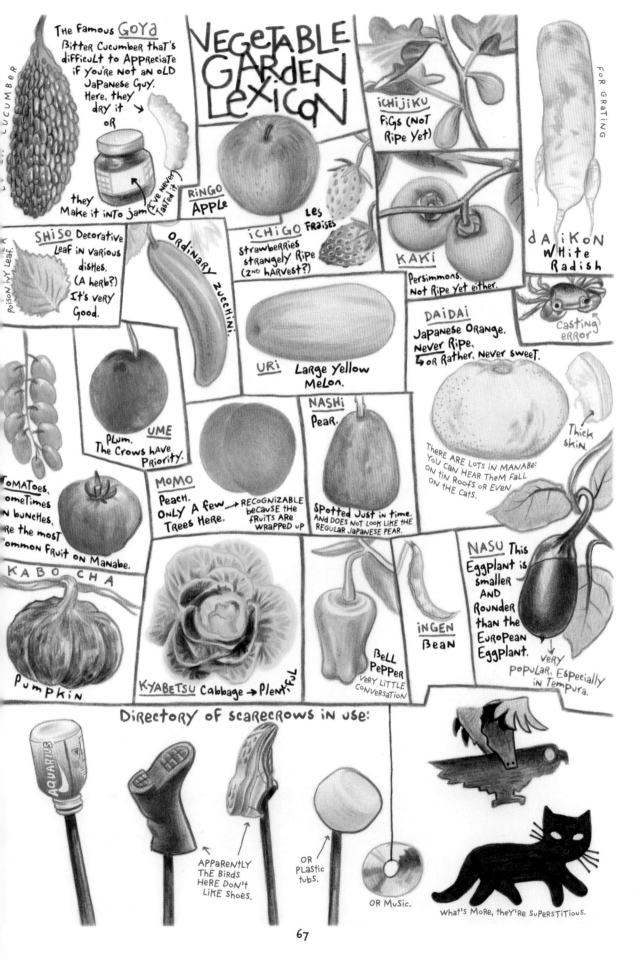

VEGETABLE GARDEN LEXICON

GOYA CUCUMBER

The Famous **GOYA** Bitter Cucumber that's difficult to Appreciate if you're not an OLD Japanese Guy. Here, they dry it or → they Make it into Jam (I've Never Tasted it)

RINGO APPLE

ICHIGO Les Fraises Strawberries strangely Ripe (2nd Harvest?)

ICHIJIKU FiGs (Not Ripe Yet)

For Grating

dAIKON White Radish

POISON IVY LEAF.

SHISO Decorative Leaf in various dishes. (A herb?) It's very Good.

ORDINARY ZUCCHINI.

KAKI Persimmons. Not Ripe Yet either.

Casting error

DAIDAI Japanese ORANGE. Never Ripe, ↳ OR Rather, Never sweet.

Thick skin.

URI Large Yellow Melon.

UME PLUM. The Crows have Priority.

MOMO Peach. ONLY A few Trees Here. → RECOGNIZABLE because the fRuits ARE WRAPPED UP

NASHI Pear. Spotted Just in time. AND DOES Not LOOK LiKE THE REGULAR JAPANESE PEAR.

There ARE LOTS in MANABE. You can HEAR THEM FALL ON TiN RoofS oR EVEN ON THE CATS.

TomAToes, sometimes in bunches, are the most common Fruit on Manabe.

KABO CHA Pumpkin

KYABETSU Cabbage → Plentiful

INGEN Bean

Bell Pepper VERY LiTTLE CONVERSATioN

NASU This Eggplant is smaller AND Rounder than the European Eggplant. ↓ VERY POPULAR, Especially in Tempura.

Directory of scarecrows in use:

AQUARIUS

APPAReNTLY THe BirdS HeRe DON't LiKE SHoes.

OR PLASTIC TUBS.

OR MUSiC.

What's More, THeY'Re SuPeRSTiTious.

67

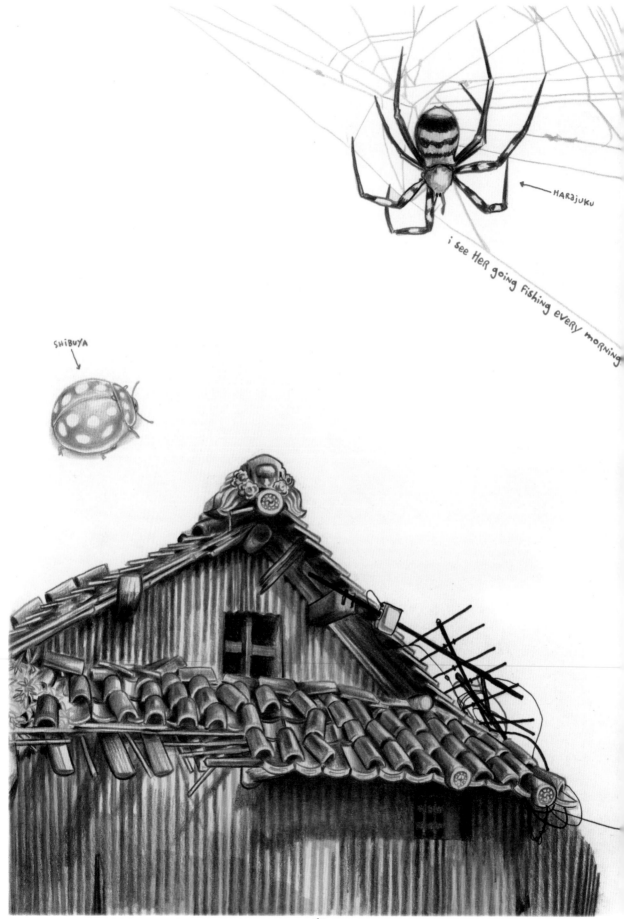

HARAJUKU

i see HeR going fishing every morning

SHIBUYA

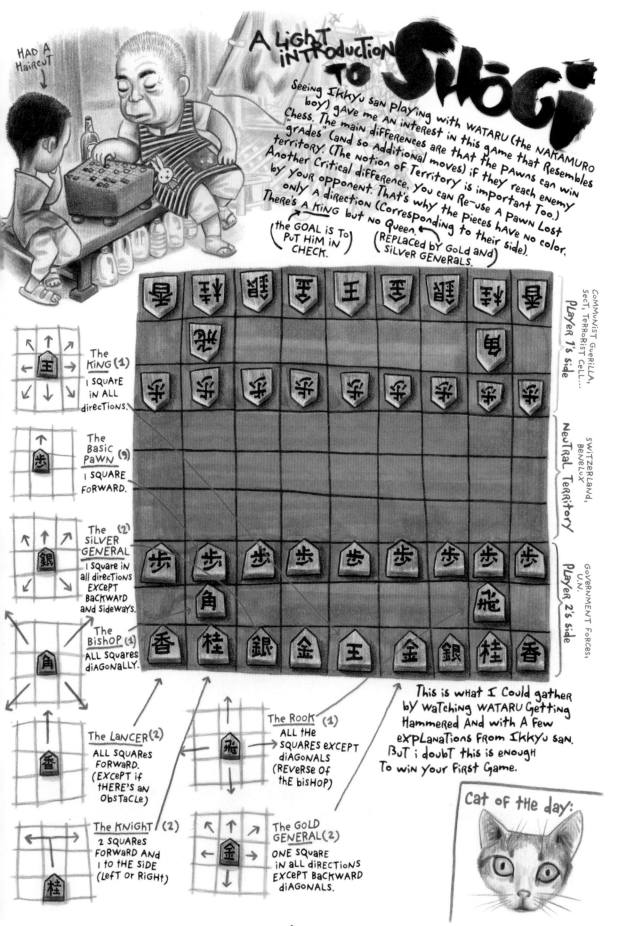

HAD A Haircut →

A LIGHT INTRODUCTION TO SHŌGI

Seeing Ikkyu san playing with WATARU (the NAKAMURO boy) gave me an interest in this game that resembles Chess. The main differences are that the pawns can win "grades" (and so additional moves) if they reach enemy territory. (The notion of Territory is important too.) Another critical difference, you can Re-use a Pawn lost by your opponent. That's why the pieces have no color, only a direction (corresponding to their side).

There's a KING but no Queen.
(the GOAL is to PUT HiM in CHECK.)
(REPLACED by Gold and SILVER GENERALs.)

COMMUNIST GUERILLA, SECT, TERRORIST CELL...
PLAYER 1's side

SWITZERLAND, BENELUX
NEUTRAL TERRITORY

GOVERNMENT FORCES, U.N.
PLAYER 2's side

The KING (1)
1 SQUARE IN ALL directions.

The Basic PAWN (9)
1 SQUARE FORWARD.

The SILVER GENERAL (2)
1 Square in all directions EXCEPT BACKWARD and SIDEWAYS.

The BiSHOP (1)
ALL SQUARES DIAGONALLY.

The LANCER (2)
ALL SQUARES FORWARD. (EXCEPT if THERE'S AN ObSTACLE)

The KNiGHT (2)
2 SQUARES FORWARD AND 1 to THE SIDE (LEFT or RiGHT)

The ROOK (1)
ALL THE SQUARES EXCEPT diAGONALS (REVERSE of tHE biSHOP)

The GOLD GENERAL (2)
ONE SQUARE IN ALL DiRECTIONS EXCEPT BACKWARD DiAGONALS.

This is wHAT I Could gather by watching WATARU Getting Hammered And with A few explanations from Ikkyu san. BuT i doubT this is enough To win your First Game.

Cat of tHe day:

69

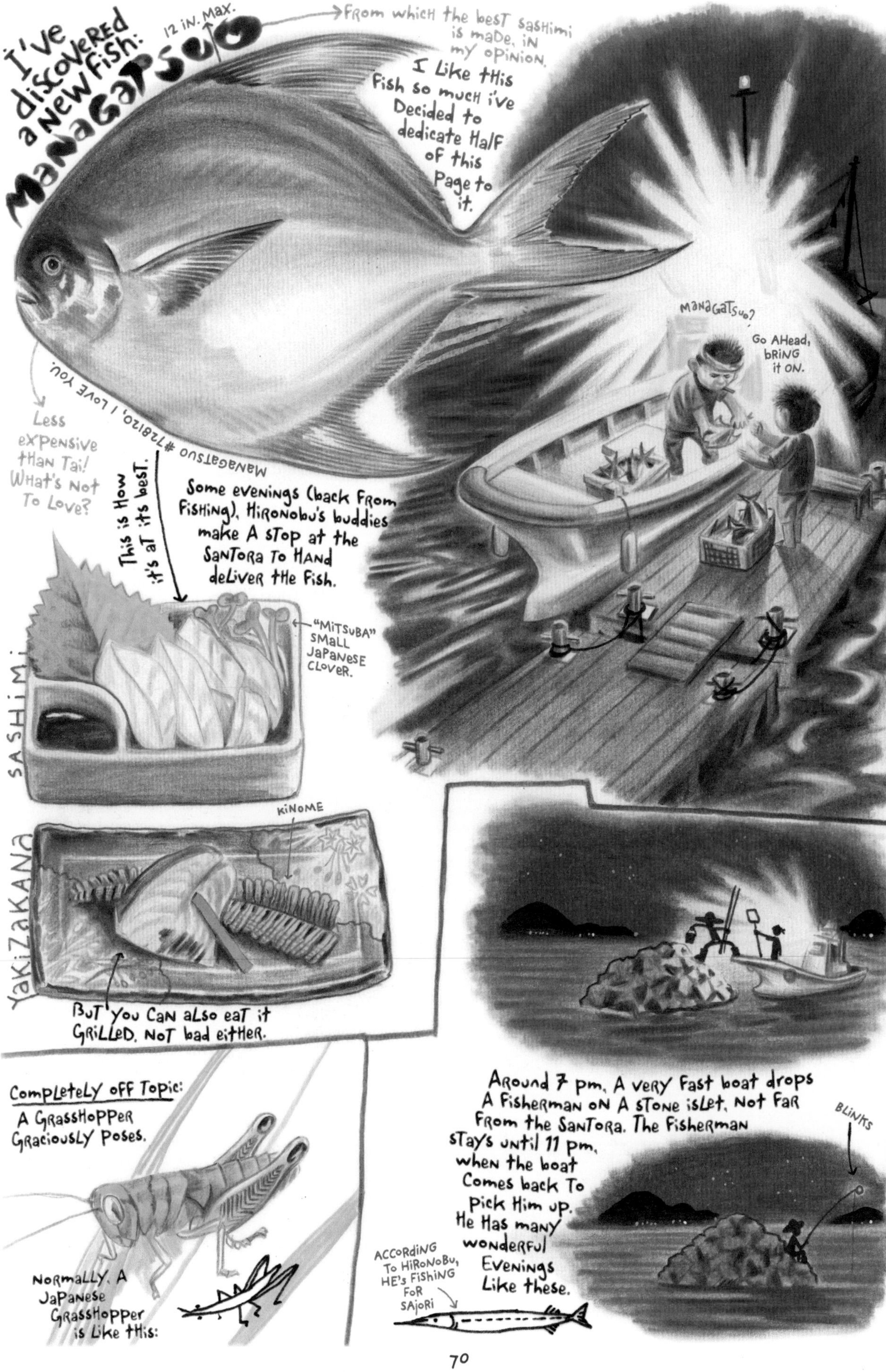
I've discovered a new fish:
Managatsuo
12 in. max.
From which the best sashimi is made, in my opinion.
I like this fish so much I've decided to dedicate half of this page to it.
Managatsuo #728120, I love you.
Less expensive than Tai! What's not to love?
This is how it's at its best.
Some evenings (back from fishing), Hironobu's buddies make a stop at the Santora to hand deliver the fish.
Managatsuo?
Go ahead, bring it on.
Sashimi
"Mitsuba" small Japanese clover.
Kinome
Yakizakana
But you can also eat it grilled, not bad either.
Completely off topic:
A grasshopper graciously poses.
Normally, a Japanese grasshopper is like this:
Around 7 pm, a very fast boat drops a fisherman on a stone islet, not far from the Santora. The fisherman stays until 11 pm, when the boat comes back to pick him up. He has many wonderful evenings like these.
Blinks
According to Hironobu, he's fishing for sajori

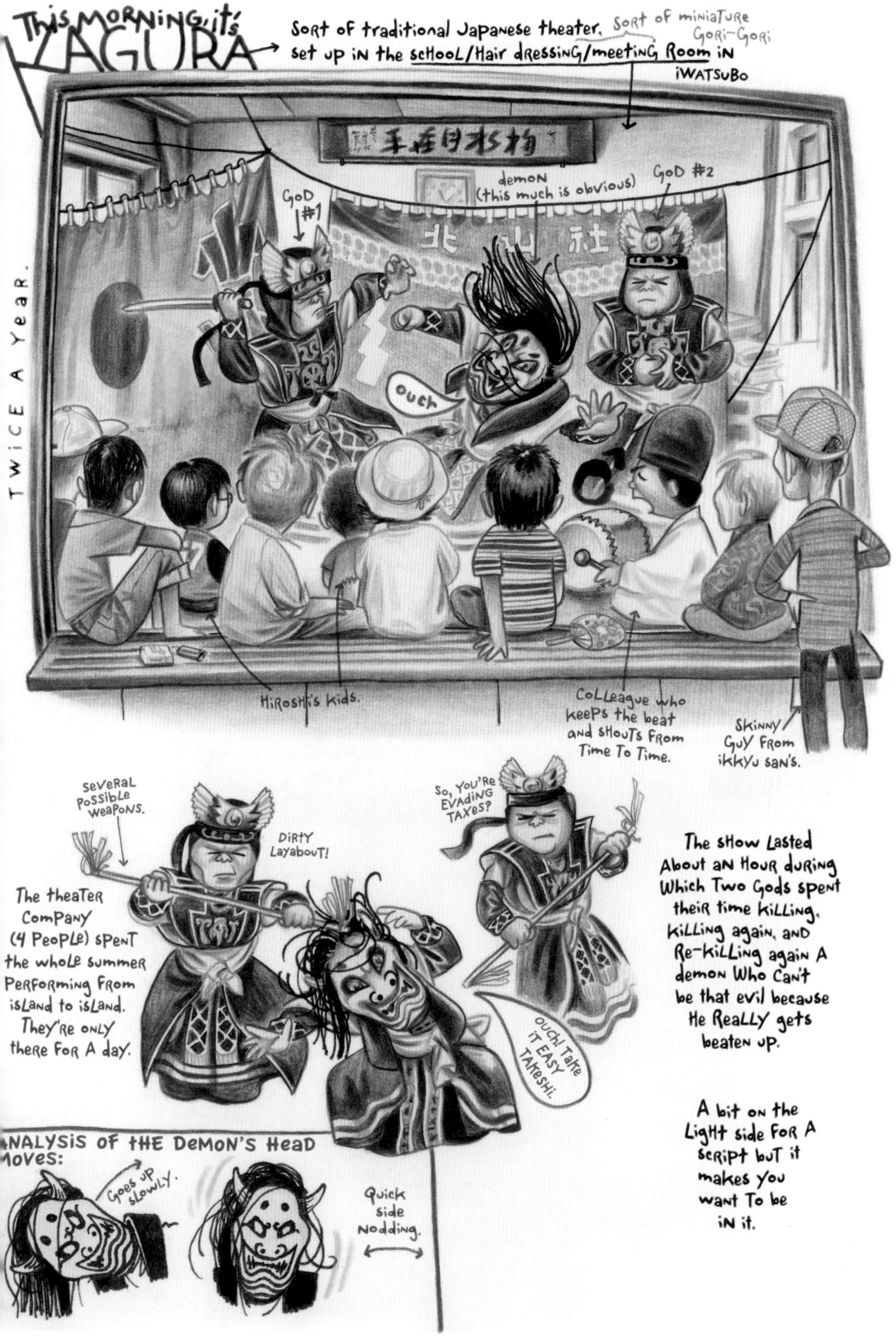
This morning, it's KAGURA
Sort of traditional Japanese theater, set up in the school/hair dressing/meeting room in iwatsubo
Sort of miniature Gori-Gori
Twice a year.
demon (this much is obvious)
GoD #1
GoD #2
ouch
Hiroshi's kids.
Colleague who keeps the beat and shouts from time to time.
Skinny guy from ikkyu san's.
several possible weapons.
Dirty layabout!
So, you're evading taxes?
The theater company (4 people) spent the whole summer performing from island to island. They're only there for a day.
The show lasted about an hour during which two gods spent their time killing, killing again, and re-killing again a demon who can't be that evil because he really gets beaten up.
Ouch! Take it easy Takeshi.
A bit on the light side for a script but it makes you want to be in it.
Analysis of the demon's head moves:
Goes up slowly.
Quick side nodding.

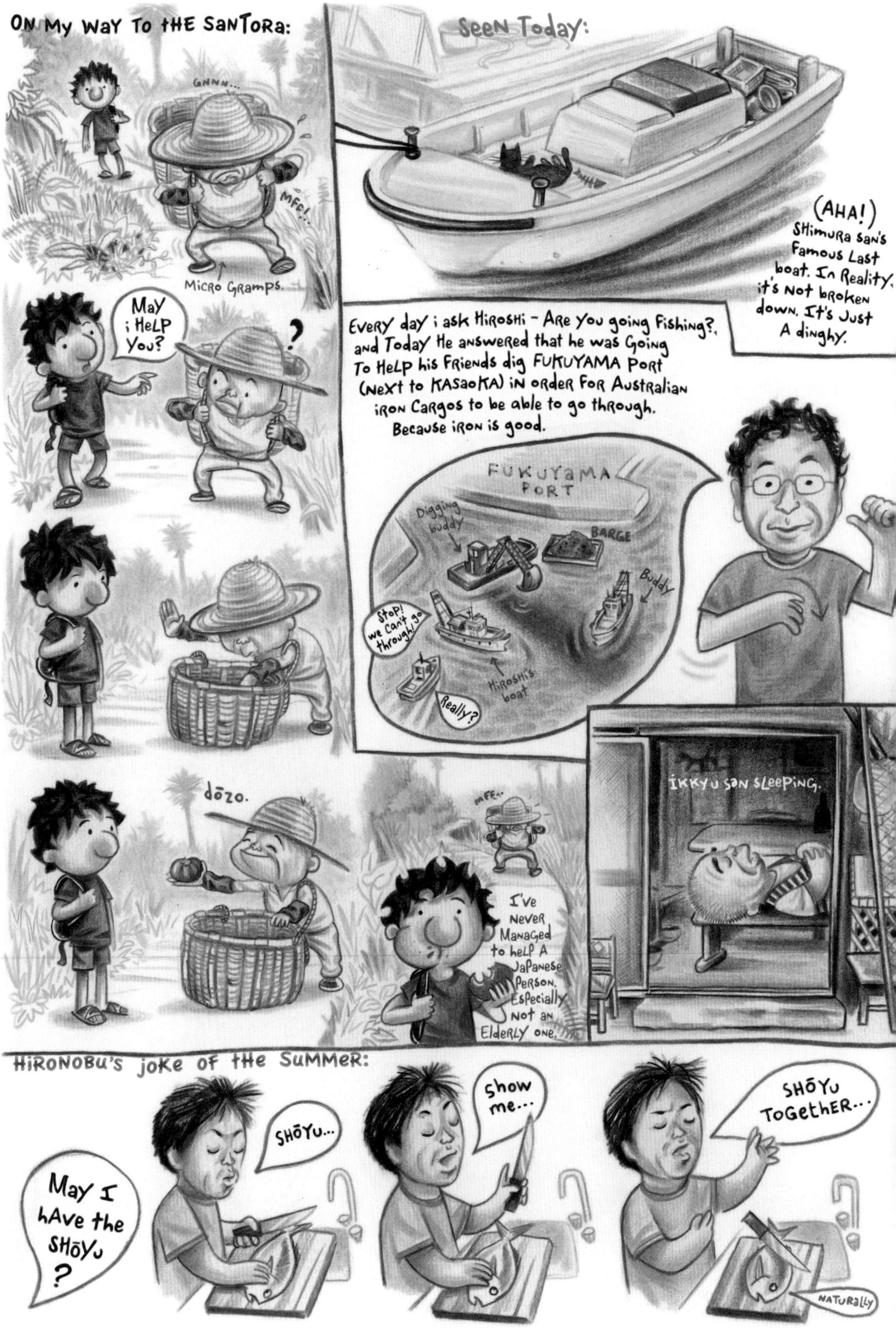
ON MY WAY TO THE SANTORA:
GNNN...
MFF!...
MICRO GRAMPS.
May i HeLP You?
?
dōzo.
MFF...
I've Never Managed to help A Japanese Person. Especially not an Elderly one.
Seen Today:
(AHA!) SHimura san's Famous Last boat. In Reality, it's Not broken down. It's Just A dinghy.
Every day i ask Hiroshi - Are you going Fishing?, and Today He answered that he was Going To HeLP his Friends dig FUKUYAMA Port (Next to KASAOKA) in order For Australian iron Cargos to be able to go through. Because iron is good.
FUKUYAMA PORT
Digging buddy
BARGE
Buddy
Stop! we can't go through!
Hiroshi's boat
Really?
IKKYU SAN SLEEPING.
HIRONOBU's joke of the summer:
May I have the SHŌYu ?
SHŌYU...
Show me...
SHŌYU TOGETHER...
NATURALLY

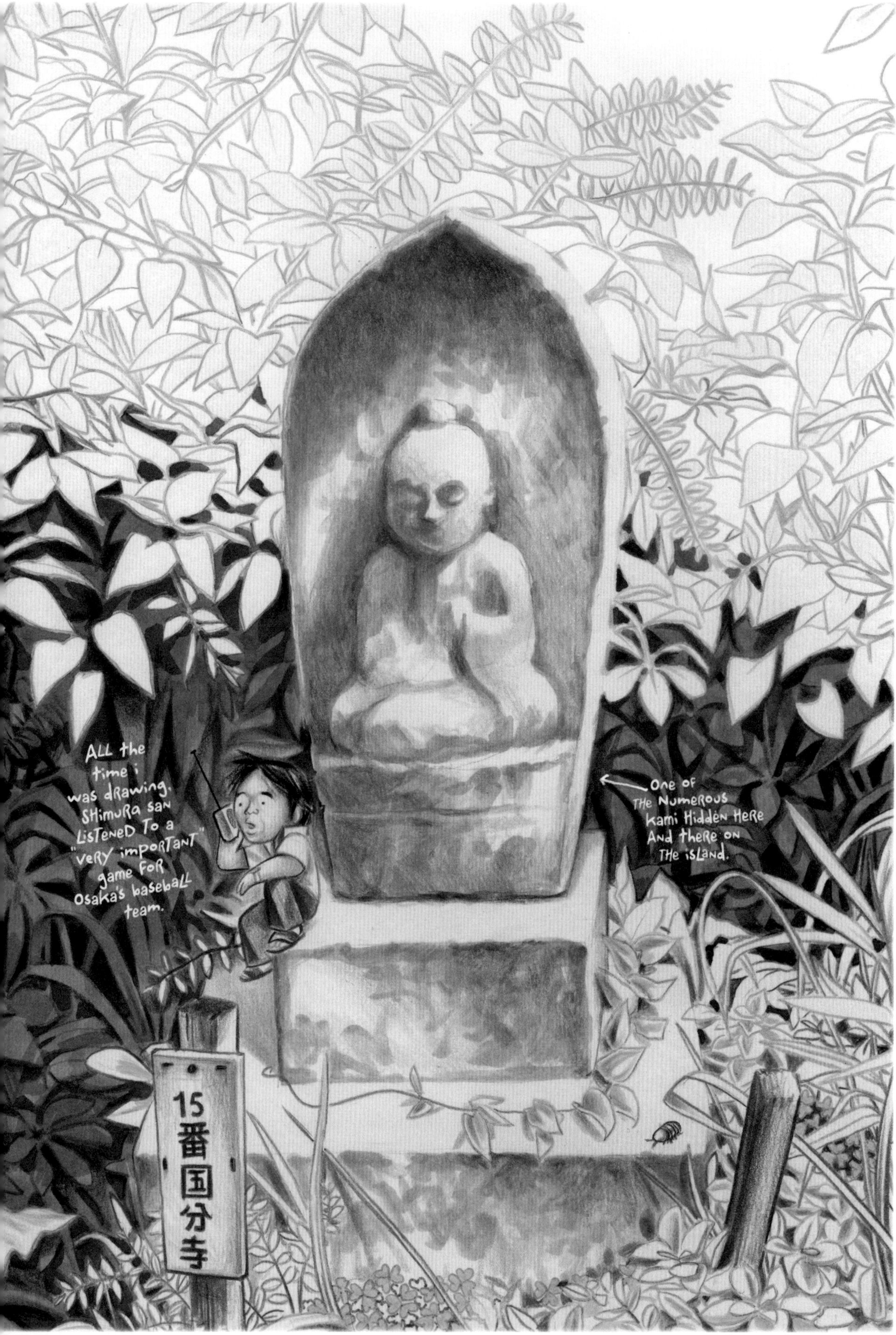
ALL the time i was drawing, SHimuRa san LisTeneD To a "very imporTanT" game FoR Osaka's baseball team.
One of The Numerous kami Hidden Here And there on The isLand.
15番国分寺

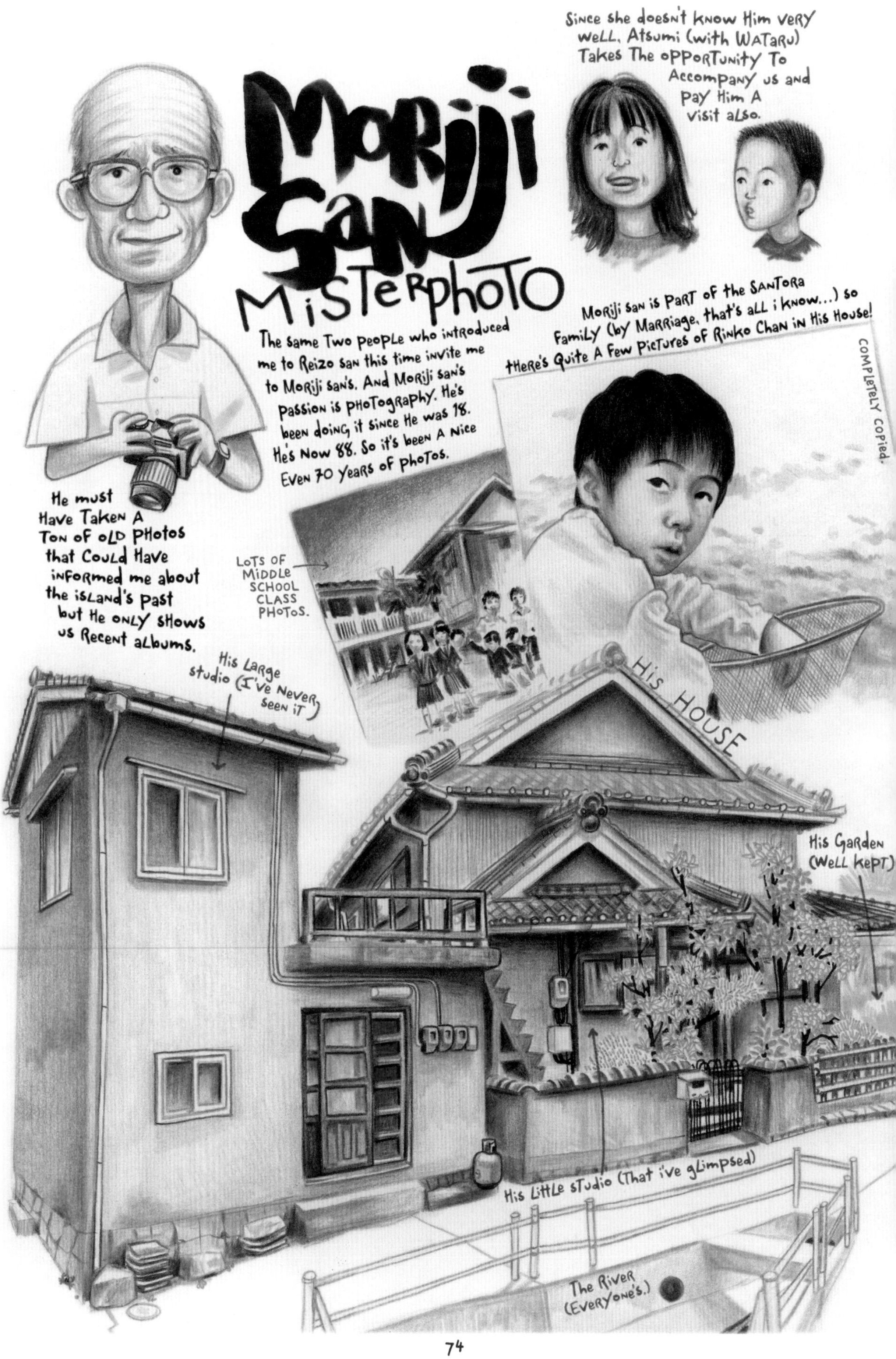
Moriji San
MisterPhoto
Since she doesn't know Him very well, Atsumi (with Wataru) Takes The opportunity To Accompany us and pay Him A visit also.
The same Two people who introduced me to Reizo san this time invite me to Moriji san's. And Moriji san's passion is photography. He's been doing it since He was 18. He's Now 88. So it's been A Nice Even 70 years of photos.
Moriji san is part of the Santora Family (by Marriage, that's all i know...) so there's Quite A Few Pictures of Rinko Chan in His House!
Completely copied.
He must Have Taken A Ton of old Photos that Could Have informed me about the island's past but He only shows us Recent albums.
Lots of Middle School Class Photos.
His Large studio (I've Never seen it)
His House
His Garden (Well kept)
His Little Studio (That i've glimpsed)
The River (Everyone's.)

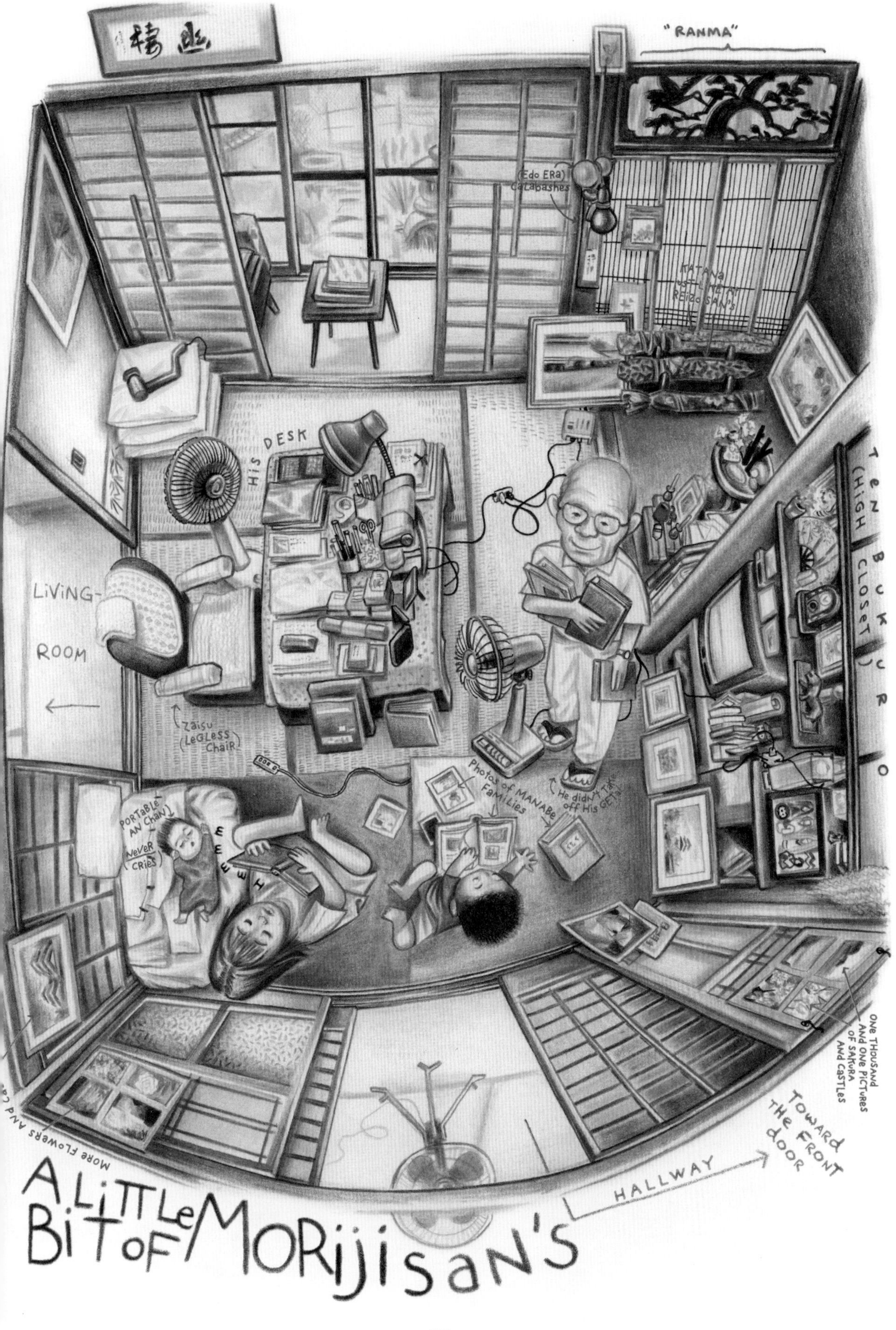
"RANMA"
(Edo ERa) Calabashes
HIS DESK
TEN BUKURO (HIGH CLOSET)
LIVING-ROOM
Zaisu (LeGLESS Chair)
PORTABLE AN CHAN NEVER CRIES
Photos of MANABE Families
He didn't take off His GETa
ONE THOUSAND AND ONE PICTURES OF SAKURA AND CASTLES
TOWARD THE FRONT door
HALLWAY
A LITTLE BIT OF MORIJISAN'S

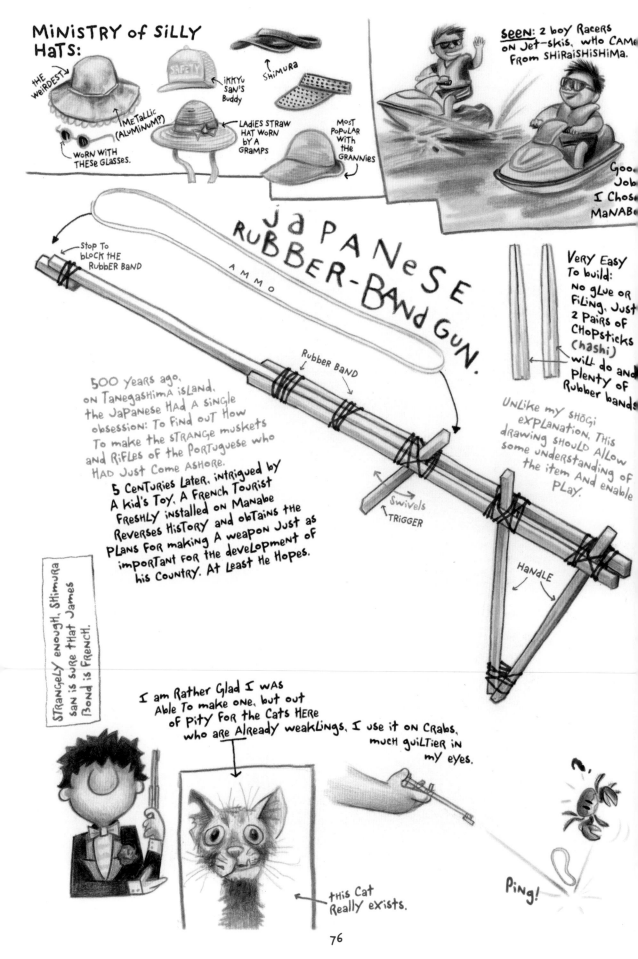

MINISTRY of SILLY HATS:

THE WEIRDEST

METALLIC (ALUMINUM?)

WORN WITH THESE GLASSES.

IKKYU SAN'S Buddy

SHIMURA

LADIES STRAW HAT WORN BY A GRAMPS

MOST POPULAR WITH THE GRANNIES

SEEN: 2 boy Racers on Jet-skis, who came from SHIRAISHISHIMA.

Good Job I Chose MANABE

JaPANeSE RUBBER-BAND GUN.

STOP TO BLOCK THE RUBBER BAND

AMMO

Rubber BAND

Swivels
TRIGGER

HANDLE

VERY Easy To build: No glue or Filing. Just 2 Pairs of CHOPSTICKS (hashi) will do and Plenty of Rubber bands

UNLIKE my shōgi explanation, This drawing should Allow some understanding of the item And enable PLAY.

500 years ago, on Tanegashima island, the Japanese HAD A single obsession: To find out How To make the STRANGE muskets and Rifles of the Portuguese who HAD Just Come ashore.

5 Centuries Later, intrigued by A kid's Toy, A French Tourist Freshly installed on Manabe Reverses History and obtains the Plans for making A weapon Just as important for the development of his Country. At Least He Hopes.

STRANGELY enough, SHimura san is sure that James Bond is French.

I am Rather Glad I was Able To make one, but out of Pity For the Cats HERE who are Already weaklings, I use it on Crabs, much guiltier in my eyes.

this Cat Really exists.

PING!

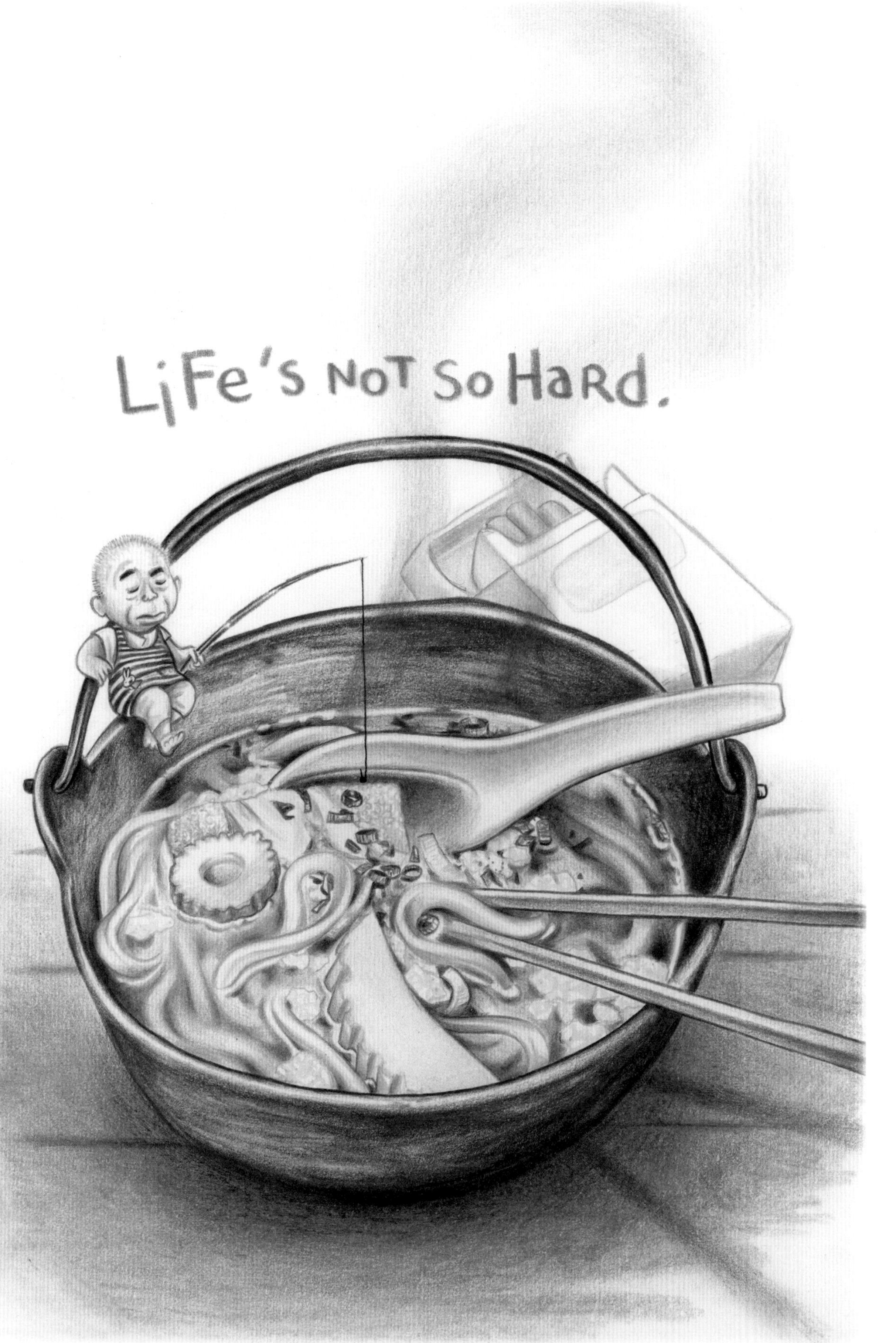
LiFe's NOT So HaRd.

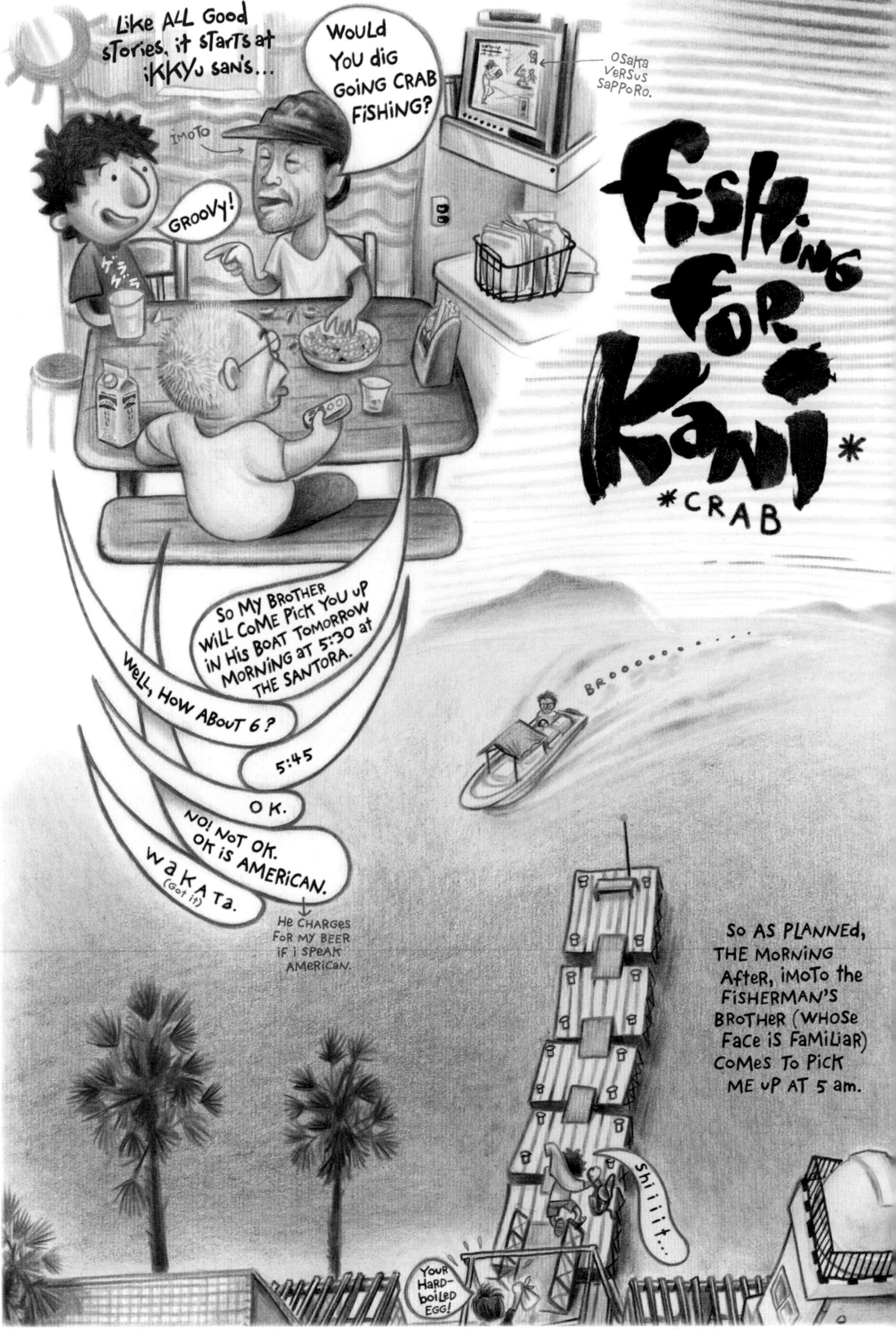

Like ALL Good stories, it starts at iKKYu san's...
WOULD YOU dig GOING CRAB FiSHiNG?
IMOTO
GROOVY!
ゲラゲラ
OSaka VeRSuS SaPPoRo.
FiSHING FOR Kani*
*CRAB
So My BROTHER WiLL COME Pick YOU uP in His BOAT TOMORROW MORNiNG at 5:30 at THE SANTORA.
WeLL, HOW ABOUT 6?
5:45
OK.
NO! NOT OK. OK iS AMERiCAN.
waKATa. (Got it)
He CHARGES FOR MY BEER iF i SPeaK AMERiCaN.
BROOOOOOO......
So AS PLANNEd, THE MORNiNG AfteR, iMoTo the FiSHERMAN'S BROTHER (WHOSe Face is FaMiLiaR) CoMes To PicK ME uP AT 5 am.
Shiiiiit...
YOUR HARD-boiLeD EGG!

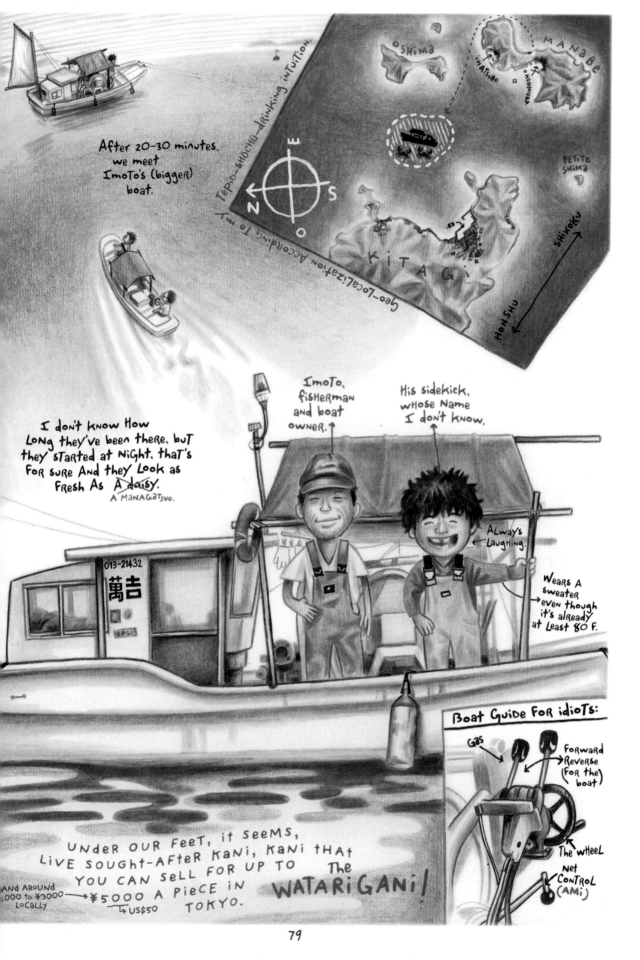

After 20-30 minutes, we meet Imoto's (bigger) boat.

Tepid-shochu-drinking intuition.

Geo-localization according to my

OSHIMA

IWATSUBO

MANABE

HONMURA

PETITE SHIMA

KITAGI

SHIKOKU

HONSHU

Imoto, fisherman and boat owner. ↑

His sidekick, whose name I don't know.

I don't know how long they've been there, but they started at night, that's for sure And they look as fresh as ~~a daisy~~. A MANAGATSUO.

Always Laughing.

Wears a sweater even though it's already at least 80 F.

013-21432
萬吉

Boat Guide for idiots:

Gas

Forward Reverse (For the boat)

The wheel

Net Control (AMI)

UNDER OUR FEET, it seems, LIVE SOUGHT-AFTER KANI, KANI THAT YOU CAN SELL FOR UP TO ¥5000 A PIECE IN TOKYO.
The WATARI GANI!

And around 1,000 to ¥3000 locally → ↳ US$50

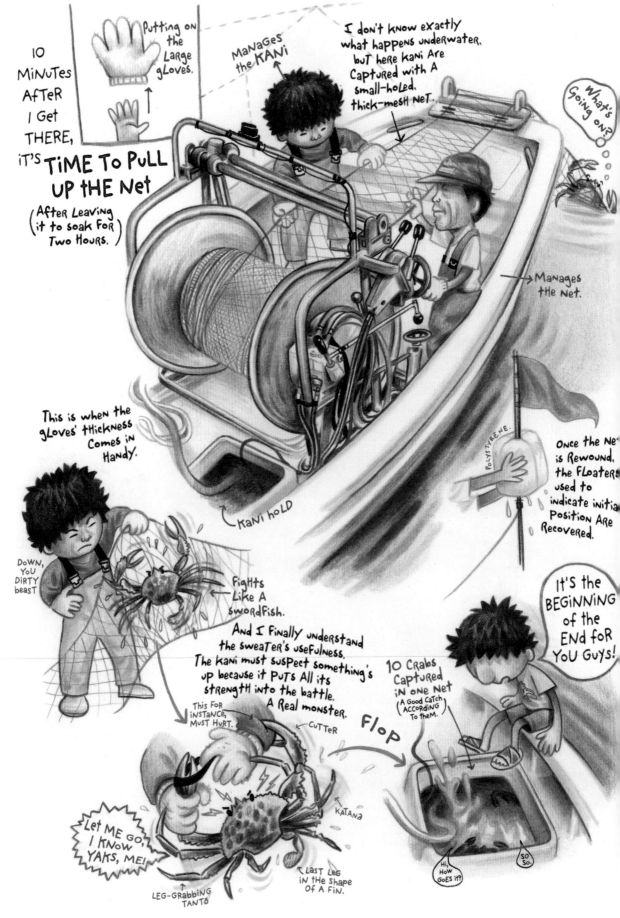

10 MINUTES AFTER I GET THERE, IT'S **TIME TO PULL UP THE NET** (After Leaving it to soak for Two Hours.)

Putting on the Large gloves.

MANAGES the KANI

I don't know exactly what happens underwater, but here kani Are Captured with A small-holed, thick-mesh Net.

What's going on?

Manages the Net.

This is when the gloves' thickness Comes in Handy.

POLYSTYRENE.

Once the Net is Rewound, the Floaters used to indicate initial Position Are Recovered.

KANI hOLD

DOWN, YOU DIRTY beast

Fights Like A swordfish.

And I Finally understand the sweater's usefulness. The kani must suspect something's up because it PuTs All its strength into the battle. A Real monster.

This FOR INSTANCE, MUST HURT.

CUTTER

Flop

It's the BEGINNING of the END FOR YOU Guys!

10 Crabs Captured IN one Net (A Good CATCH ACCORDING To them.)

KATANA

Let ME GO, I KNOW YAKS, ME!

LEG-GRABBING TANTO

LAST LEG IN THE SHAPE OF A FIN.

Hi, HOW GOES it?

SO SO.

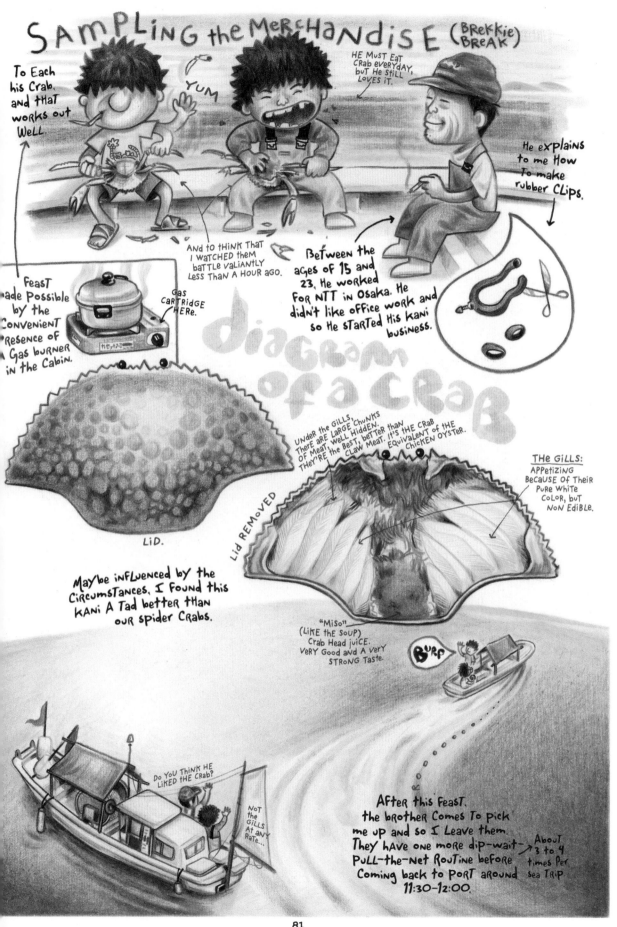

SAMPLING the MERCHANDISE (BREKKIE BREAK)

To Each his Crab. and that works out well.

YUM

HE MUST Eat Crab everyday, but He still loves it.

He explains to me How To make rubber Clips.

AND TO THINK THAT I WATCHED THEM BATTLE VALIANTLY LESS THAN A HOUR AGO.

Between the ages of 15 and 23, He worked for NTT in Osaka. He didn't like office work and so He started His kani business.

Feast ade Possible by the Convenient Resence of Gas burner in the Cabin.

GAS CARTRIDGE HERE.

Diagram of a Crab

LID.

Lid REMOVED

UNDER the GILLS, THERE ARE LARGE CHUNKS OF MEAT, WELL HIDDEN. THEY'RE the BEST, BETTER THAN CLAW MEAT. IT'S THE CRAB EQUIVALENT OF THE CHICKEN OYSTER.

THE GILLS: APPETIZING BECAUSE OF THEIR PURE WHITE COLOR, BUT NON EDIBLE.

Maybe influenced by the circumstances, I found this KANI A Tad better than our spider Crabs.

"Miso" (LIKE the SOUP) Crab Head juice. VERY Good and A very STRONG Taste.

BURP

Do you Think He LIKED THE Crab?

NOT the GILLS At any Rate...

After this Feast. the brother Comes To pick me up and so I Leave them. They have one more dip-wait-PULL-the-Net Routine before Coming back to PORT around 11:30-12:00.

About 3 to 4 times Per sea Trip

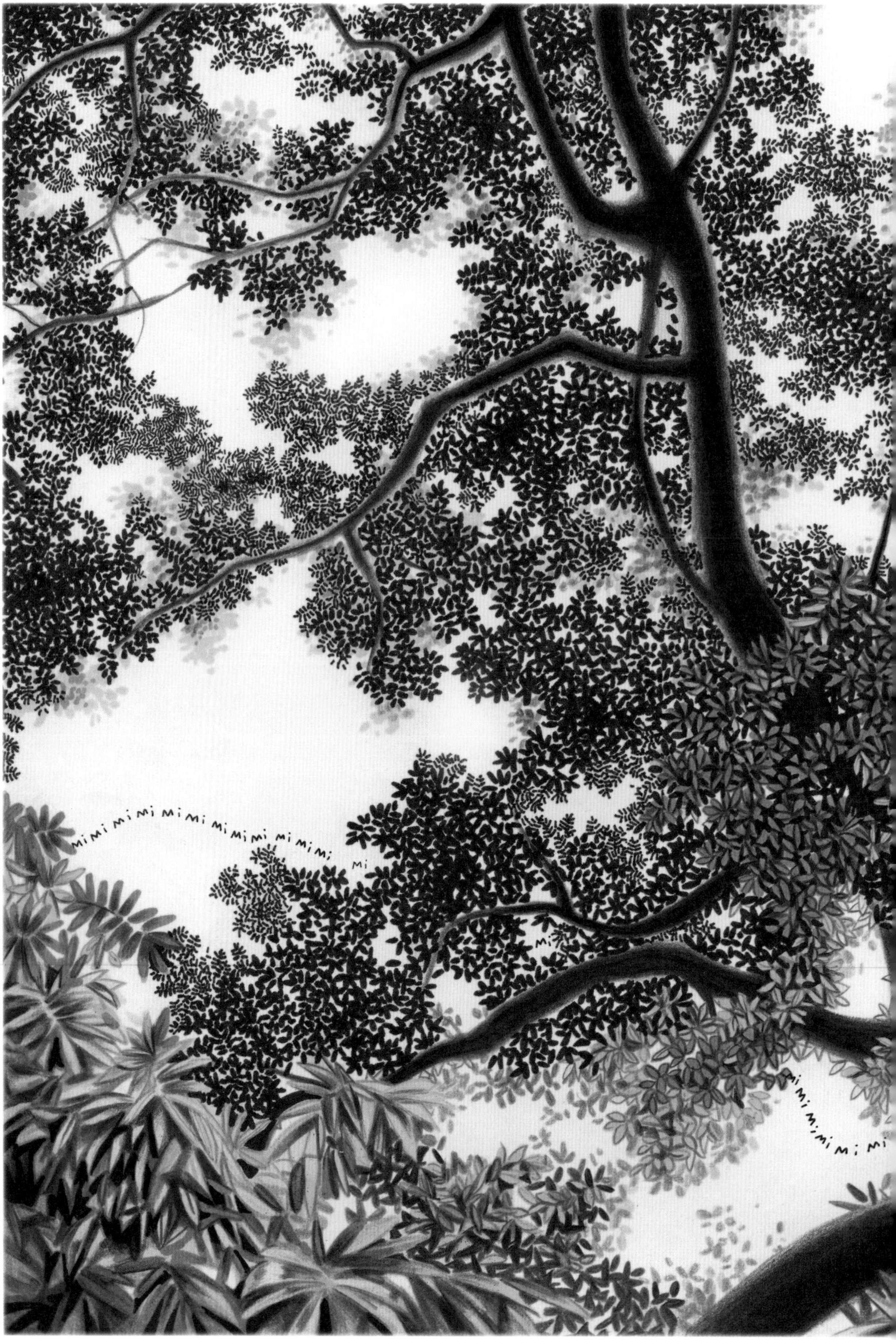
MiMi MiMiMi Mi Mi Mi MiMiMi Mi MiMi Mi
Mi
mi Mi MiMi Mi Mi

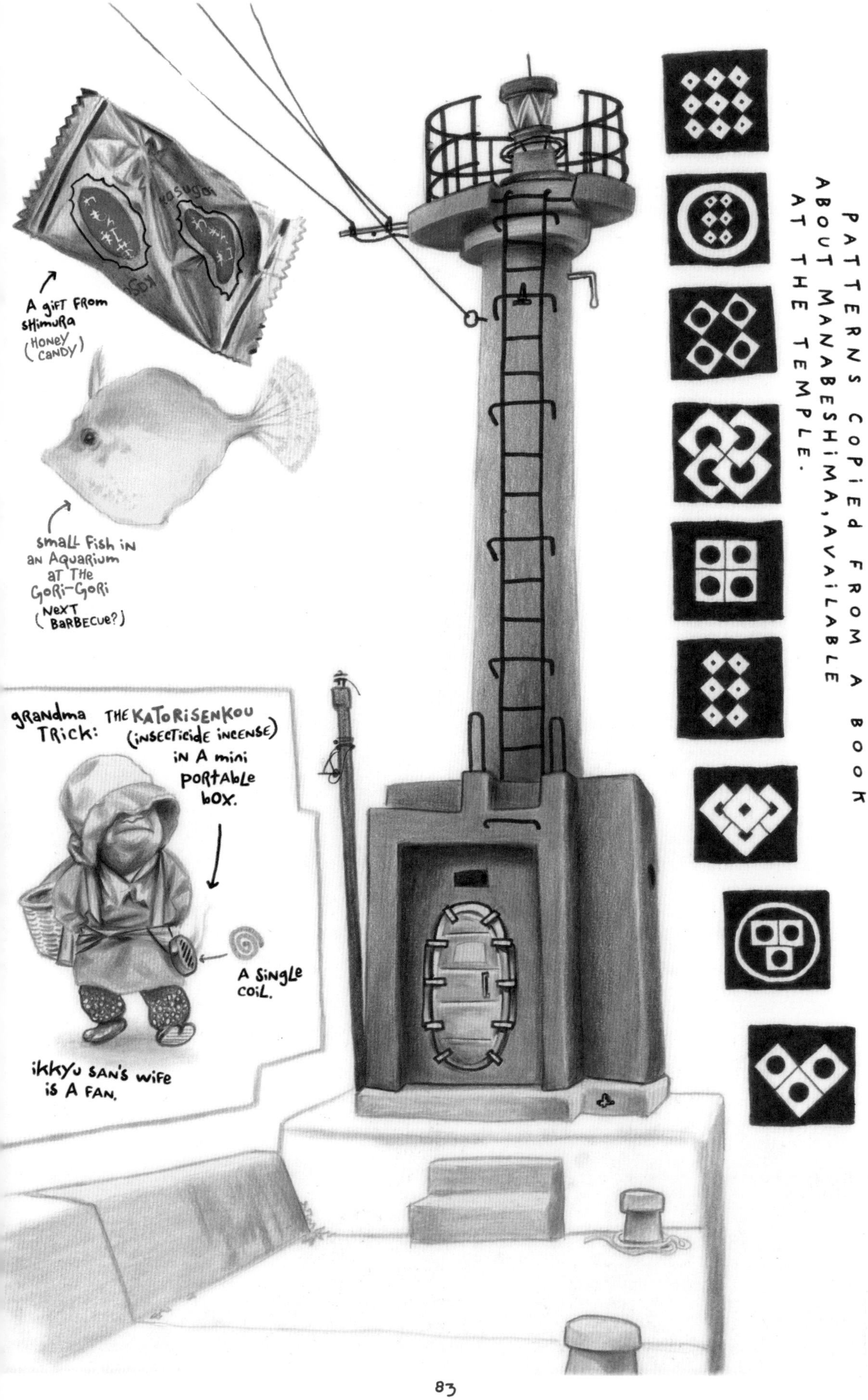

kasugai
A gift from shimura (Honey candy)
small fish in an Aquarium at The Gori-Gori (Next Barbecue?)
grandma Trick: The Katorisenkou (insecticide incense) in A mini portable box.
A single coil.
ikkyu san's wife is A fan.
PATTERNS COPIED FROM A BOOK ABOUT MANABESHIMA, AVAILABLE AT THE TEMPLE.

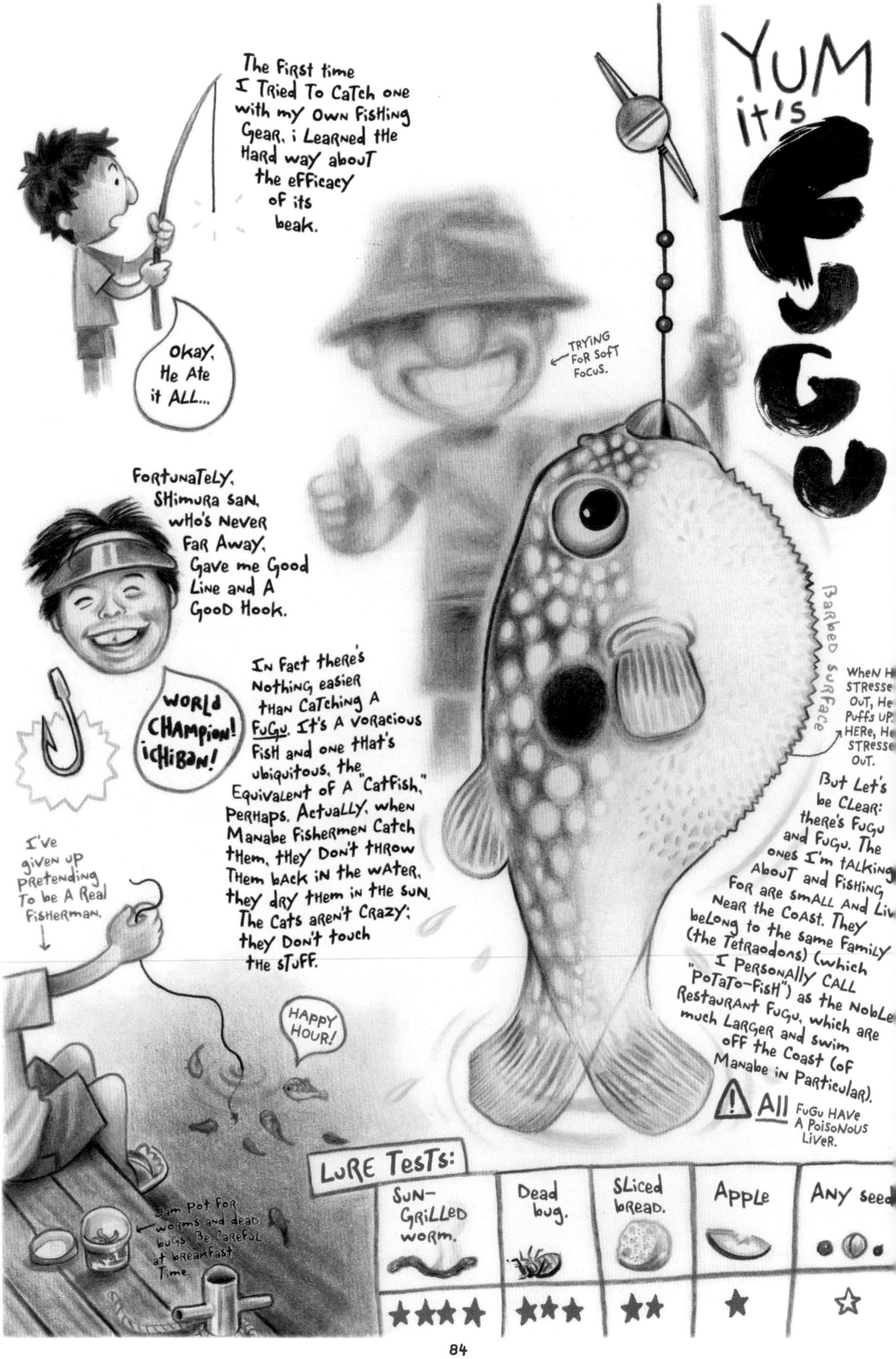
YUM it's FUGU
The First time I Tried To Catch one with my own Fishing Gear, i Learned the Hard way about the efficacy of its beak.
Okay, He Ate it ALL...
TRYING FOR SOFT FOCUS.
Fortunately, Shimura San, who's Never Far Away, Gave me Good Line and A Good Hook.
WORLD CHAMPION! ICHIBAN!
In Fact there's Nothing easier than Catching A Fugu. It's A voracious Fish and one that's ubiquitous, the Equivalent of A "Catfish," Perhaps. Actually, when Manabe Fishermen Catch them, they Don't throw them back in the water, they dry them in the sun. The Cats aren't Crazy; they Don't touch the stuff.
BARBED SURFACE
When H STRESSE OUT, He Puffs UP. HERE, He STRESSE OUT.
But Let's be Clear: there's Fugu and Fugu. The ones I'm talking About and Fishing For are small And Liv Near the Coast. They belong to the same Family (the Tetraodons) (which I Personally CALL "Potato-Fish") as the Noble Restaurant Fugu, which are much Larger and swim off the Coast (of Manabe in Particular).
⚠ All Fugu HAVE A Poisonous Liver.
I've given up pretending To be A Real Fisherman.
HAPPY HOUR!
Jam pot for worms and dead bugs. Be Careful at breakfast Time.
LURE TESTS:
SUN-GRILLED WORM. ★★★★
Dead bug. ★★★
Sliced bread. ★★
Apple ★
Any seed ☆

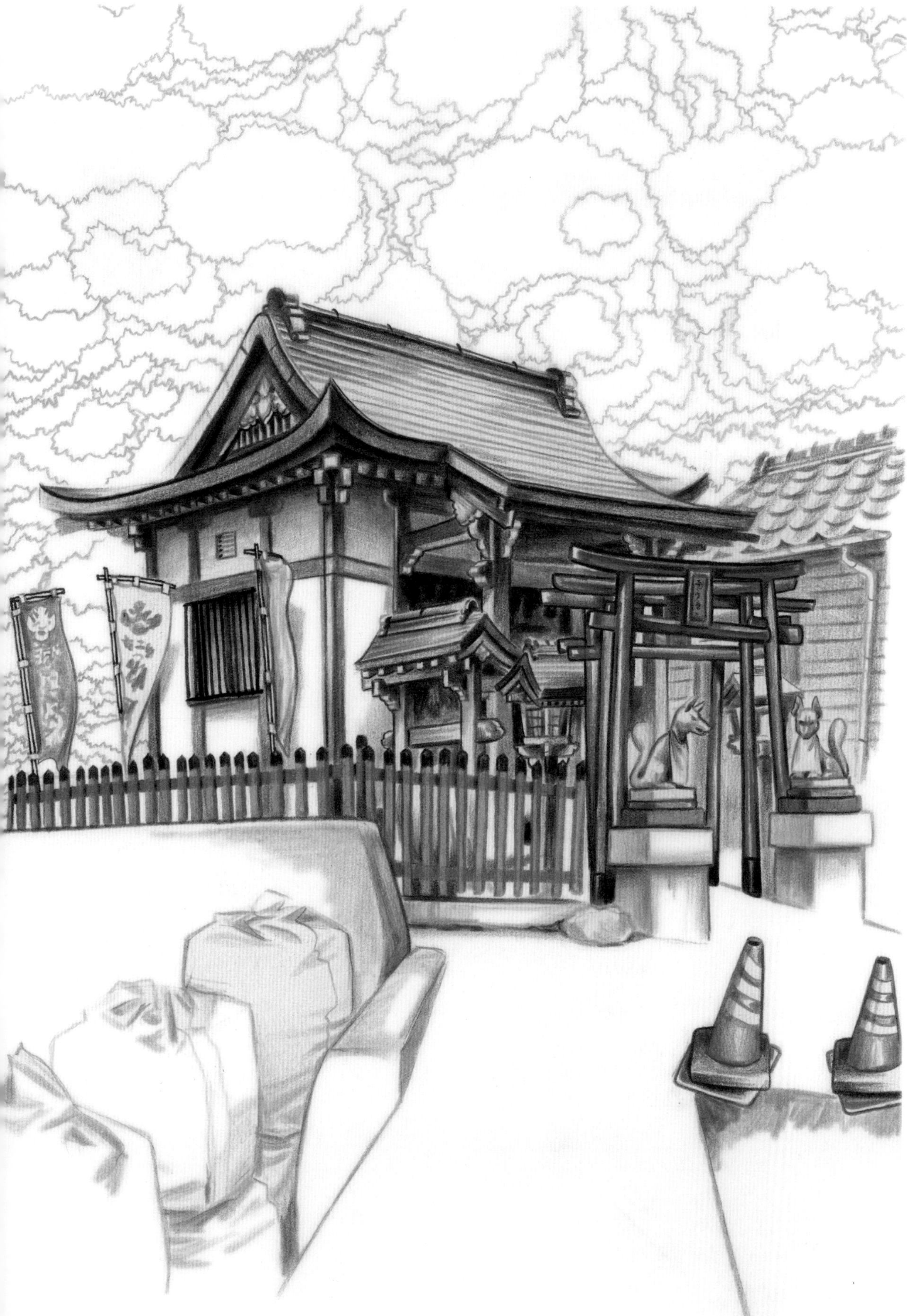

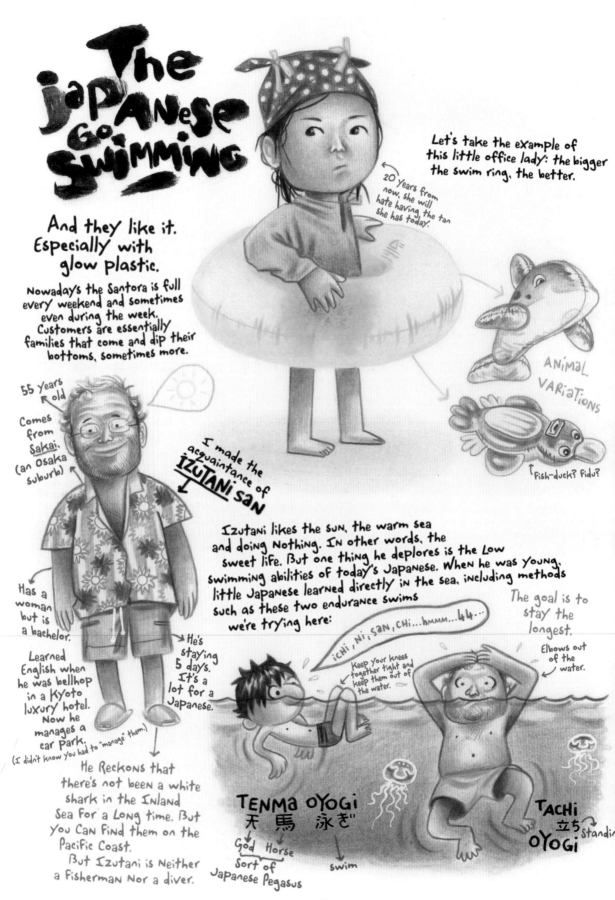

The Japanese Go Swimming

Let's take the example of this little office lady: the bigger the swim ring, the better.

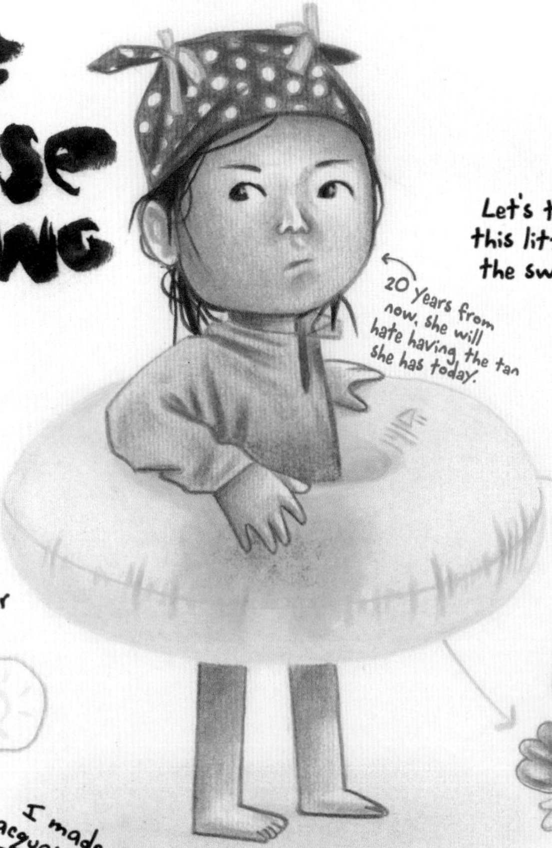
20 years from now, she will hate having the tan she has today.

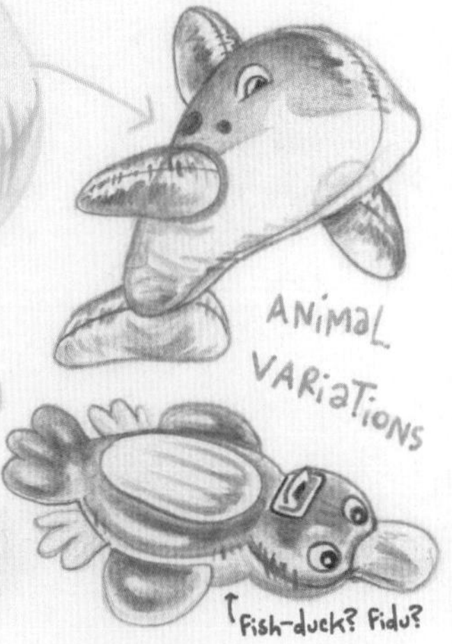
ANIMAL VARIATIONS
Fish-duck? Fidu?

And they like it. Especially with glow plastic.

Nowadays the Santora is full every weekend and sometimes even during the week. Customers are essentially families that come and dip their bottoms, sometimes more.

I made the acquaintance of **IZUTANI SAN**

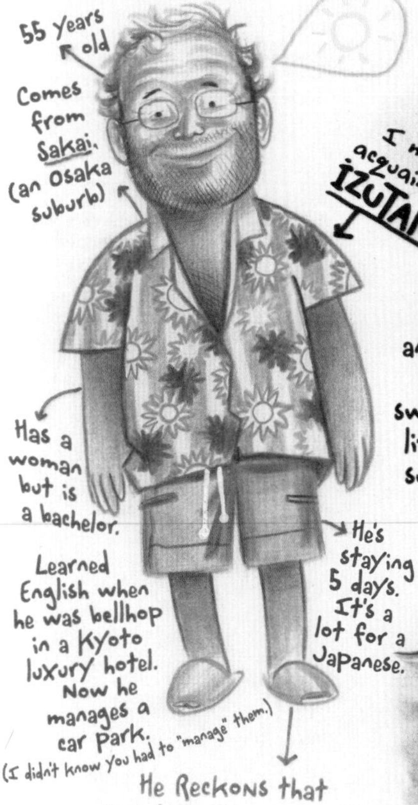
55 years old
Comes from Sakai. (an Osaka suburb)
Has a woman but is a bachelor.
He's staying 5 days. It's a lot for a Japanese.
Learned English when he was bellhop in a Kyoto luxury hotel. Now he manages a car park.
(I didn't know you had to "manage" them.)

He Reckons that there's not been a white shark in the Inland Sea For a Long time. But You Can Find them on the Pacific Coast. But Izutani is Neither a Fisherman Nor a diver.

Izutani likes the sun, the warm sea and doing Nothing. In other words, the sweet life. But one thing he deplores is the Low swimming abilities of today's Japanese. When he was young, little Japanese learned directly in the sea, including methods such as these two endurance swims we're trying here:

The goal is to stay the longest.

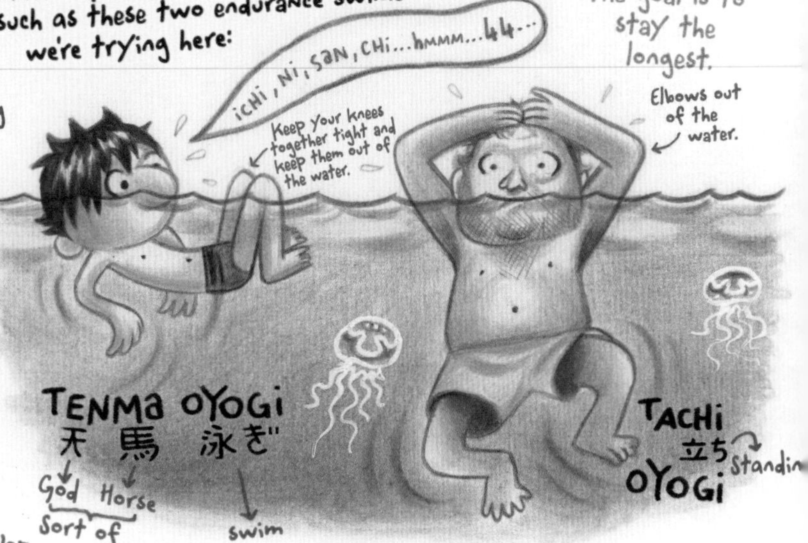
ICHI, NI, SAN, CHI... hmmm... 44...
Keep your knees together tight and keep them out of the water.
Elbows out of the water.
TENMA OYOGI
天馬泳ぎ
God Horse
Sort of Japanese Pegasus
swim
TACHI OYOGI
立ち
Standin

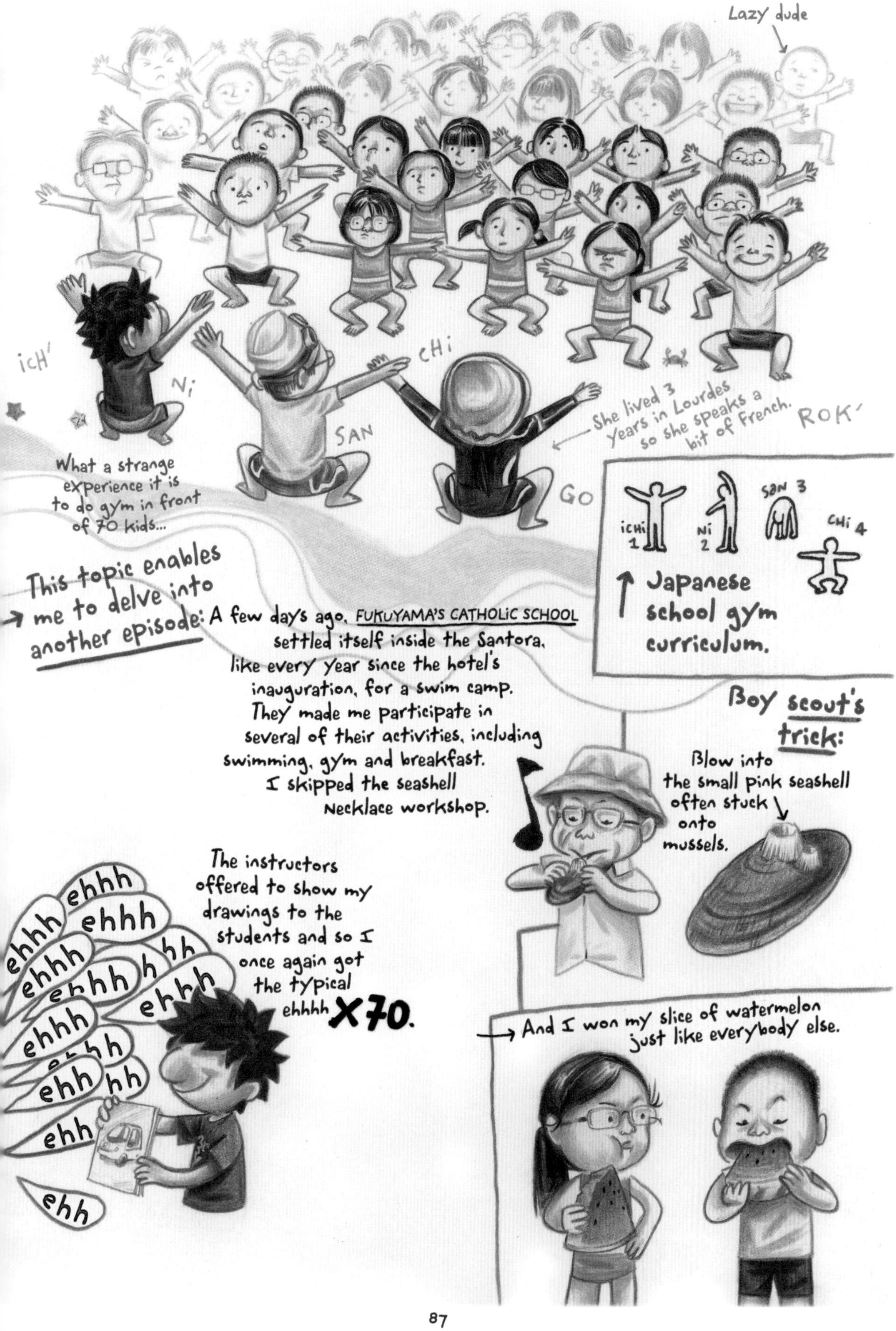
Lazy dude
iCH'
Ni
SAN
CHi
GO
ROK'
She lived 3 years in Lourdes so she speaks a bit of French.
What a strange experience it is to do gym in front of 70 kids...
iCHi 1
Ni 2
SAN 3
CHi 4
↑ Japanese school gym curriculum.
This topic enables me to delve into another episode: A few days ago, FUKUYAMA'S CATHOLIC SCHOOL settled itself inside the Santora, like every year since the hotel's inauguration, for a swim camp. They made me participate in several of their activities, including swimming, gym and breakfast. I skipped the seashell Necklace workshop.
Boy scout's trick:
Blow into the small pink seashell often stuck onto mussels.
The instructors offered to show my drawings to the students and so I once again got the typical ehhhh X70.
ehhh
ehhh
ehhh
ehhh
ehhh
ehhh
ehhh
ehh
ehh
ehh
And I won my slice of watermelon just like everybody else.

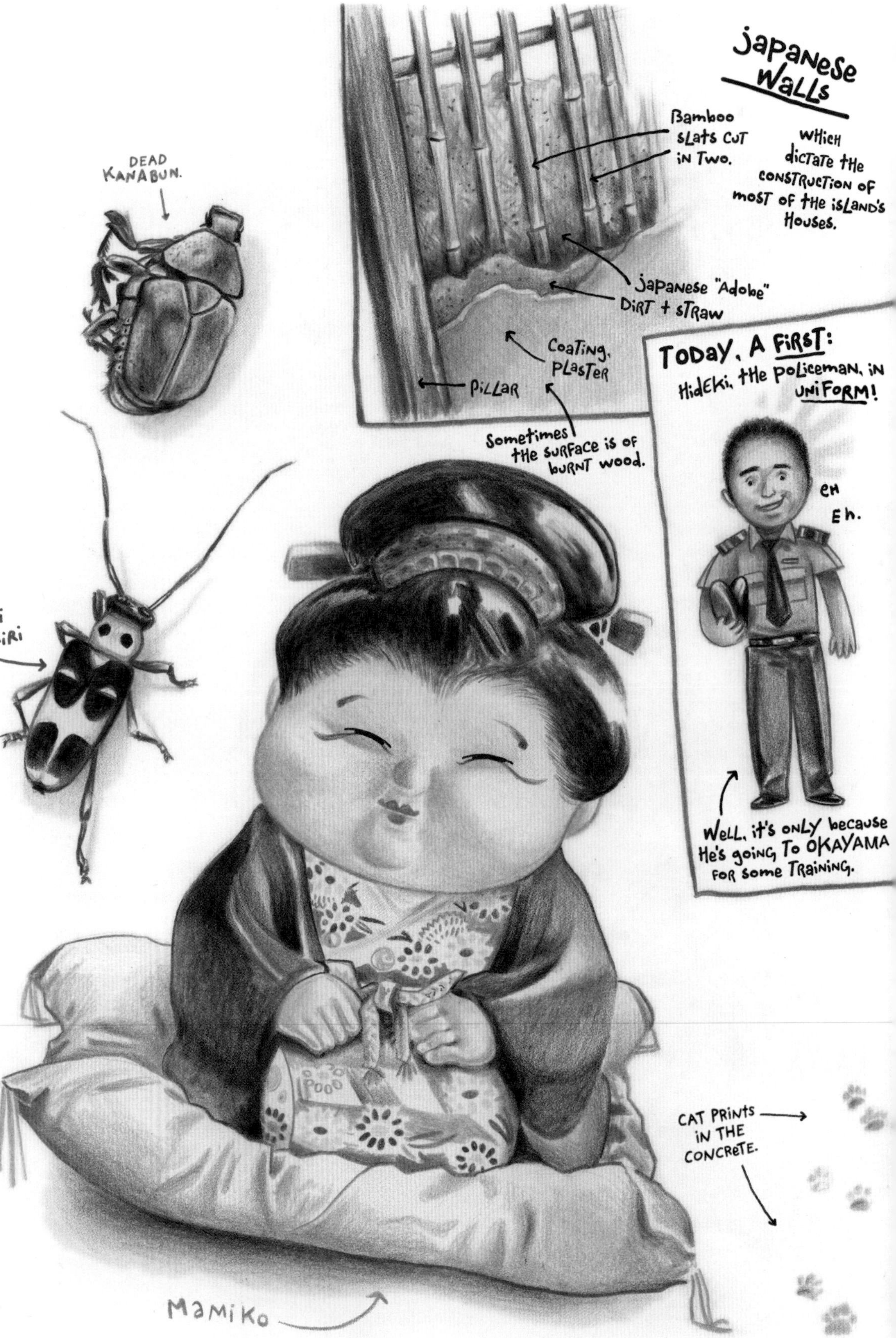
Japanese WALLS
which dictate the construction of most of the island's Houses.
Bamboo slats cut in Two.
Japanese "Adobe" DiRT + sTRaw
Coating, PLasTeR
piLLaR
Sometimes the surface is of burnt wood.
DEAD KANABUN.
RAMii KAMiKiRi
TODAY, A FiRST:
HidEKi, the policeman, in UNiFORM!
eh
Eh.
WeLL, it's ONLY because He's going TO OKAYAMA FOR some TRAINING.
CAT PRINTS IN THE CONCRETE.
MAMiKo

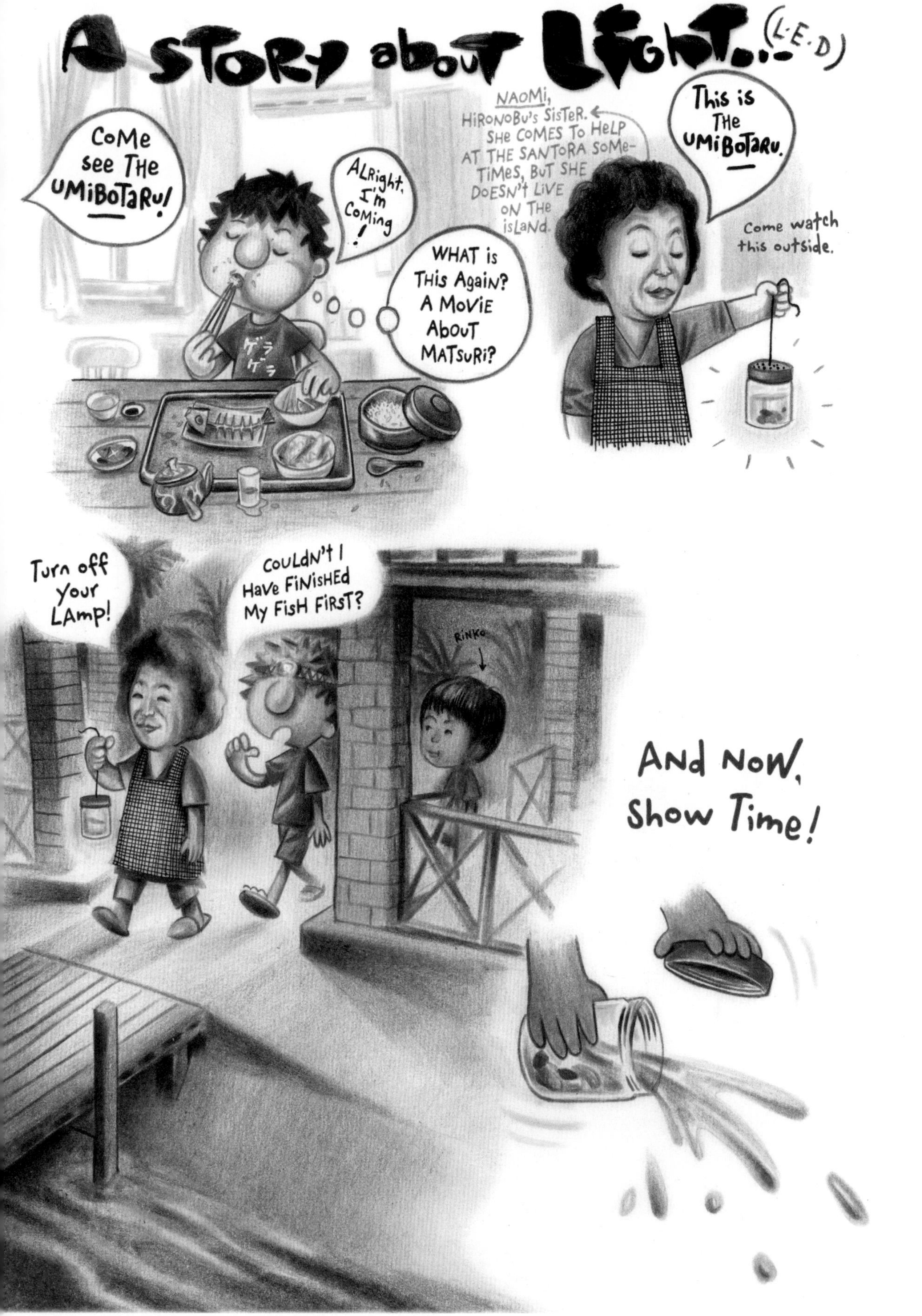
A STORY about LIGHT... (L.E.D)
Come see The UMiBOTARU!
ALright, I'm Coming!
WHAT is This Again? A Movie About MATSURi?
ゲラゲラ
NAOMi, HiRONOBu's SisTeR. SHe COMES To HeLP AT THE SANTORA SoMe-TiMes, BuT SHE DOESN't LiVE ON The isLand.
This is The UMiBoTaRu.
Come watch this outside.
Turn off your LAmp!
CouLdN't I Have FiNisHed My FisH FirsT?
RiNKo
ANd Now, Show Time!

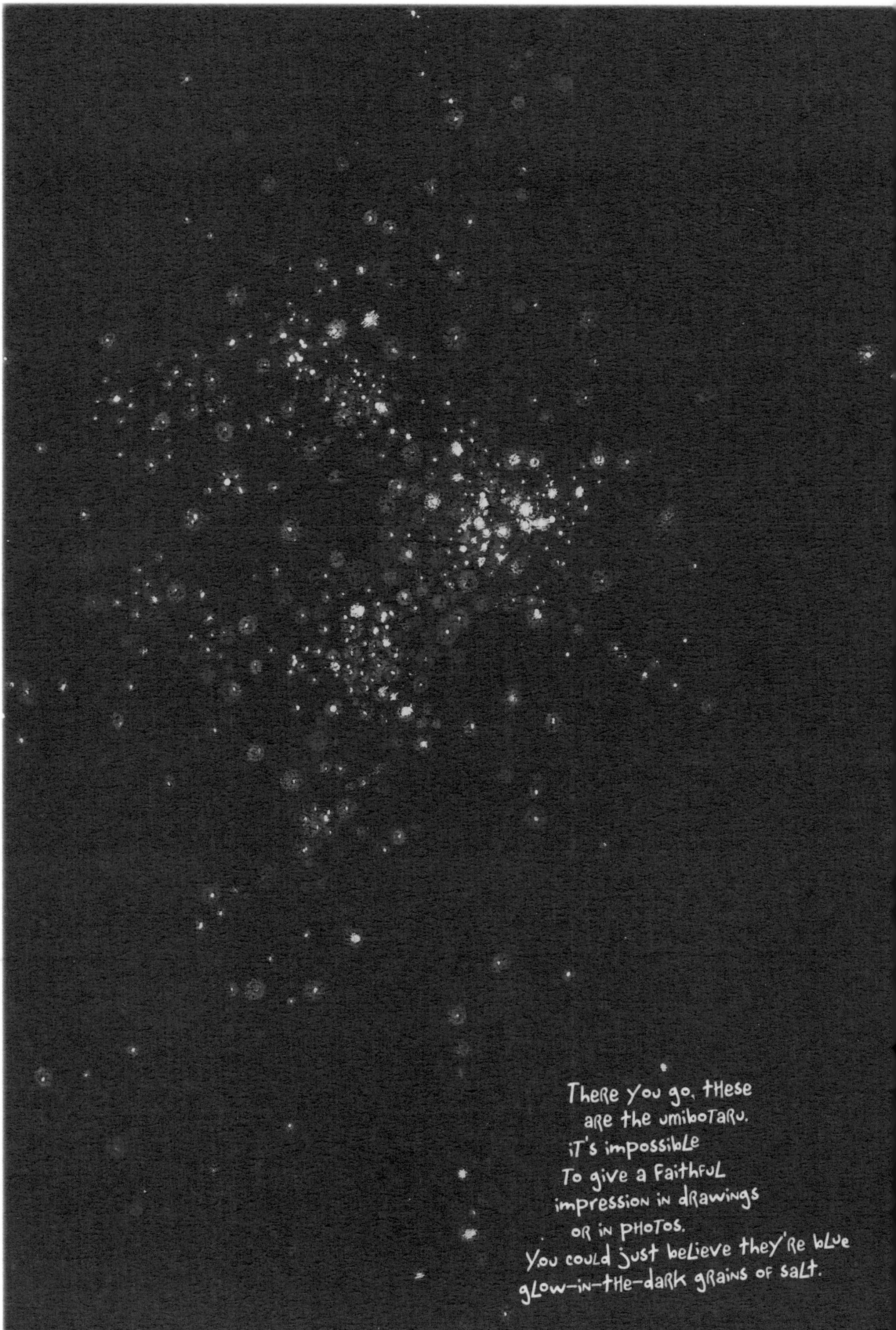
There you go, these
are the umibotaru.
it's impossible
to give a faithful
impression in drawings
or in photos.
You could just believe they're blue
glow-in-the-dark grains of salt.

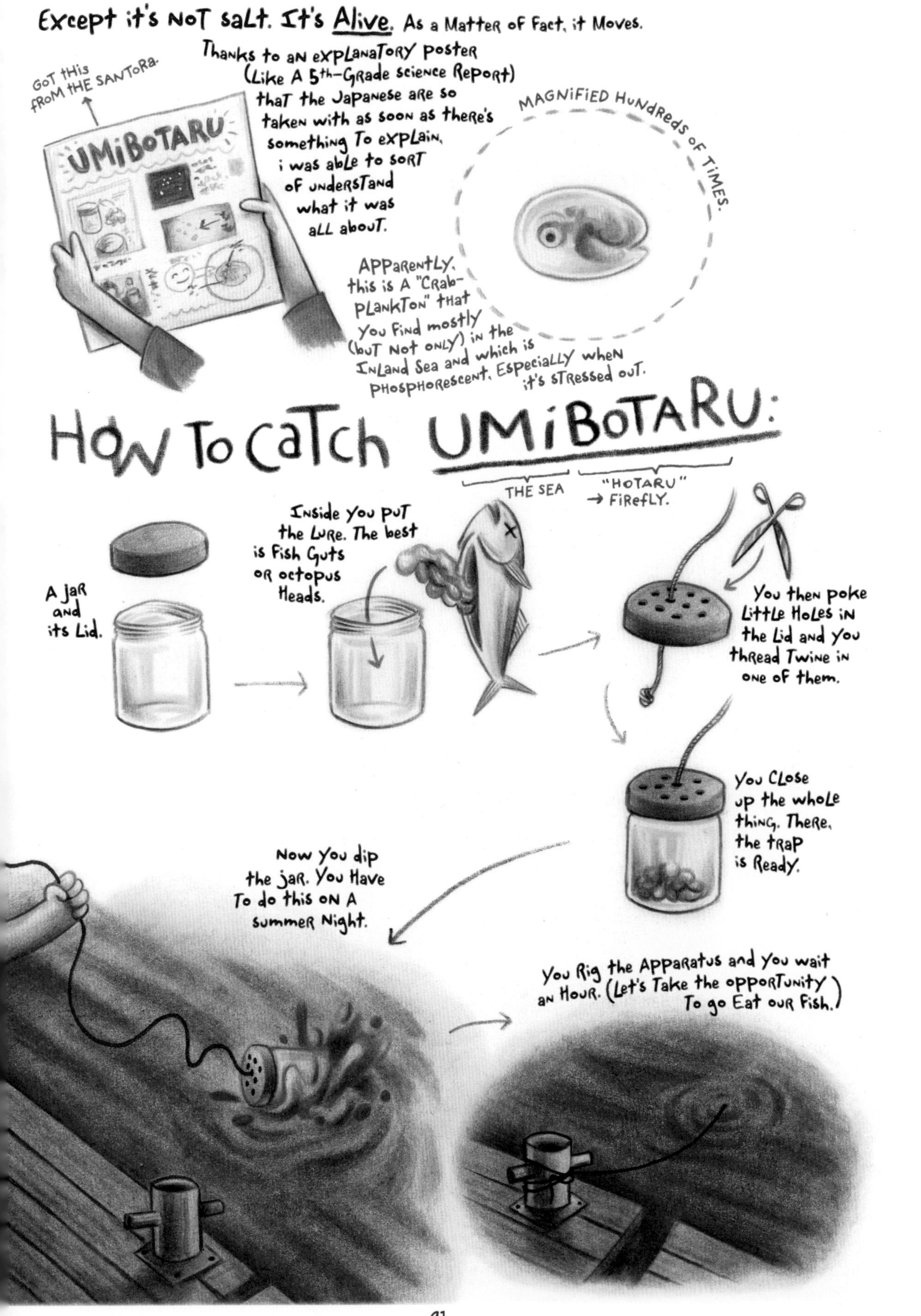
Except it's NOT salt. It's Alive. As a Matter of Fact, it Moves.
GOT THIS FROM THE SANTORA
UMIBOTARU
Thanks to an explanatory poster (Like A 5th-Grade science Report) that the Japanese are so taken with as soon as there's something To explain, i was able to sort of understand what it was all about.
MAGNIFIED HUNDREDS OF TIMES.
APPARENTLY, this is A "Crab-plankton" that you find mostly (but Not only) in the Inland Sea and which is phosphorescent, Especially when it's stressed out.
HOW TO CATCH UMIBOTARU:
THE SEA
"HOTARU" → FIREFLY.
A jar and its Lid.
Inside you put the Lure. The best is fish Guts or octopus Heads.
You then poke Little Holes in the Lid and you thread Twine in one of them.
You Close up the whole thing. There, the trap is Ready.
Now you dip the jar. You Have To do this on A summer Night.
You Rig the Apparatus and you wait an Hour. (Let's Take the opportunity To go Eat our Fish.)

You come back, it's harvest time and, surprise, the jar is already aglow.

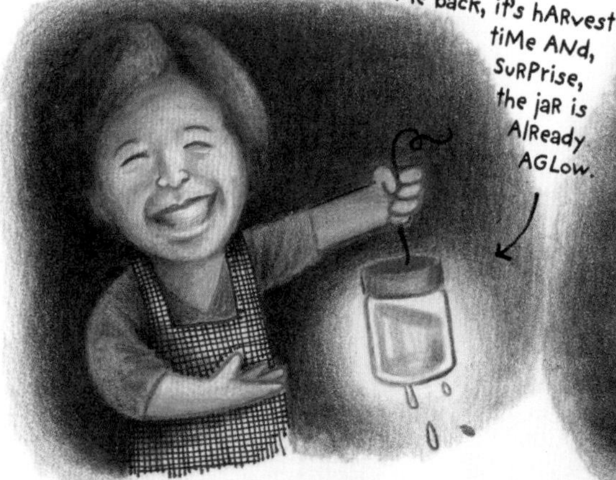

The umibotaru have come in, but not the fis (who woul hav like to.

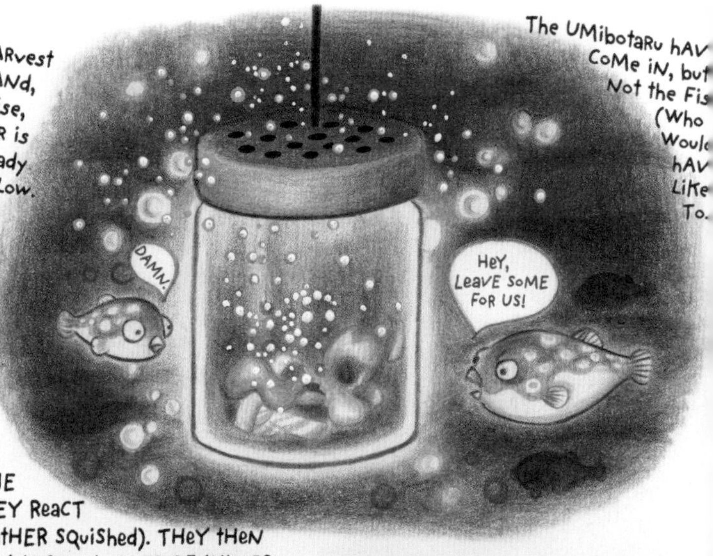
DAMN.
HEY, LEAVE SOME FOR US!

So, you can not only rest your gaze on the umibotaru but also your finger. Indeed, they react especially when they are stimulated (or rather squished). They then ooze out a glowing blue liquid with which you can do lots of things:

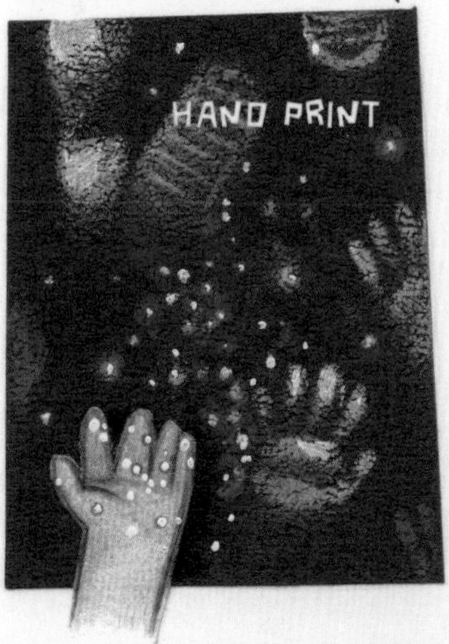
HAND PRINT

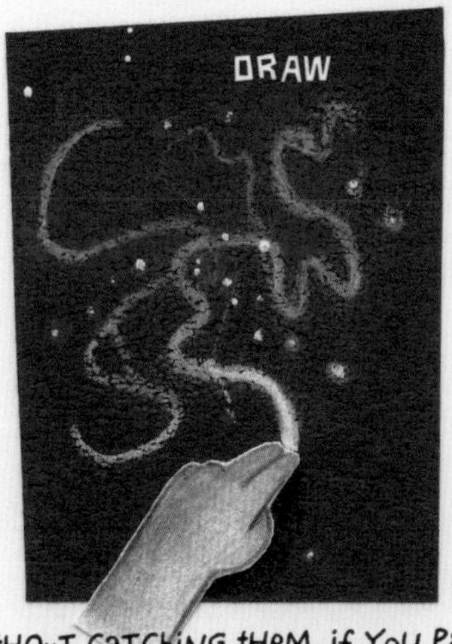
DRAW

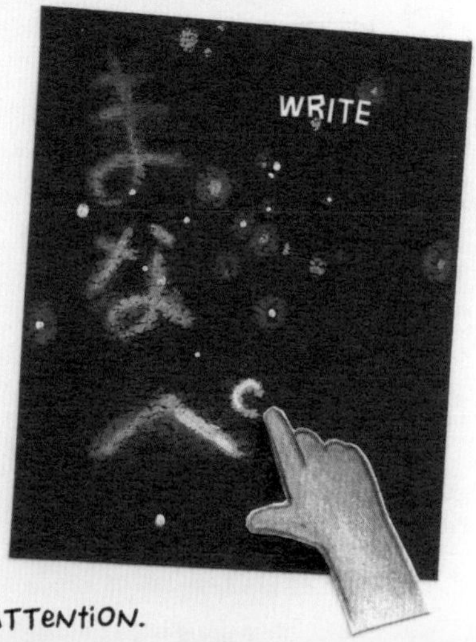
WRITE

But you can also watch them without catching them, if you pay attention. Each diffuse light means umibotaru are being attacked by fish.

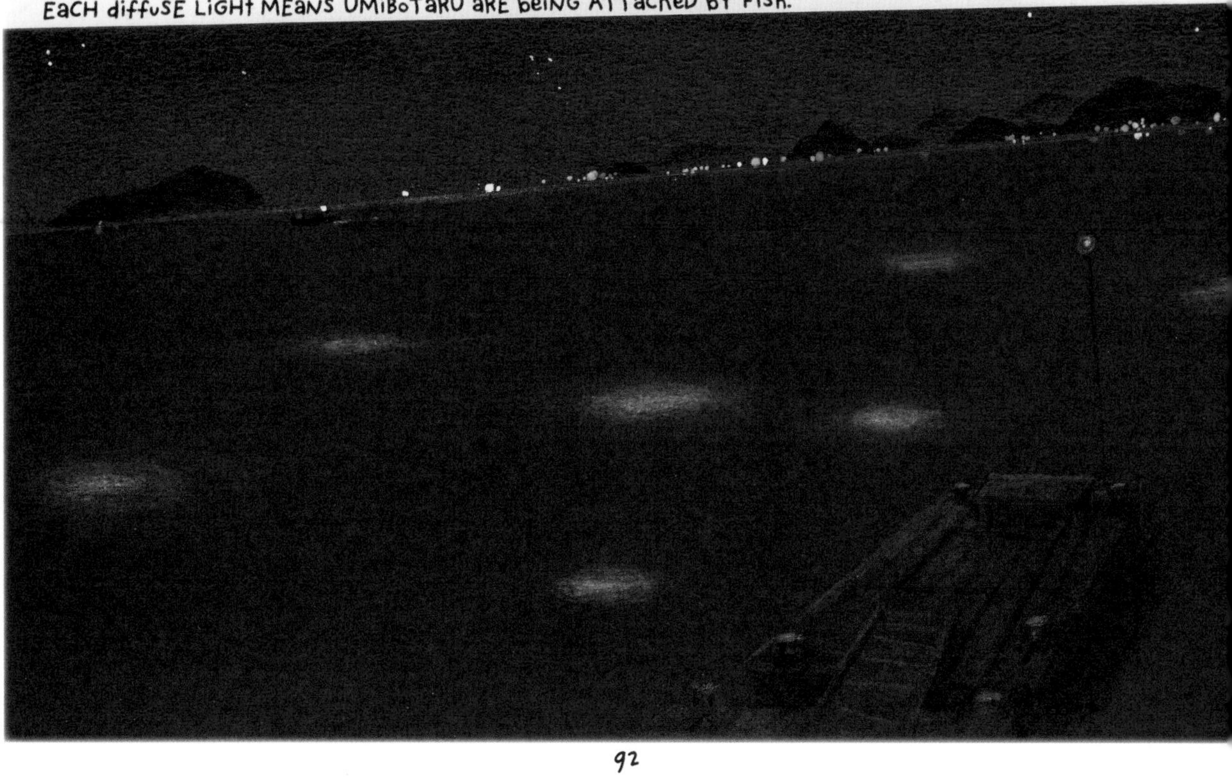

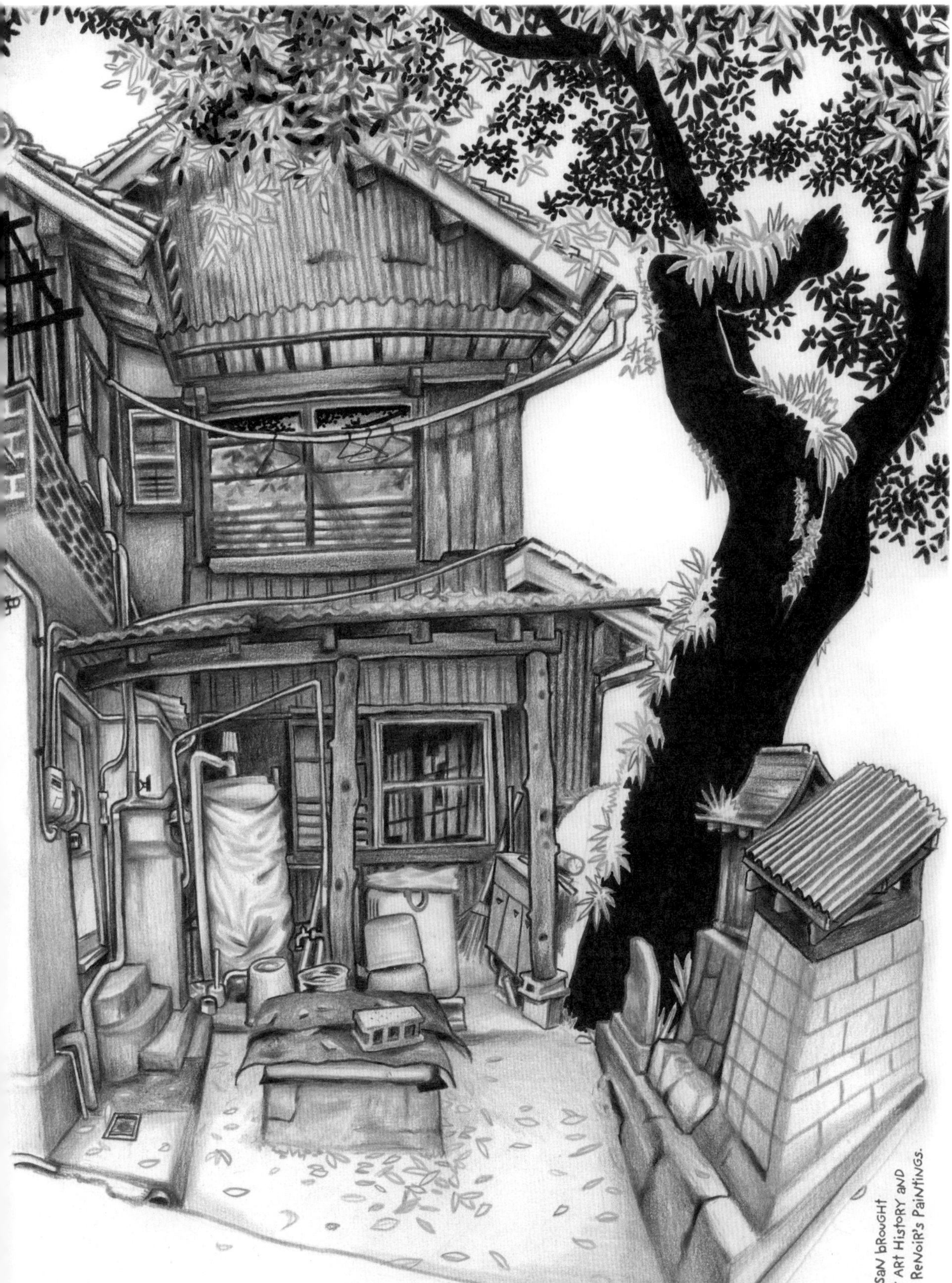

Today, SHIMURA SAN bROUGHT Me A book about ART History and ONly SHOWED Me RENOIR's PAINTINGS.

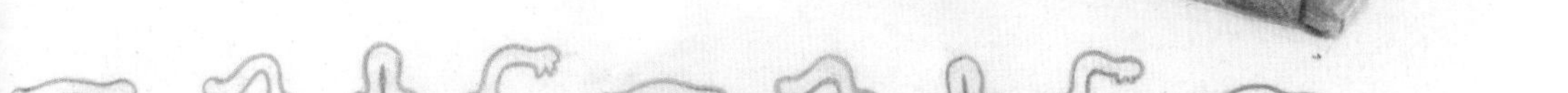

FELLOW TRAVELER →

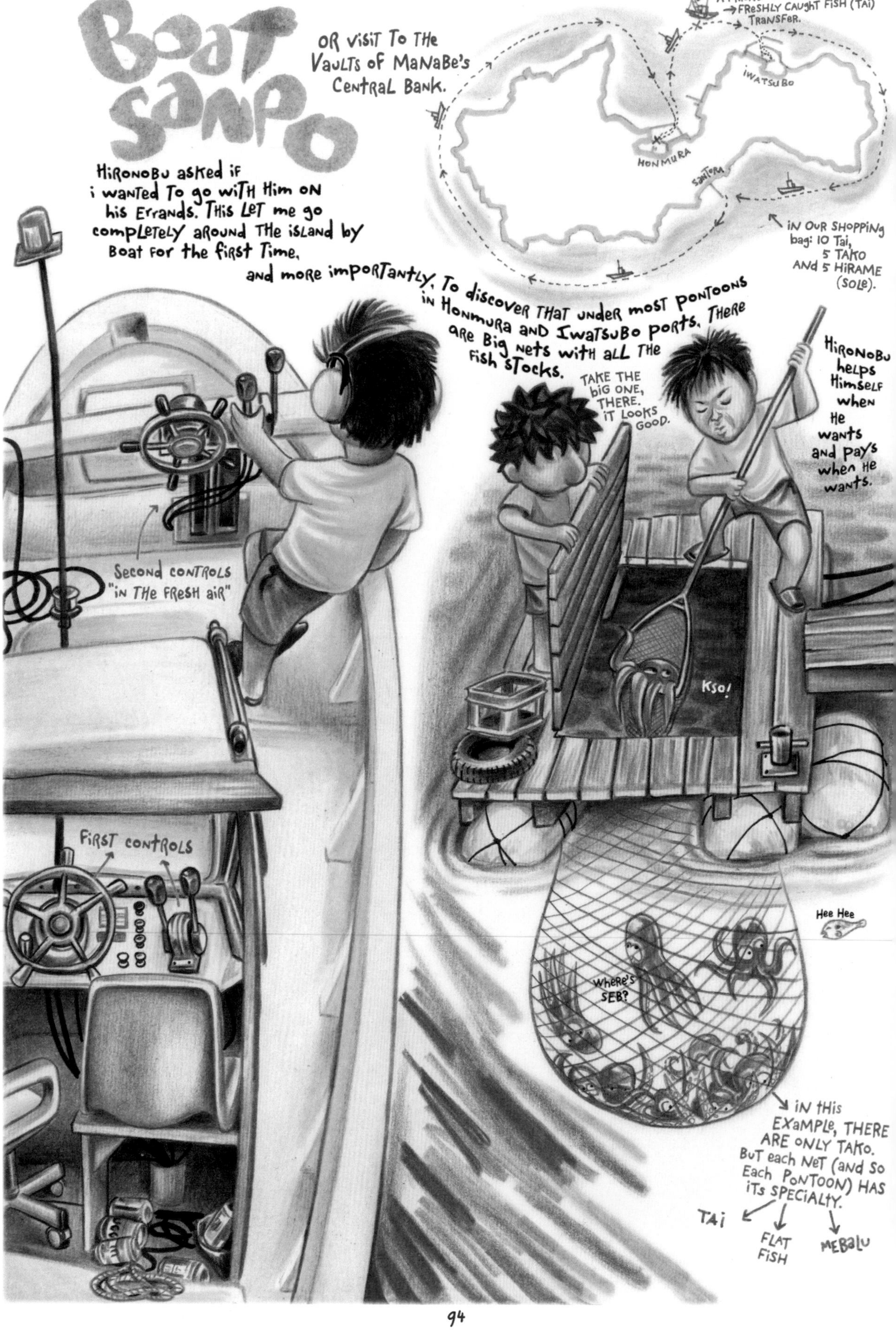
Boat Sanpo
OR VISIT TO THE VAULTS OF MANABE's CENTRAL BANK.
MEETING WITH A FRIEND OF HIRONOBU's.
FRESHLY CAUGHT FISH (TAI) TRANSFER.
IWATSUBO
HONMURA
SANTORA
IN OUR SHOPPING bag: 10 Tai, 5 TAKO AND 5 HIRAME (SOLE).
HIRONOBU asked if i wanted to go with him on his Errands. This let me go completely around the island by Boat for the first Time,
and more importantly, to discover that under most pontoons in Honmura and Iwatsubo ports, there are Big nets with all the fish stocks.
TAKE THE big ONE, THERE. IT LOOKS GOOD.
HIRONOBU helps himself when he wants and pays when he wants.
Second controls "in the fresh air"
KSO!
FIRST CONTROLS
Hee Hee
Where's SEB?
IN THIS EXAMPLE, THERE ARE ONLY TAKO. BUT each NET (and so Each PONTOON) HAS ITS SPECIALTY.
TAI
FLAT FISH
MEBALU

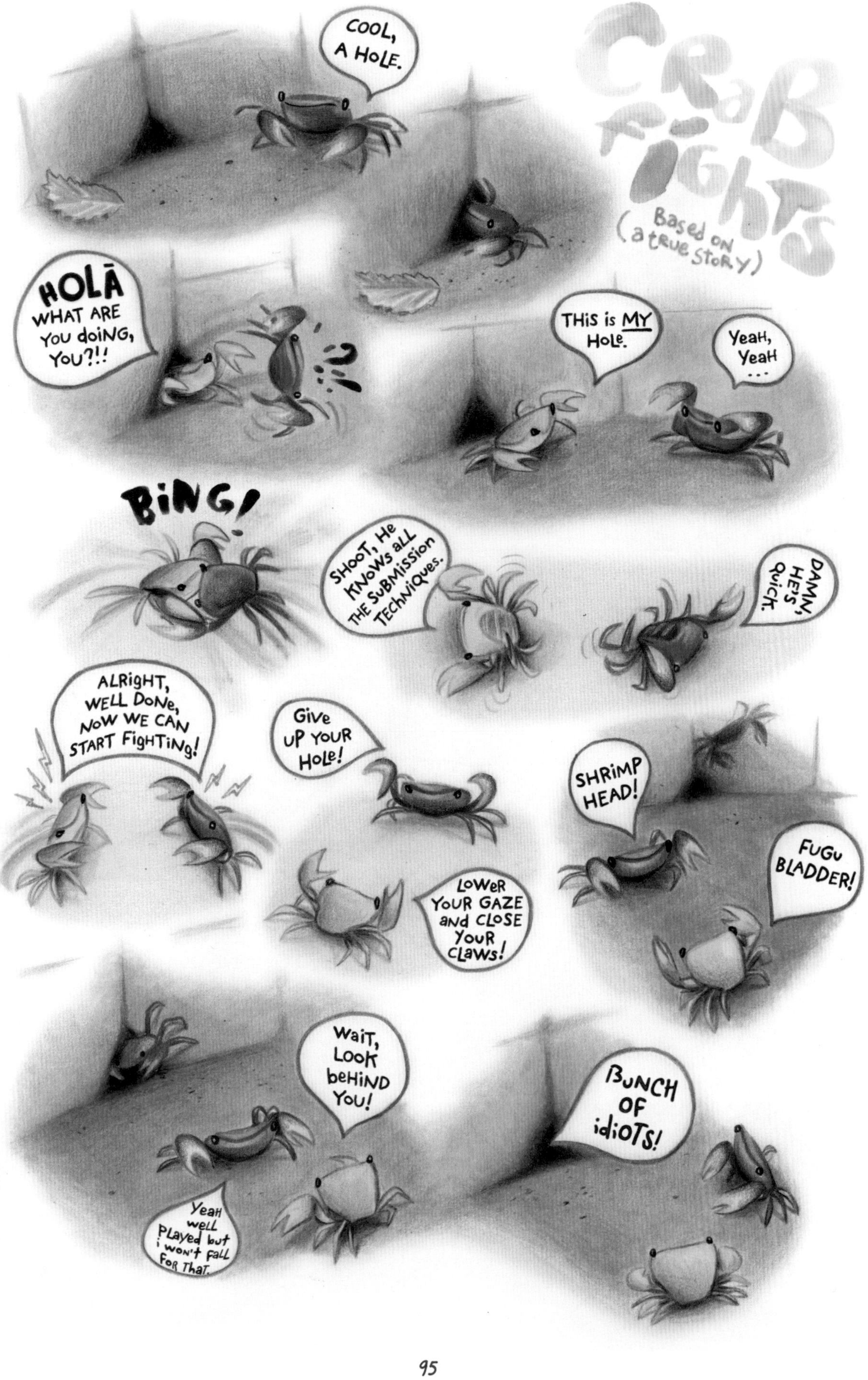
Crab Fights
(Based on a true story)
COOL, A HOLE.
HOLĀ WHAT ARE YOU doiNG, YOU?!!
?
THIS is MY HOLE.
YeaH, YeaH ...
BING!
SHOOT, He KNOWS aLL THE SUBMISSION TECHNIQUES.
DAMN, HE'S Quick.
ALRIGHT, WELL DONE, NOW WE CAN START FIGHTING!
Give uP YOUR HOLE!
LOWER YOUR GAZE and CLOSE YOUR CLAWS!
SHRIMP HEAD!
FUGU BLADDER!
Wait, LOOK beHIND YOU!
YeaH well PLayed but i won't fall for THAT.
BUNCH OF idiOTS!

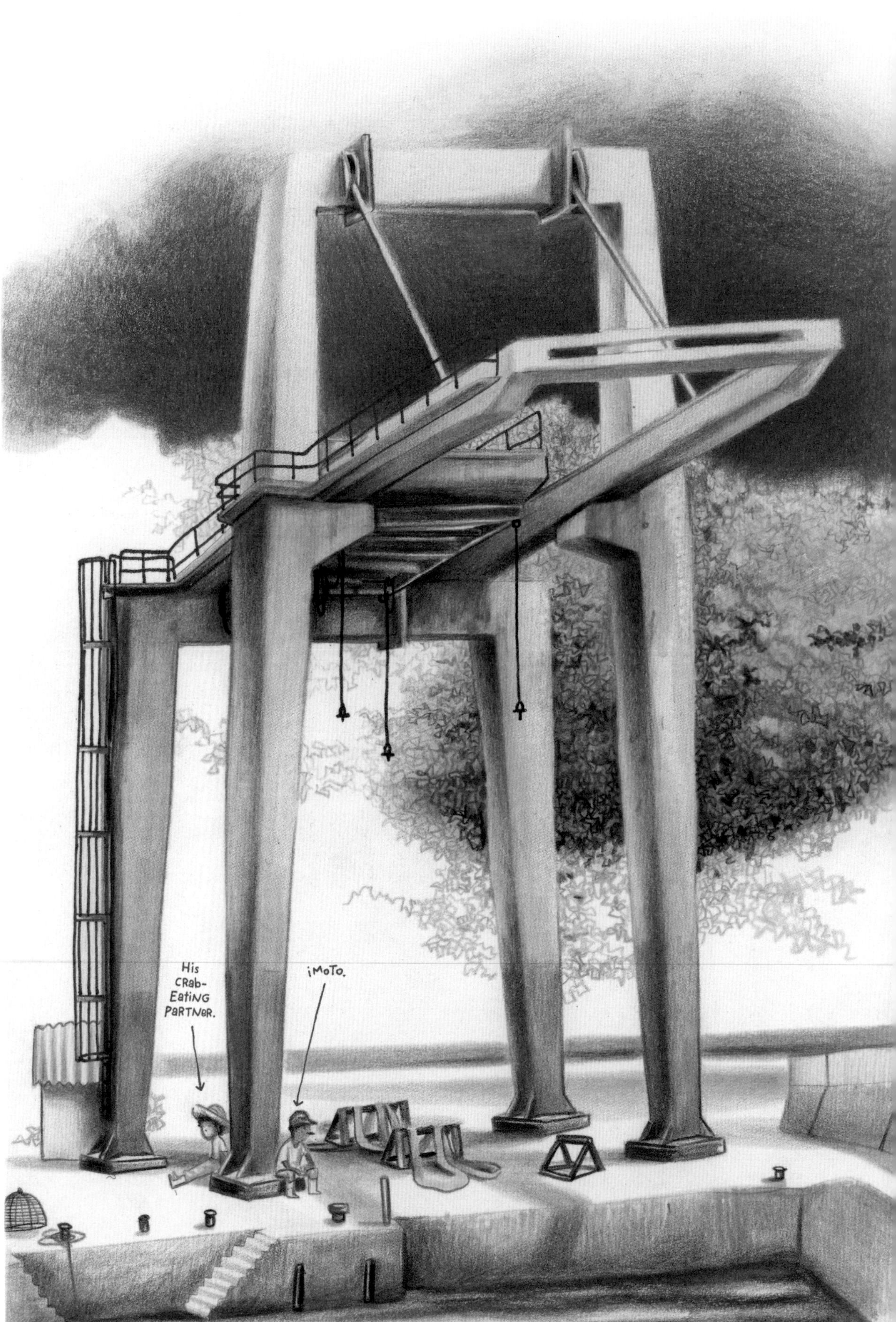
His crab-eating partner.
iMoto.

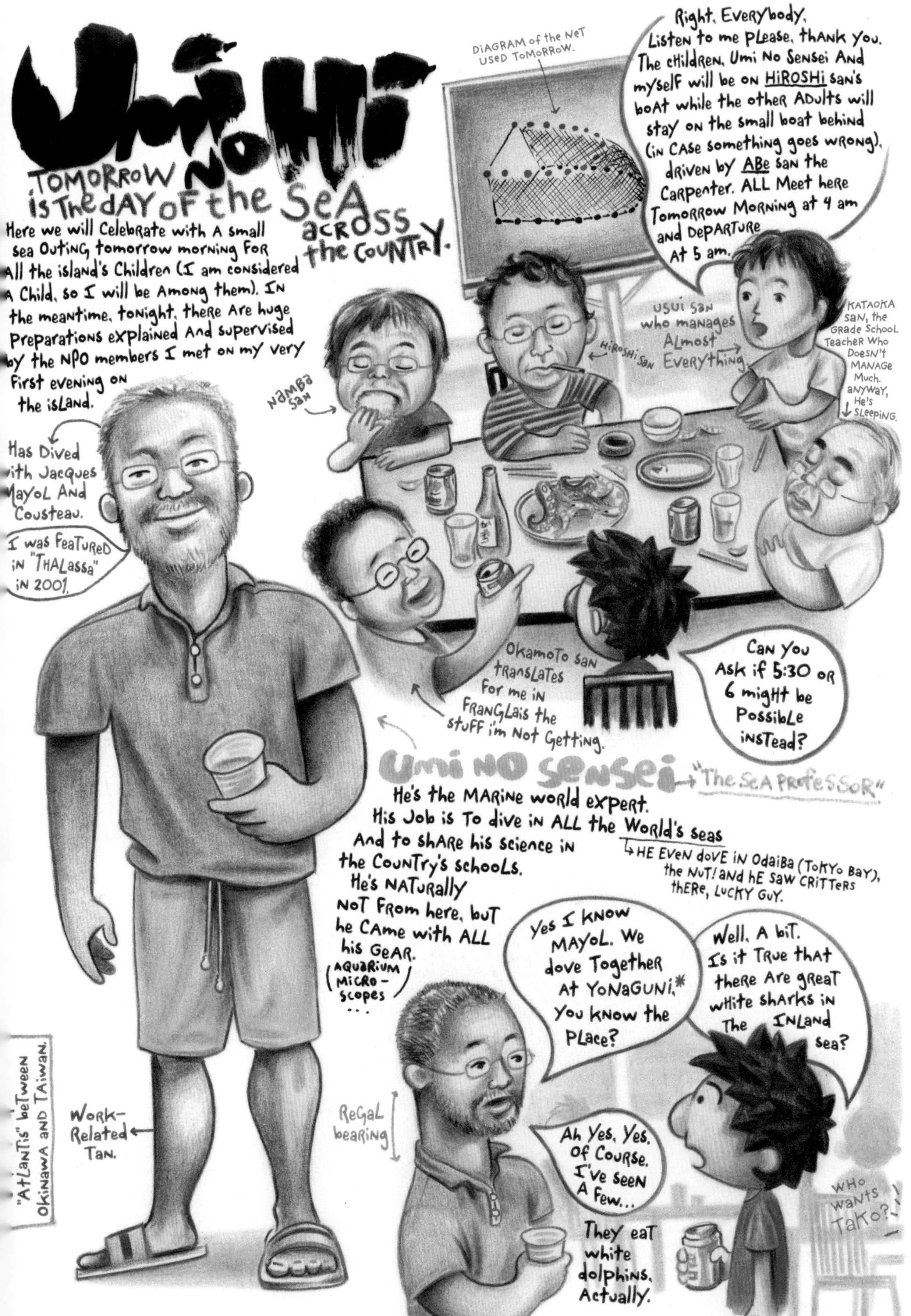

UMI NO HI
TOMORROW is the DAY of the SeA ACROSS the COUNTRY.
Here we will Celebrate with A small sea Outing tomorrow morning for All the island's Children (I am considered A Child, so I will be Among them). In the meantime, tonight, there Are huge Preparations explained And supervised by the NPO members I met on my very first evening on the isLand.
DIAGRAM of the NeT USED TOMORROW.
Right, Everybody, Listen to me Please, thank you. The children, Umi No Sensei And myself will be on HIROSHI san's boAt while the other ADults will stay on the small boat behind (in CAse something goes wrong), driven by ABe san the Carpenter. ALL Meet here Tomorrow Morning at 4 am and DePARTURE At 5 am.
USUI SAN who manages ALmost Everything
KATAOKA SAN, the Grade School TeacheR Who DOESN'T MANAGE Much, anyway, He's SLEEPING.
HiROSHi SAN
NAMBA SAN
Has Dived with Jacques Mayol And Cousteau.
I was FeaTuReD in "THALassa" in 2001.
Okamoto San transLates for me in FRangLais the stuff i'm Not Getting.
Can you Ask if 5:30 or 6 might be Possible instead?
Umi NO sensei → "The SeA PRofeSSoR"
He's the MARINE world expert. His Job is To dive in ALL the World's seas And to shaRe his science in the Country's schooLs.
↳ HE EVEN doVE IN OdaiBa (ToKYo BAY), the NuT! and hE SAW CRITTeRS thERe, LUCKY GuY.
He's NATURALLY NOT From here, but he CAme with ALL his GeAR. (AQUARIUM MICRO-SCOPES . . .
Yes I KNOW MAYoL. We dove Together At YoNaGUNi.* You know the PLace?
Well, A bit. Is it True that there Are great white sharks in The INLand sea?
WORK-Related TAN.
ReGaL bearing
Ah Yes, Yes, Of Course. I've seen A Few...
They eat white dolphins, Actually.
WHO wants TaKo?!
* "AtLanTis" between OKINAWA AND TAiwan.

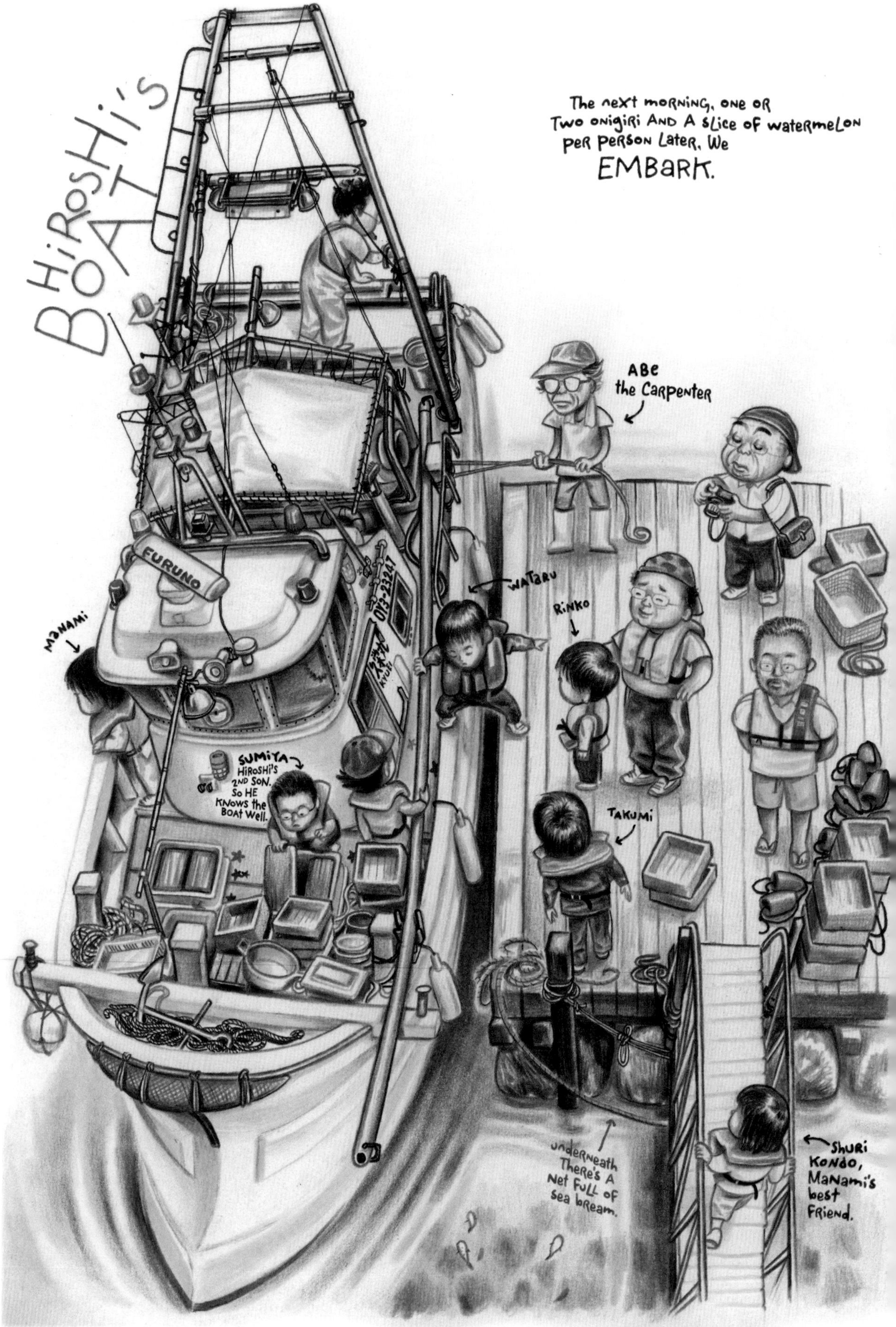
HiRoSHi's BOAT
The next morning, one or Two onigiri And A slice of watermelon per person Later, We EMBark.
ABe the CarPenter
WaTaRU
RiNKO
MaNaMi
SUMiYa HiRoSHi's 2ND SON. So HE KNOWS the BOAT Well.
TaKUMi
underneath There's A Net FULL of sea bream.
SHURi KONDO, MaNaMi's best FRiend.
FURUNO

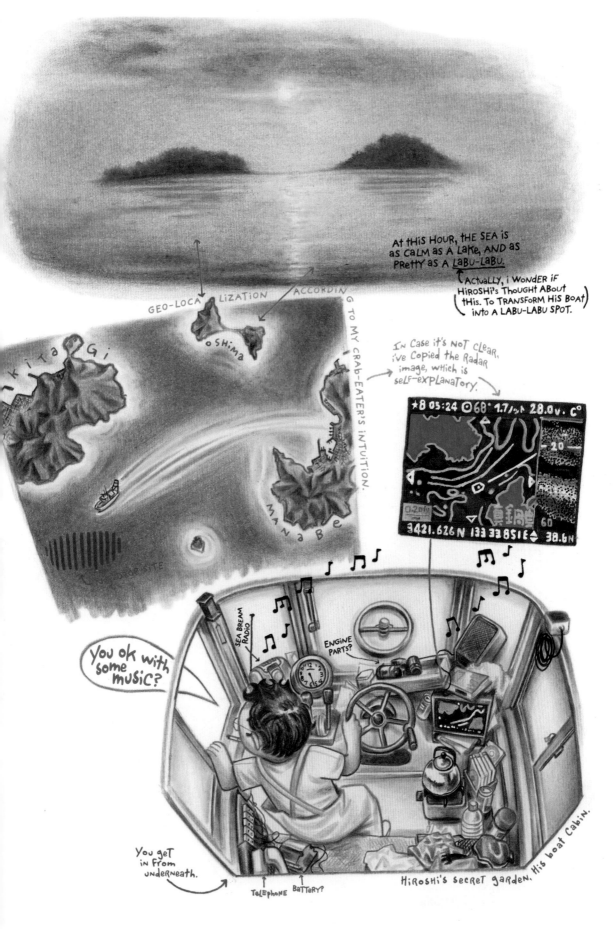

At this hour, the sea is as calm as a lake, and as pretty as a LABU-LABU.

(Actually, i wonder if Hiroshi's thought about this. To transform his boat into a LABU-LABU spot.)

GEO-LOCA LIZATION ACCORDING TO MY CRAB-EATER'S INTUITION.

o SHiMA

KiTaGi

MaNaBe

In case it's not clear, i've copied the radar image, which is self-explanatory.

★8 05:24 ⊙68° 1.7 ₁/ᴵ 28.0v. C°
− 20
Ö·2ᴹ
60
3421.626 N 133 33 851E ⊿ 38.6 N

you ok with some music?

SEA BREAM RADIO

ENGINE PARTS?

You get in from underneath.

TELEPHONE BATTERY?

HIROSHI'S SECRET GARDEN. His boat cabin.

99

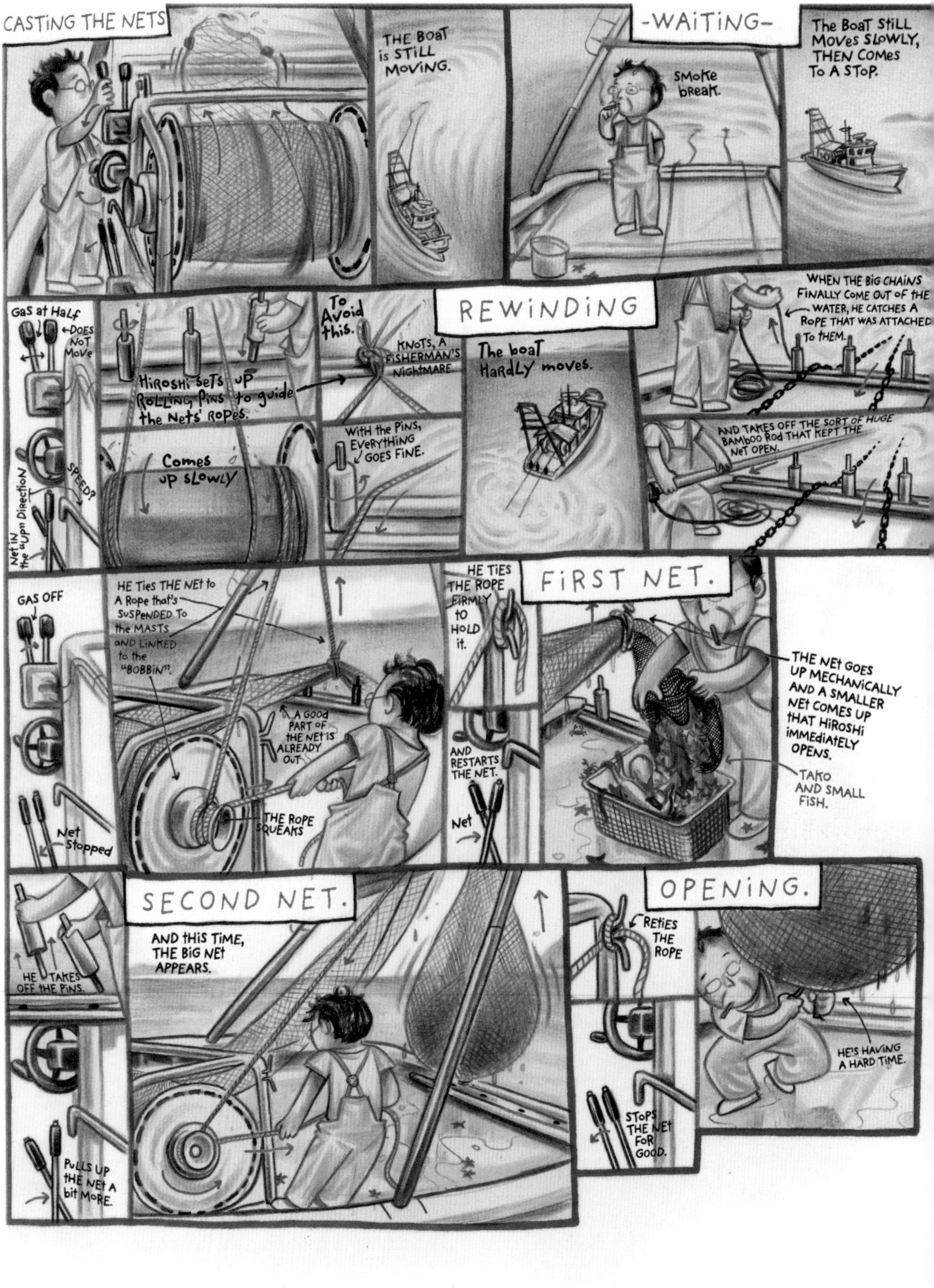
CASTING THE NETS
THE BOAT is STILL MOVING.
-WAITING-
SMOKE break.
The BOAT STILL MOVES SLOWLY, THEN COMES TO A STOP.
Gas at Half
DOES NOT MOVE
SPEED?
Net IN the "up" Direction
Hiroshi sets up Rolling Pins to guide the Nets' ropes.
Comes up slowly
To Avoid this.
KNOTS, A FISHERMAN'S NIGHTMARE.
WITH the PINS, EVERYTHING GOES FINE.
REWINDING
The boat hardly moves.
WHEN THE BIG CHAINS FINALLY COME OUT OF THE WATER, HE CATCHES A ROPE THAT WAS ATTACHED TO THEM.
AND TAKES OFF THE SORT OF HUGE BAMBOO ROD THAT KEPT THE NET OPEN.
GAS OFF
Net Stopped
HE TIES THE NET to A Rope that's SUSPENDED to the MASTS AND LINKED to the "BOBBIN".
A GOOD PART OF THE NET IS ALREADY OUT
THE ROPE SQUEAKS
HE TIES THE ROPE FIRMLY to HOLD it.
AND RESTARTS THE NET.
Net
FIRST NET.
THE NET GOES UP MECHANICALLY AND A SMALLER NET COMES UP THAT HIROSHI IMMEDIATELY OPENS.
TAKO AND SMALL FISH.
HE TAKES OFF THE PINS.
PULLS UP THE NET A bit MORE.
SECOND NET.
AND THIS TIME, THE BIG NET APPEARS.
OPENING.
RETIES THE ROPE
STOPS THE NET FOR GOOD.
HE'S HAVING A HARD TIME.

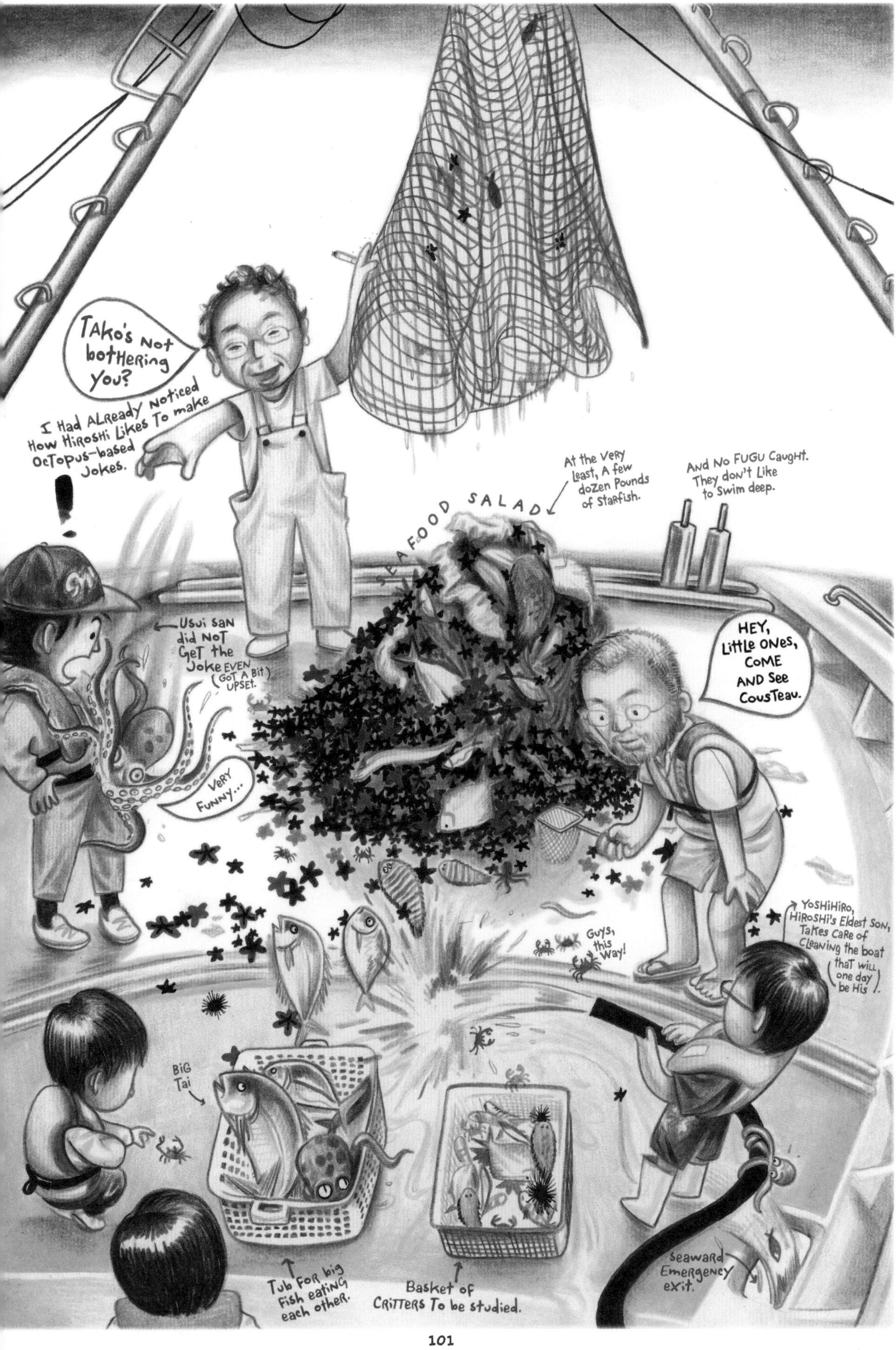

Tako's Not bothering you?
I Had ALready Noticed How Hiroshi Likes To make Octopus-based Jokes.
!
SEAFOOD SALAD
At the Very Least, A few dozen Pounds of Starfish.
And No FUGU Caught. They don't Like to Swim deep.
Usui SAN did NOT Get the Joke EVEN (GOT A Bit UPSET.)
HEY, Little ONes, COME AND See Cousteau.
Very Funny...
Guys, this Way!
YOSHIHIRO, HIROSHI's Eldest SON, Takes Care of Cleaning the boat (that will one day be His).
BIG Tai
Tub FOR big Fish eating each other.
Basket of CRITTERS To be studied.
Seaward Emergency exit.

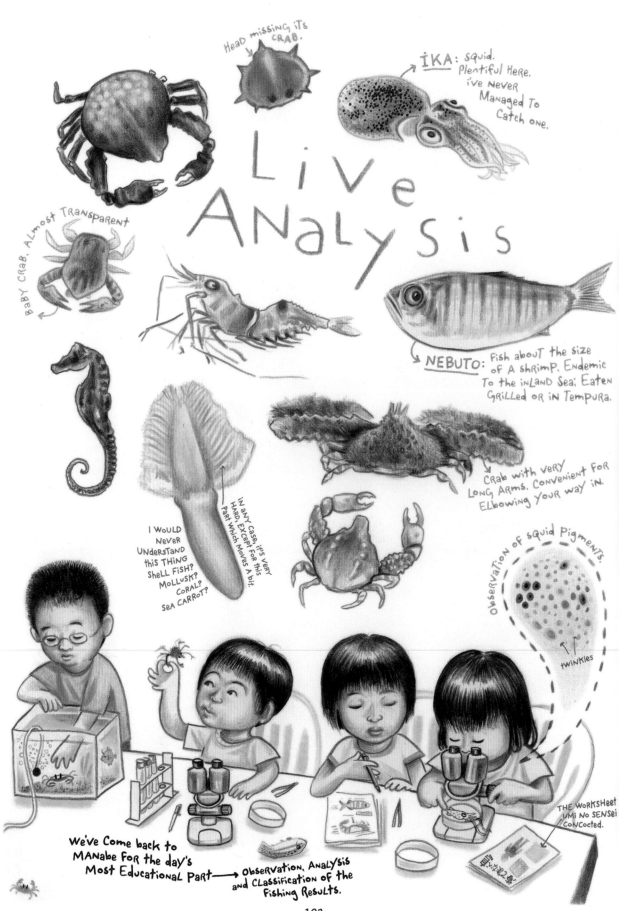

Head missing its CRAB.

ĪKA: Squid. Plentiful here. I've never managed to catch one.

Live Analysis

BABY CRAB. Almost Transparent

NEBUTO: Fish about the size of a shrimp. Endemic to the inland sea; Eaten grilled or in Tempura.

Crab with very long arms. Convenient for elbowing your way in.

In any case, it's very hard, except for this part which moves a bit.

I would never understand this thing. Shell fish? Mollusk? Coral? Sea carrot?

Observation of squid pigments.

Twinkles

We've come back to Manabe for the day's most educational part → Observation, analysis and classification of the fishing results.

THE Worksheet Umi no Sensei concocted.

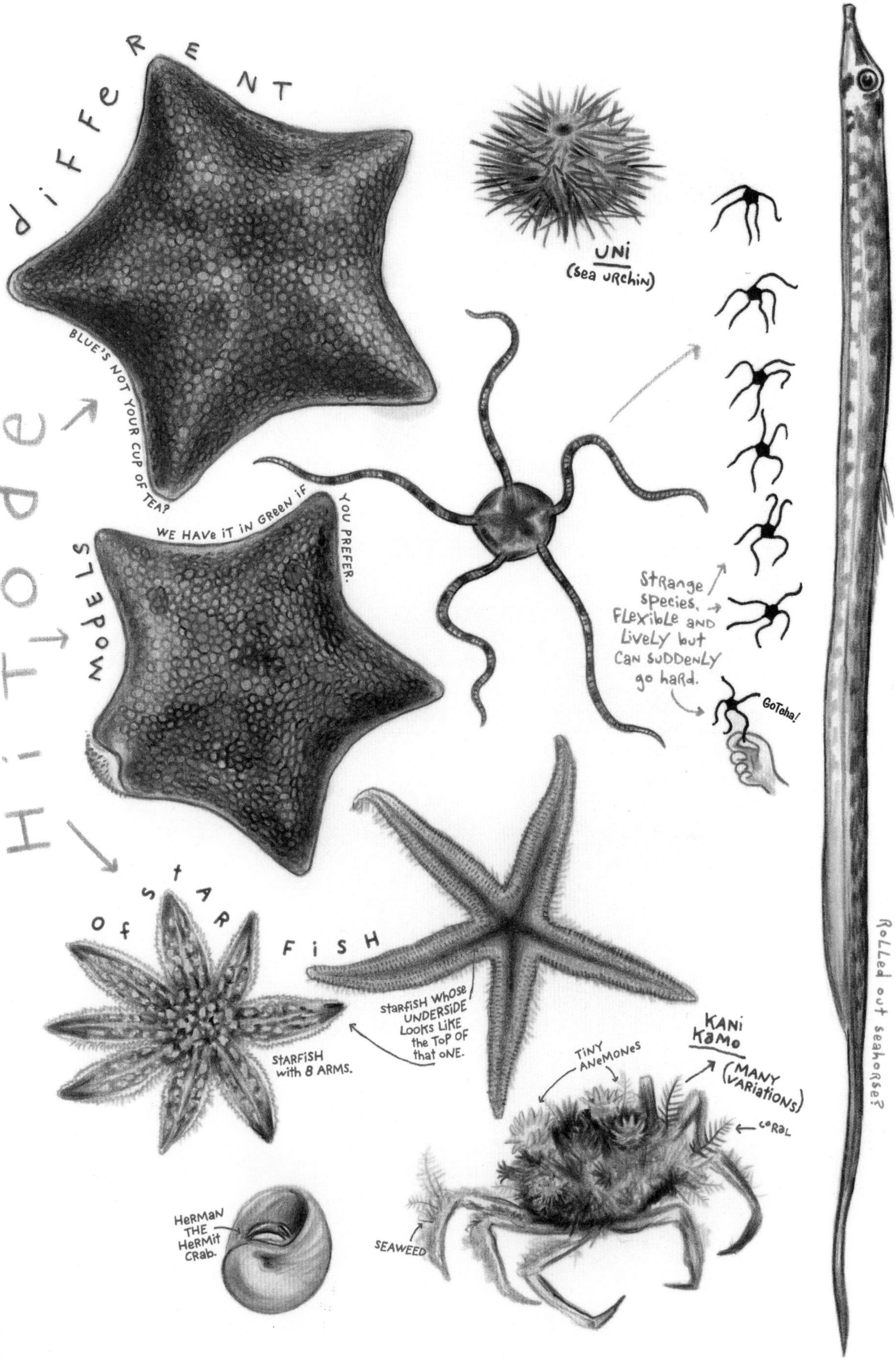
Hi Tide
different
models
of starfish
BLUE'S NOT YOUR CUP OF TEA?
WE HAVE IT IN GREEN IF YOU PREFER.
UNi
(sea uRchin)
Strange species, FLEXibLe and LiveLy but can suddenLy go hard.
GoTcha!
RoLLed out seahorse?
starFiSH whose UNDERSIDE Looks LiKE the Top OF that oNE.
STARFISH with 8 ARMS.
KANi KaMo
(MANY VARIATIONS)
TiNY ANeMONeS
coRaL
SEAWEED
HeRMan THE HeRMit CRab.

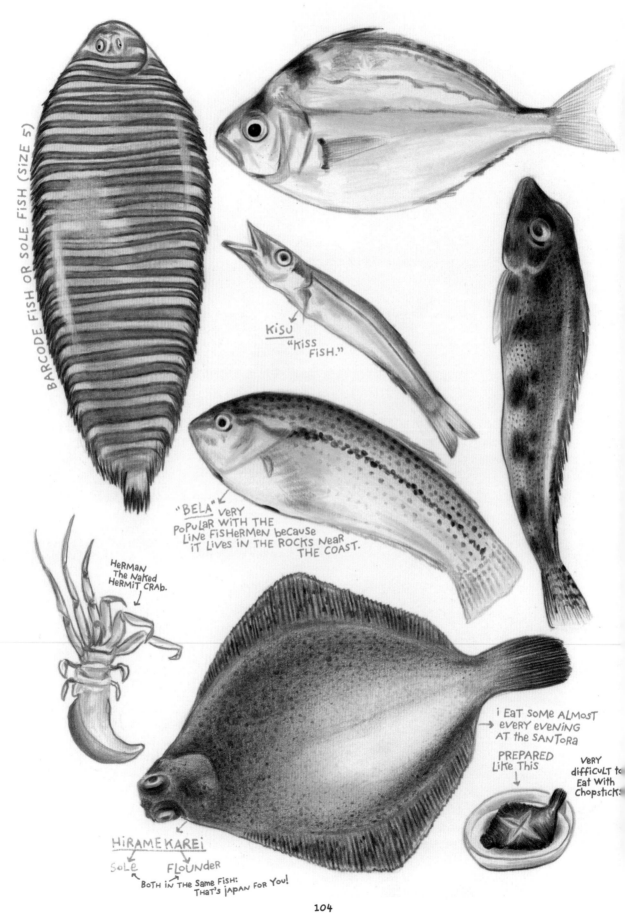

BARCODE FISH OR SOLE FISH (SIZE 5)

KISU
"KISS FISH."

"BELA" VERY
POPULAR WITH THE
LINE FISHERMEN because
iT LiVES iN THE ROCKS NEAR
THE COAST.

HERMAN
The Naked
HERMiT CRAb.

i EAT SOME ALMOST
EVERY EVENiNG
AT the SANToRA

PREPARED
Like THiS

VERY
diffiCULT to
EAT With
Chopsticks

HiRAME KAREi

SOLE   FLOUNDER

BOTH iN THE SAME FiSH:
THAT's jApAN FoR You!

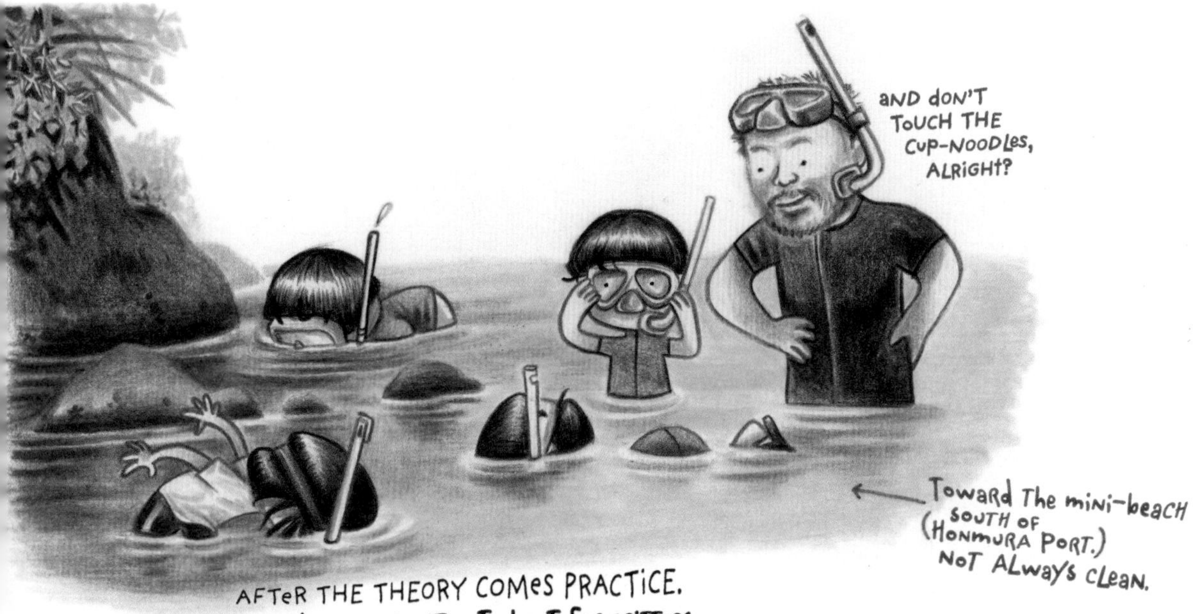
AND DON'T TOUCH THE CUP-NOODLES, ALRIGHT?
TOWARD THE MINI-BEACH SOUTH OF (HONMURA PORT.) NOT ALWAYS CLEAN.

AFTER THE THEORY COMES PRACTICE.
THE CHILDREN ARE INVITED TO HUNT FOR CRITTERS IN THE ROCKS AS AN INTRODUCTION TO DIVING.

I STAY IN THE COMPANY OF SOME PARENTS, HIROSHI, OKAMOTO AND HIDEKI, WHO DISCOVERS THE TEKO PRINCIPLE:

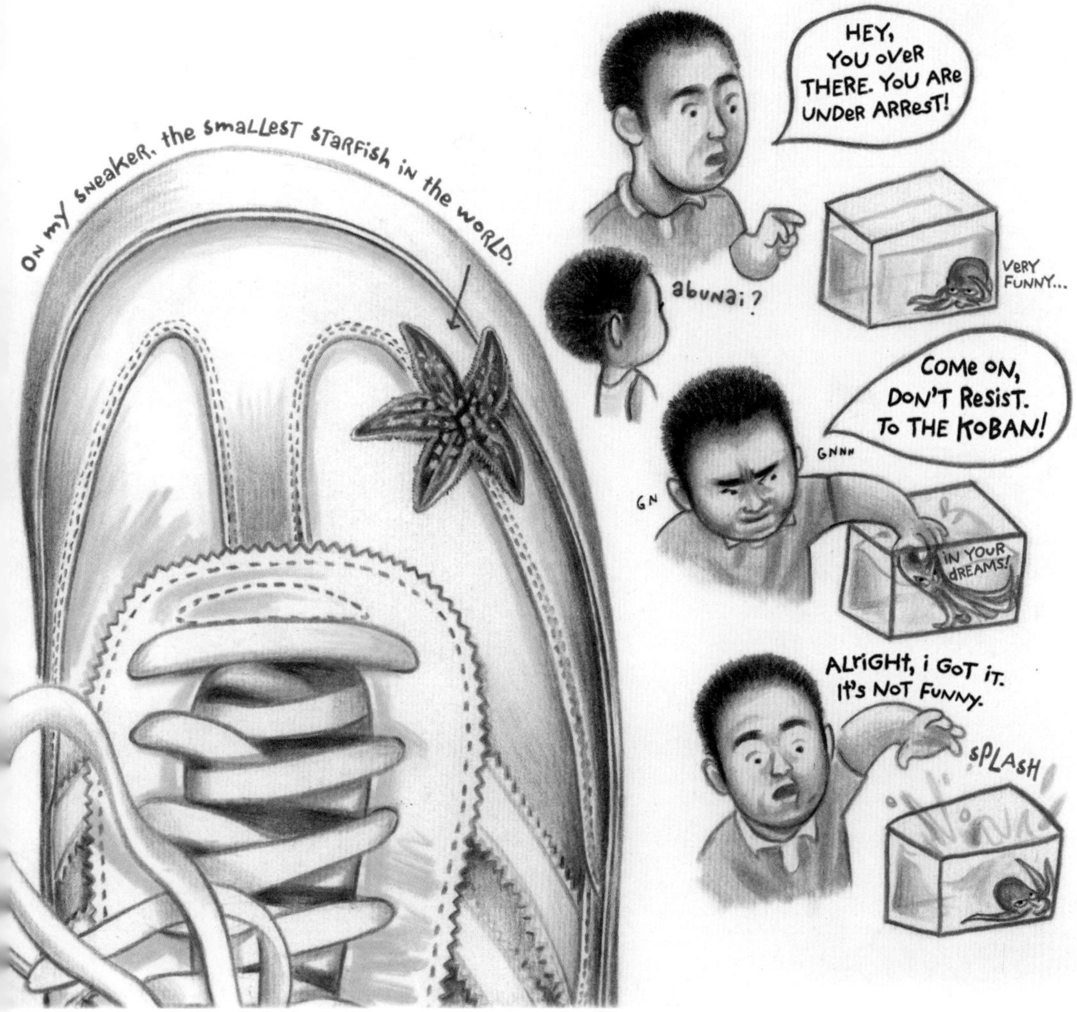
ON MY SNEAKER, THE SMALLEST STARFISH IN THE WORLD.
HEY, YOU OVER THERE. YOU ARE UNDER ARREST!
VERY FUNNY...
ABUNAI?
COME ON, DON'T RESIST. TO THE KOBAN!
GNNN
GN
IN YOUR DREAMS!
ALRIGHT, I GOT IT. IT'S NOT FUNNY.
SPLASH

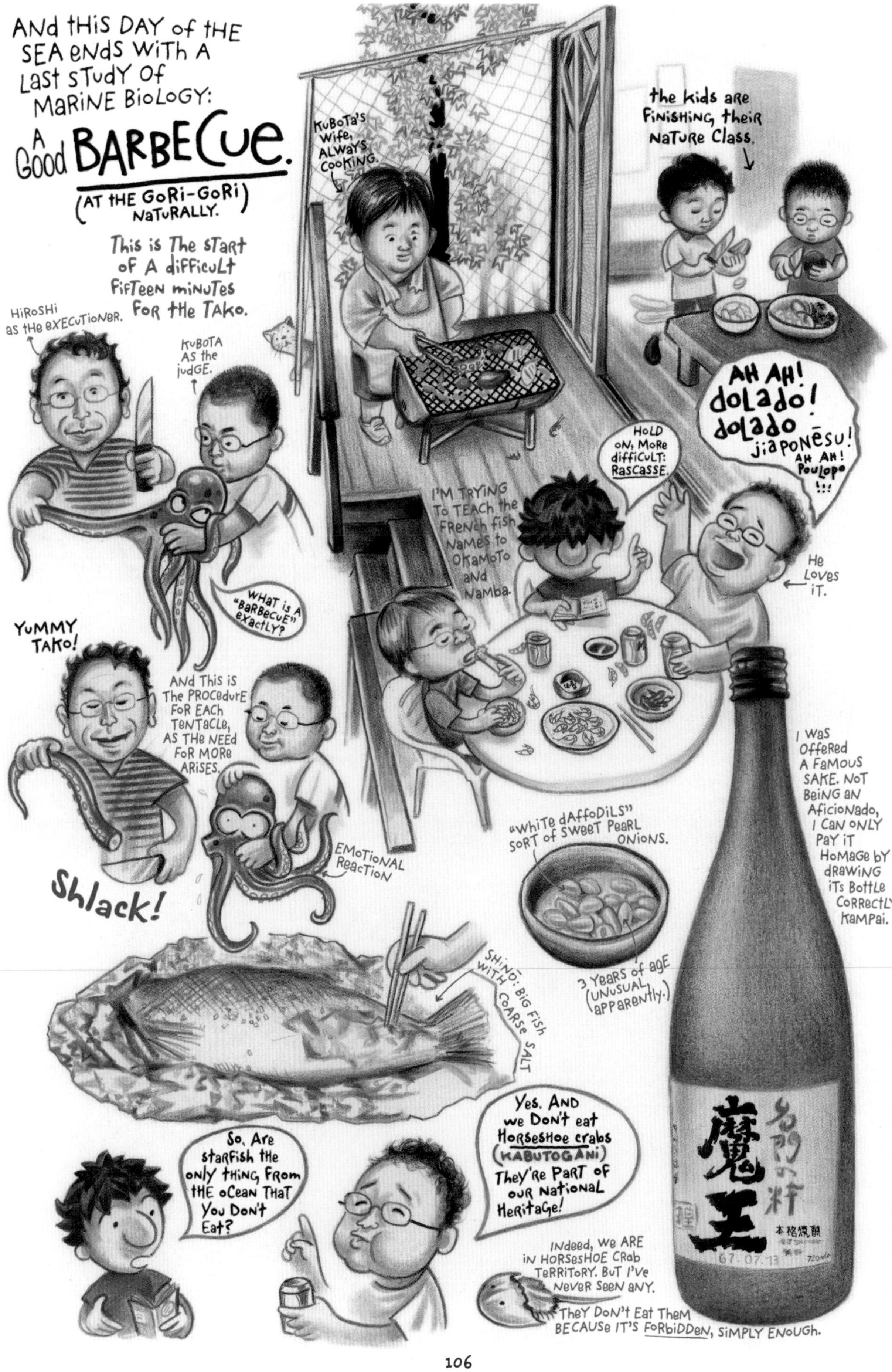
And this day of the sea ends with a last study of marine biology:
A Good BARBECUE.
(At the Gori-Gori naturally.)
This is the start of a difficult fifteen minutes for the Tako.
Hiroshi as the executioner.
Kubota as the judge.
"What is a "barbecue" exactly?
Yummy Tako!
And this is the procedure for each tentacle, as the need for more arises.
Emotional reaction
Shlack!
Kubota's wife, always cooking.
the kids are finishing their nature class.
AH AH! dolado! dolado jiaponēsu! AH AH! Poulopo !!!
Hold on, more difficult: Rascasse.
I'm trying to teach the French fish names to Okamoto and Namba.
He loves it.
"White daffodils" sort of sweet pearl onions.
3 years of age (unusual apparently.)
Shino: big fish with coarse salt
I was offered a famous sake. Not being an aficionado, I can only pay it homage by drawing its bottle correctly. Kampai.
魔王
So, are starfish the only thing from the ocean that you don't eat?
Yes. And we don't eat horseshoe crabs (Kabutogani) They're part of our national heritage!
Indeed, we are in horseshoe crab territory. But I've never seen any.
They don't eat them because it's forbidden, simply enough.

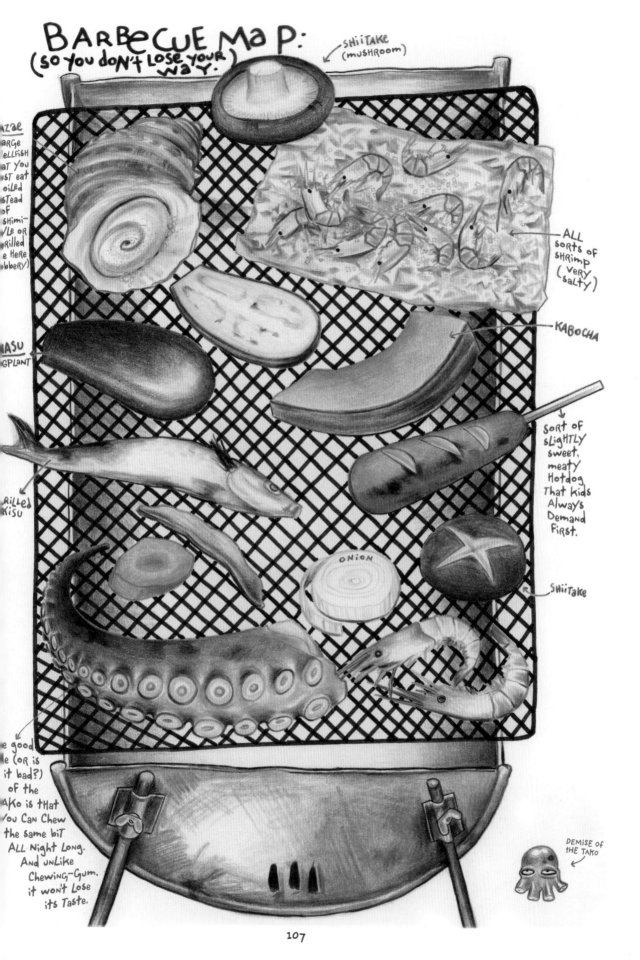

BARBECUE MaP:
(SO YOU DON'T LOSE YOUR WaY.)

SHiiTAKE
(MUSHROOM)

...ZAE
...ARGE
...ELLFISH
...AT YOU
...ST EAT
...OILED
...STEAD
...OF
...SHIMI-
...LE OR
...RILLED
... E HERE
...BBERY)

ALL SORTS OF SHRIMP (VERY SALTY)

KABOCHA

...ASU
...GPLANT

SORT OF SLIGHTLY SWEET, MEATY HOTDOG THAT KIDS ALWAYS DEMAND FIRST.

...RILLED
...KISU

ONION

SHiiTAKE

...E GOOD
...LE (OR IS
... IT BAD?)
... OF THE
...AKO IS THAT
...OU CAN CHEW
... THE SAME BIT
... ALL NIGHT LONG.
... AND UNLIKE
... CHEWING-GUM.
... IT WON'T LOSE
... ITS TASTE.

DEMISE OF THE TAKO

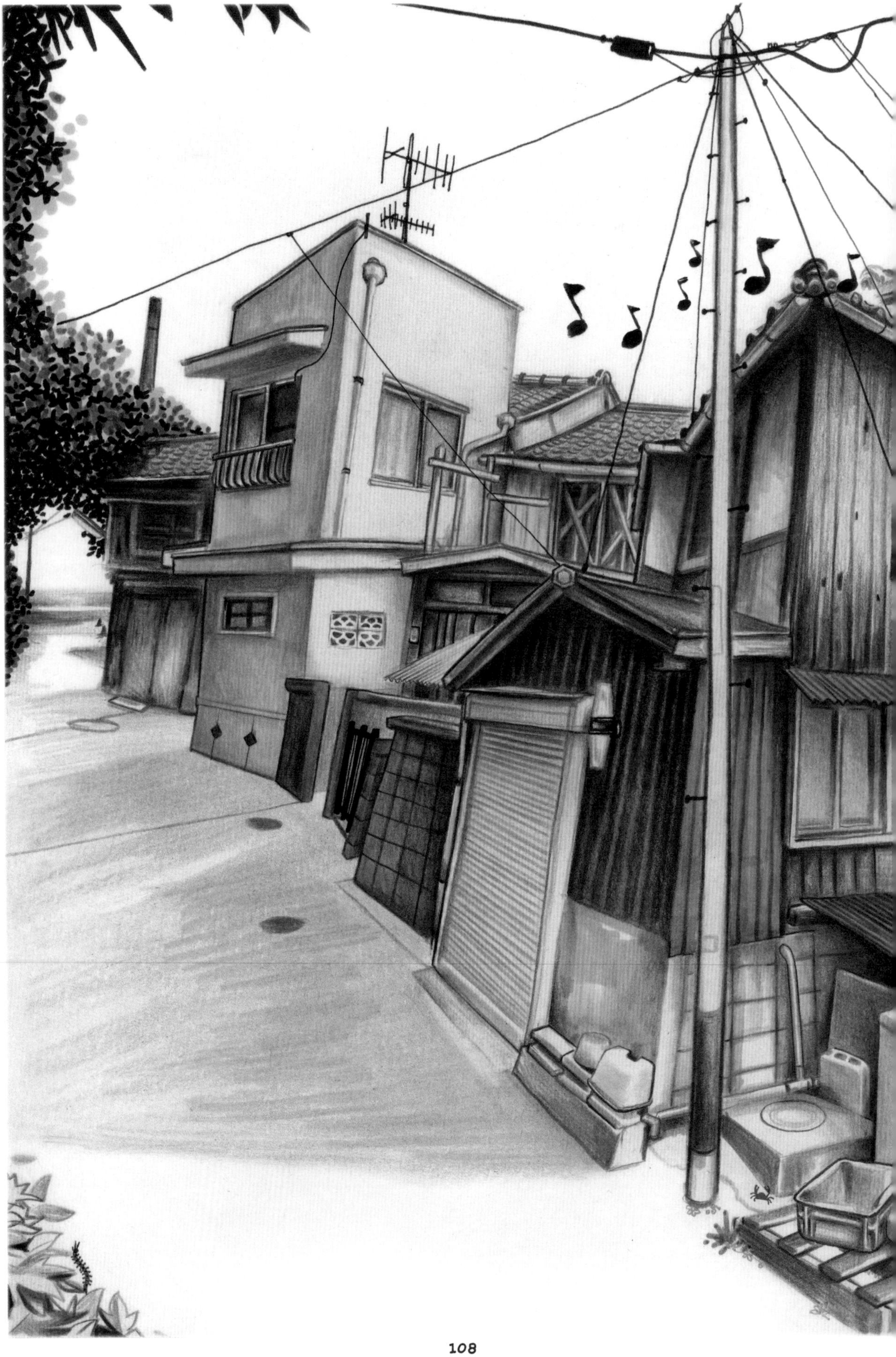

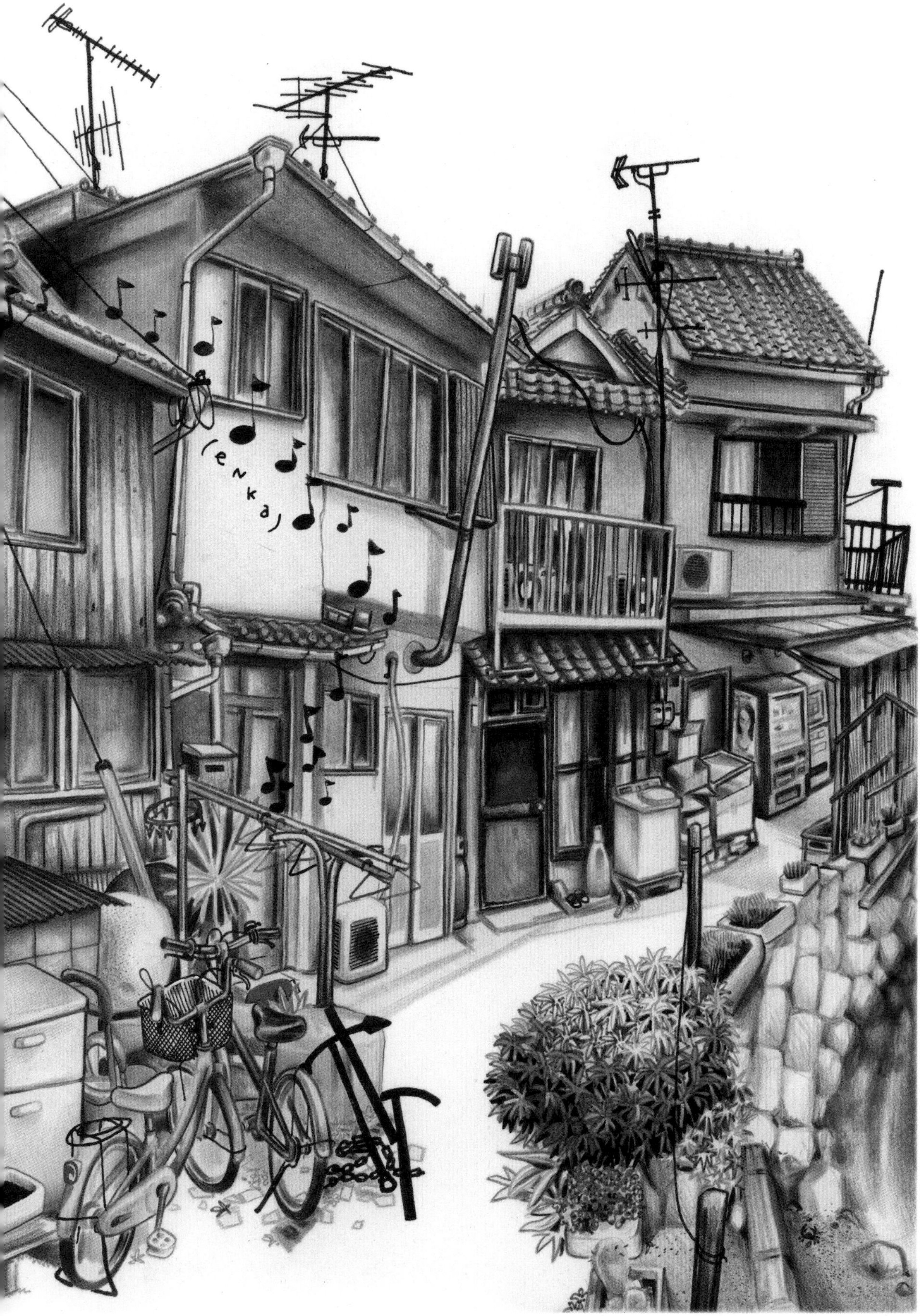
(enka)

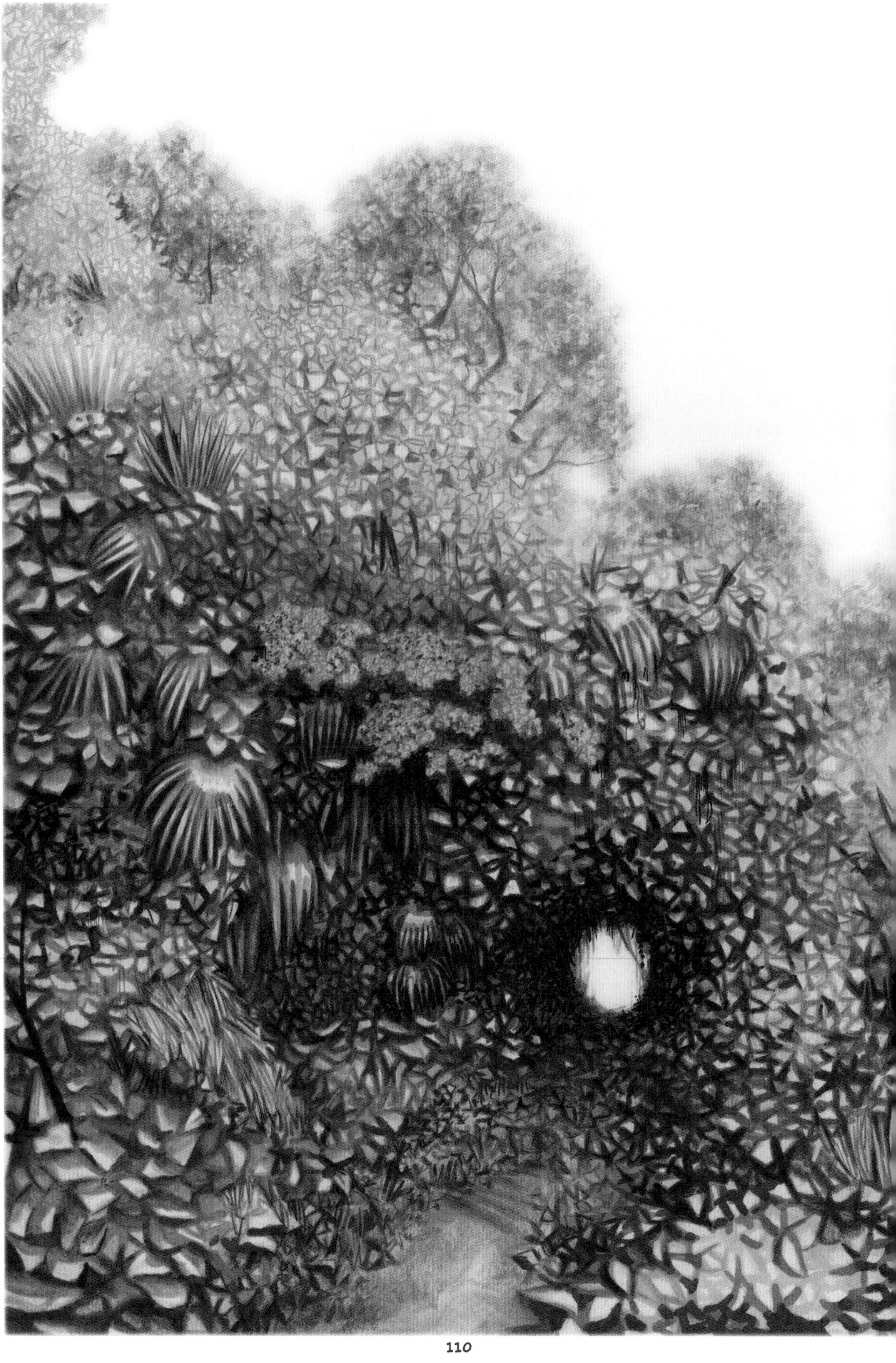

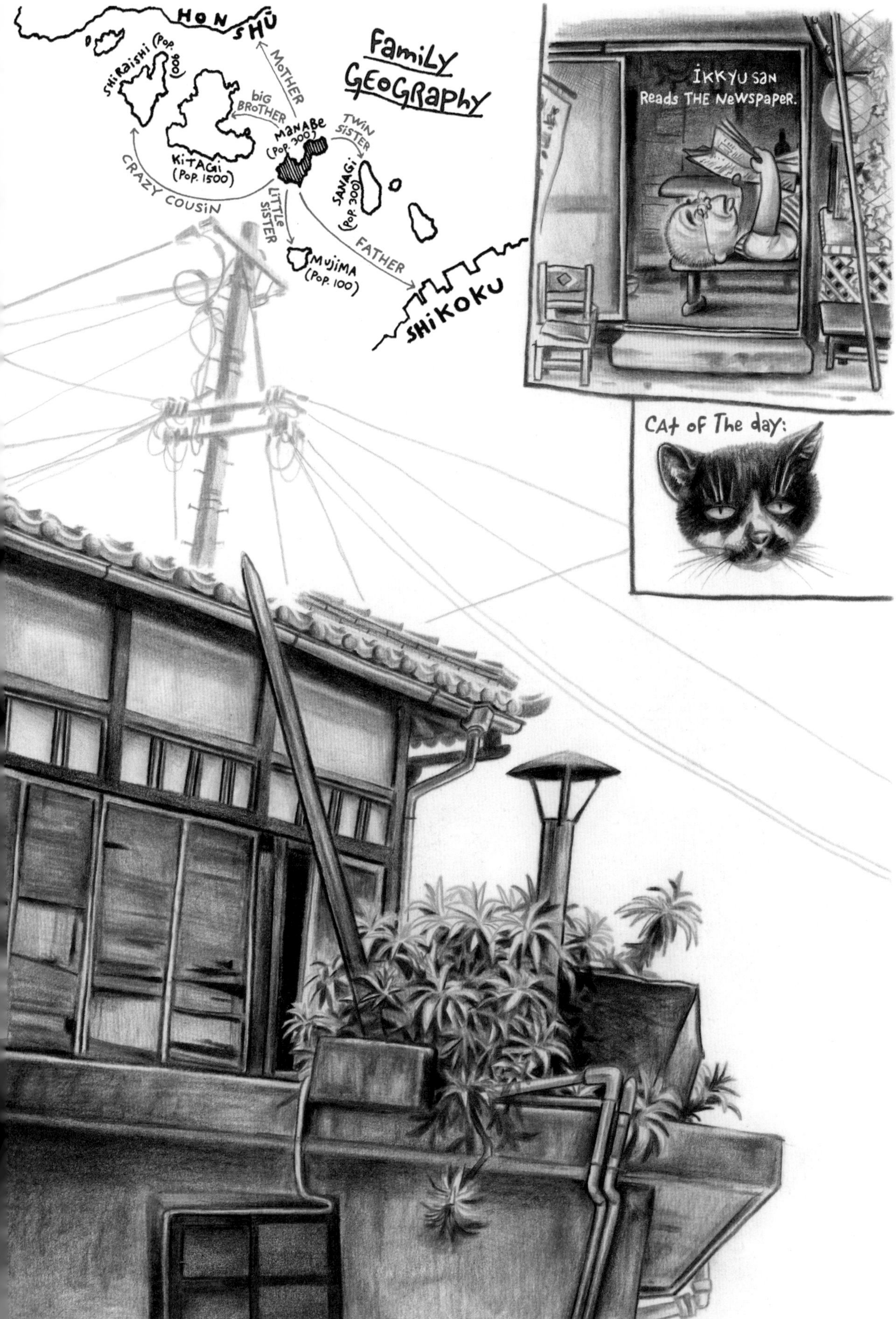

Family Geography
HONSHŪ
SHIRAISHI (POP. 900)
MOTHER
big BROTHER
MANABE (POP. 300)
TWIN SISTER
KITAGI (POP. 1500)
CRAZY COUSIN
LITTLE SISTER
SANAGI (POP. 300)
MUJIMA (POP. 100)
FATHER
SHIKOKU
IKKYU SAN Reads THE NEWSPAPER.
CAT of The day:

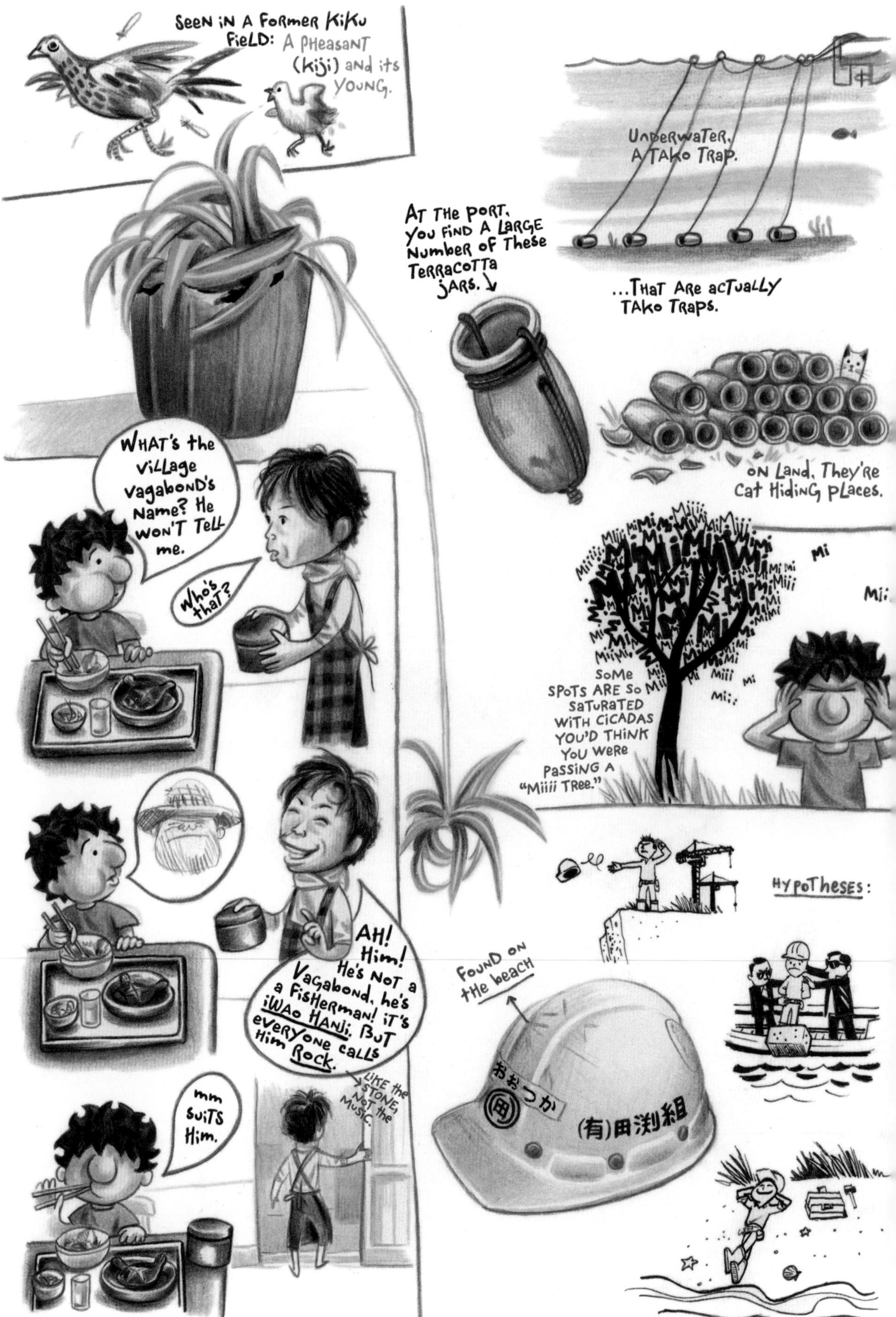
SEEN IN A FORMER KIKU FIELD: A PHEASANT (KIJI) AND ITS YOUNG.
WHAT'S THE VILLAGE VAGABOND'S NAME? HE WON'T TELL ME.
WHO'S THAT?
AH! HIM! HE'S NOT A VAGABOND, HE'S A FISHERMAN! IT'S IWAO HANJI. BUT EVERYONE CALLS HIM ROCK.
LIKE THE STONE, NOT THE MUSIC.
MM SUITS HIM.
AT THE PORT, YOU FIND A LARGE NUMBER OF THESE TERRACOTTA JARS.
UNDERWATER, A TAKO TRAP.
...THAT ARE ACTUALLY TAKO TRAPS.
ON LAND, THEY'RE CAT HIDING PLACES.
SOME SPOTS ARE SO SATURATED WITH CICADAS YOU'D THINK YOU WERE PASSING A "MIIII TREE."
MI
MI
HYPOTHESES:
FOUND ON THE BEACH
おおつか
(有)田渕組

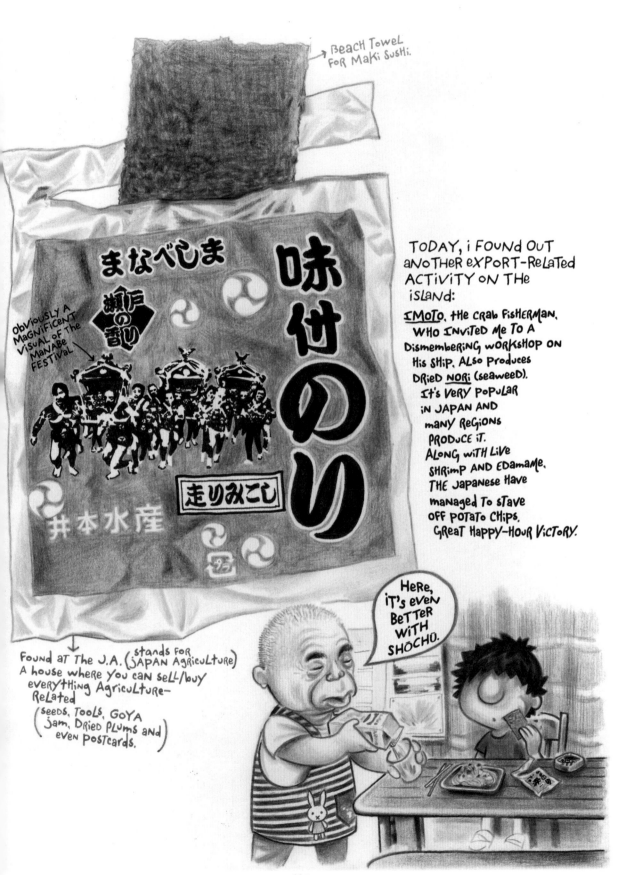

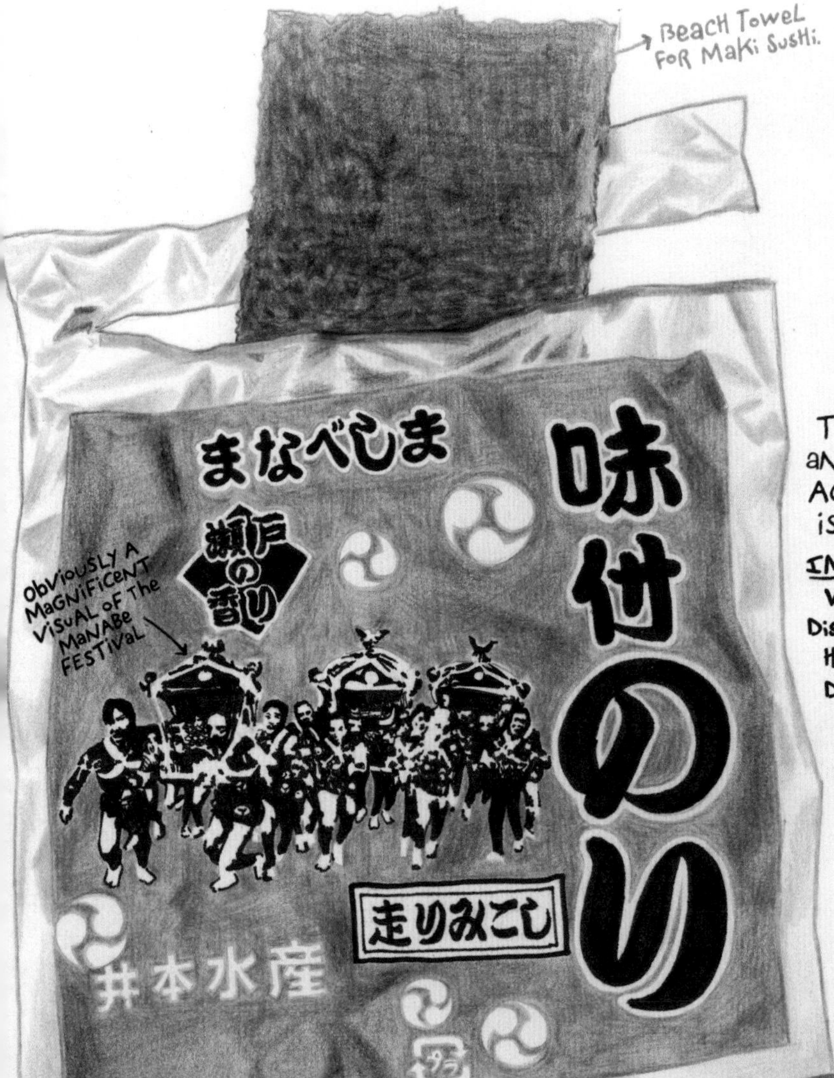
Beach Towel for Maki Sushi.
まなべしま
瀬戸の香り
味付のり
Obviously a magnificent visual of the Manabe festival
走りみこし
井本水産

Found at the J.A. (stands for Japan Agriculture)
A house where you can sell/buy everything agriculture-related
(seeds, tools, goya jam, dried plums and even postcards.)

TODAY, I FOUND OUT ANOTHER EXPORT-RELATED ACTIVITY ON THE ISLAND:

IMOTO, THE CRAB FISHERMAN, WHO INVITED ME TO A DISMEMBERING WORKSHOP ON HIS SHIP, ALSO PRODUCES DRIED NORI (SEAWEED). IT'S VERY POPULAR IN JAPAN AND MANY REGIONS PRODUCE IT. ALONG WITH LIVE SHRIMP AND EDAMAME, THE JAPANESE HAVE MANAGED TO STAVE OFF POTATO CHIPS. GREAT HAPPY-HOUR VICTORY.

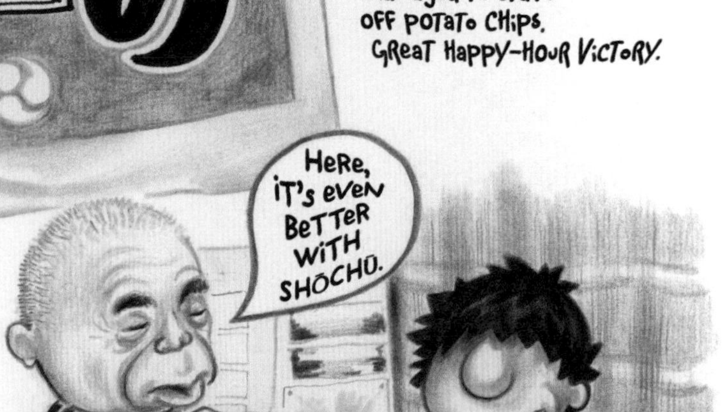
Here, it's even better with shochū.

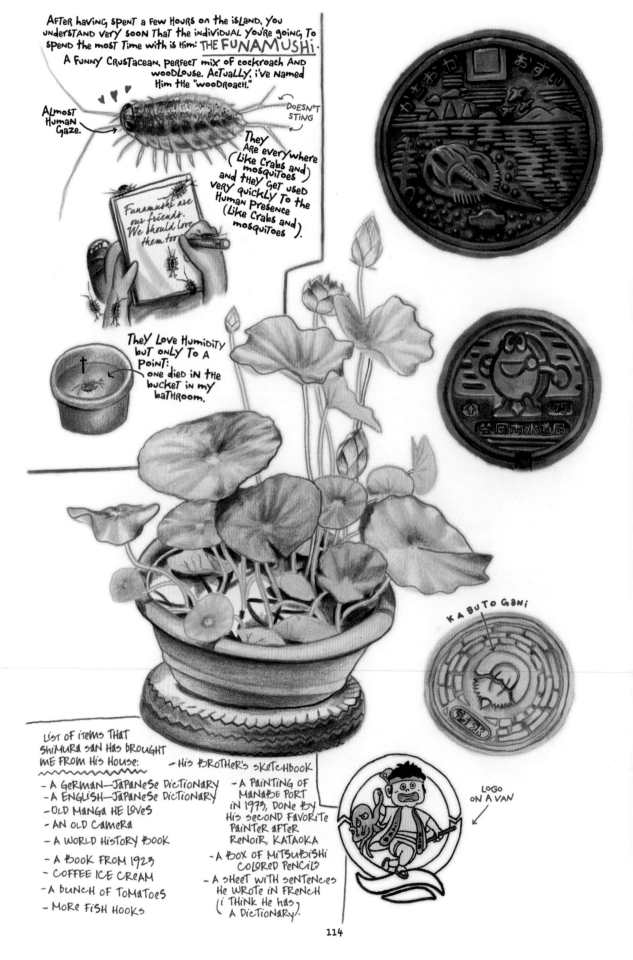

After having spent a few hours on the island, you understand very soon that the individual you're going to spend the most time with is him: THE FUNAMUSHI.

A funny crustacean, perfect mix of cockroach and woodlouse. Actually, i've named him the "woodroach."

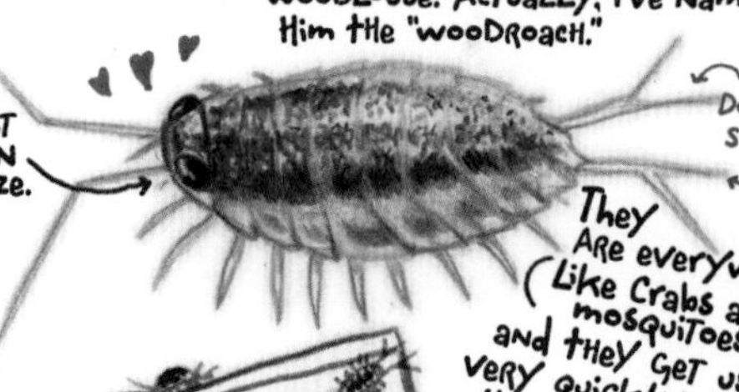
Almost Human Gaze.
Doesn't sting

They are everywhere (like crabs and mosquitoes) and they get used very quickly to the human presence (like crabs and mosquitoes).

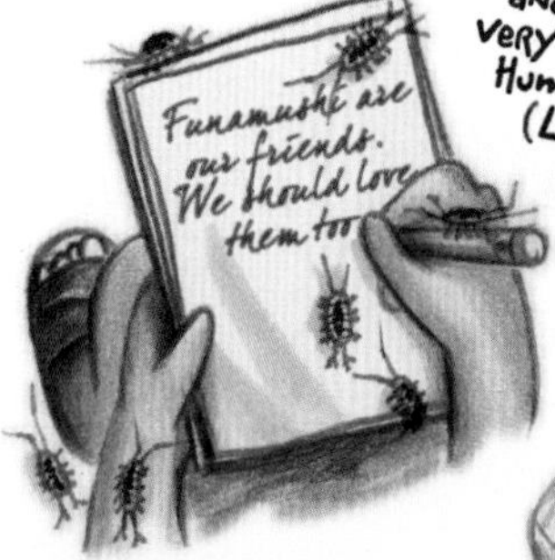
Funamushi are our friends. We should love them too

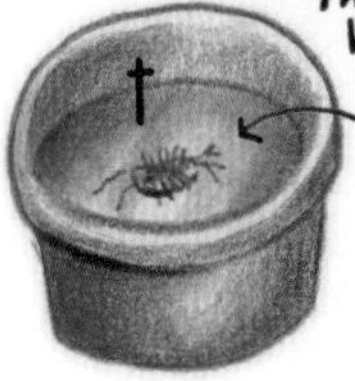

They love humidity but only to a point: one died in the bucket in my bathroom.

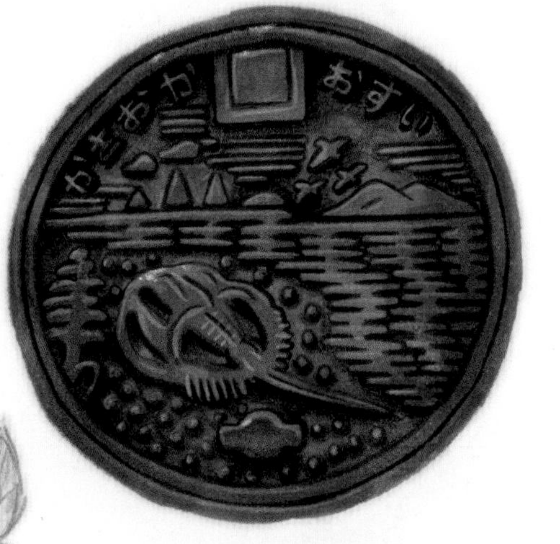
おすい

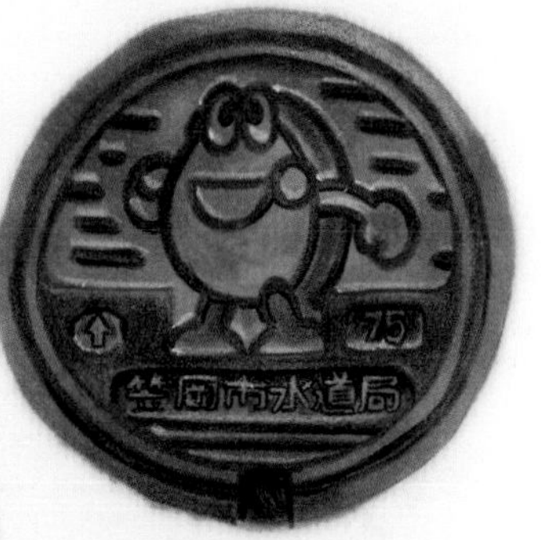
笠岡市水道局

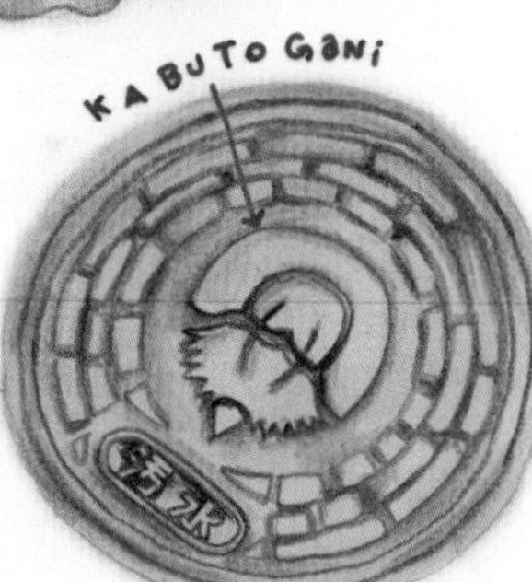
KABUTO GANi

List of items that Shimura san has brought me from his house:

- A German—Japanese dictionary
- A English—Japanese dictionary
- Old manga he loves
- An old camera
- A world history book
- A book from 1923
- Coffee ice cream
- A bunch of tomatoes
- More fish hooks
- His brother's sketchbook
- A painting of Manabe Port in 1973, done by his second favorite painter after Renoir, Kataoka
- A box of Mitsubishi colored pencils
- A sheet with sentences he wrote in French (i think he has a dictionary).

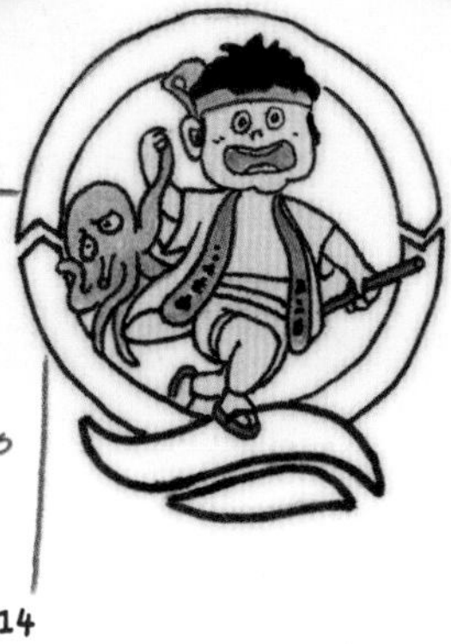

Logo on a van

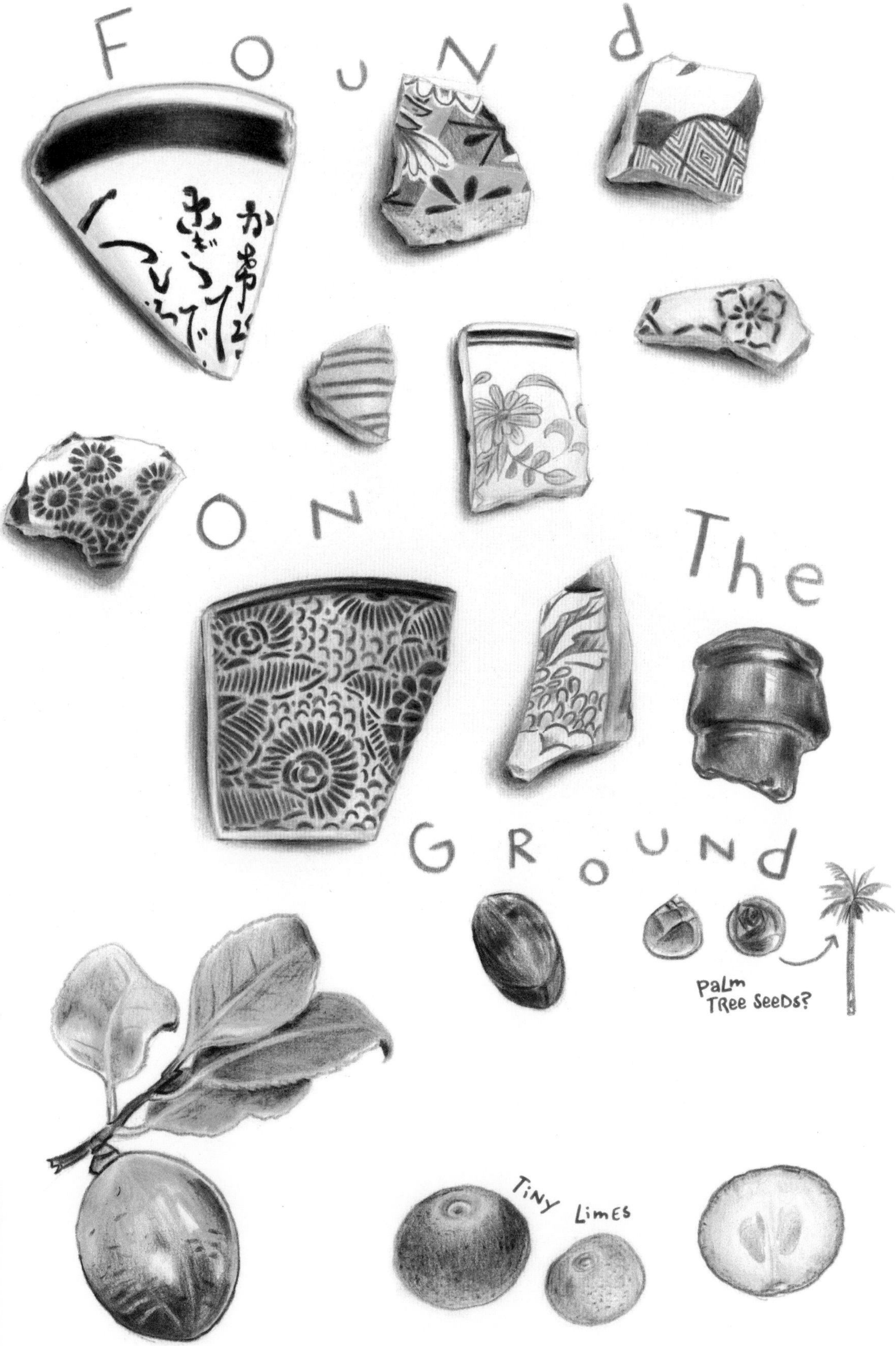
Found
On
The
Ground
Palm Tree Seeds?
Tiny Limes

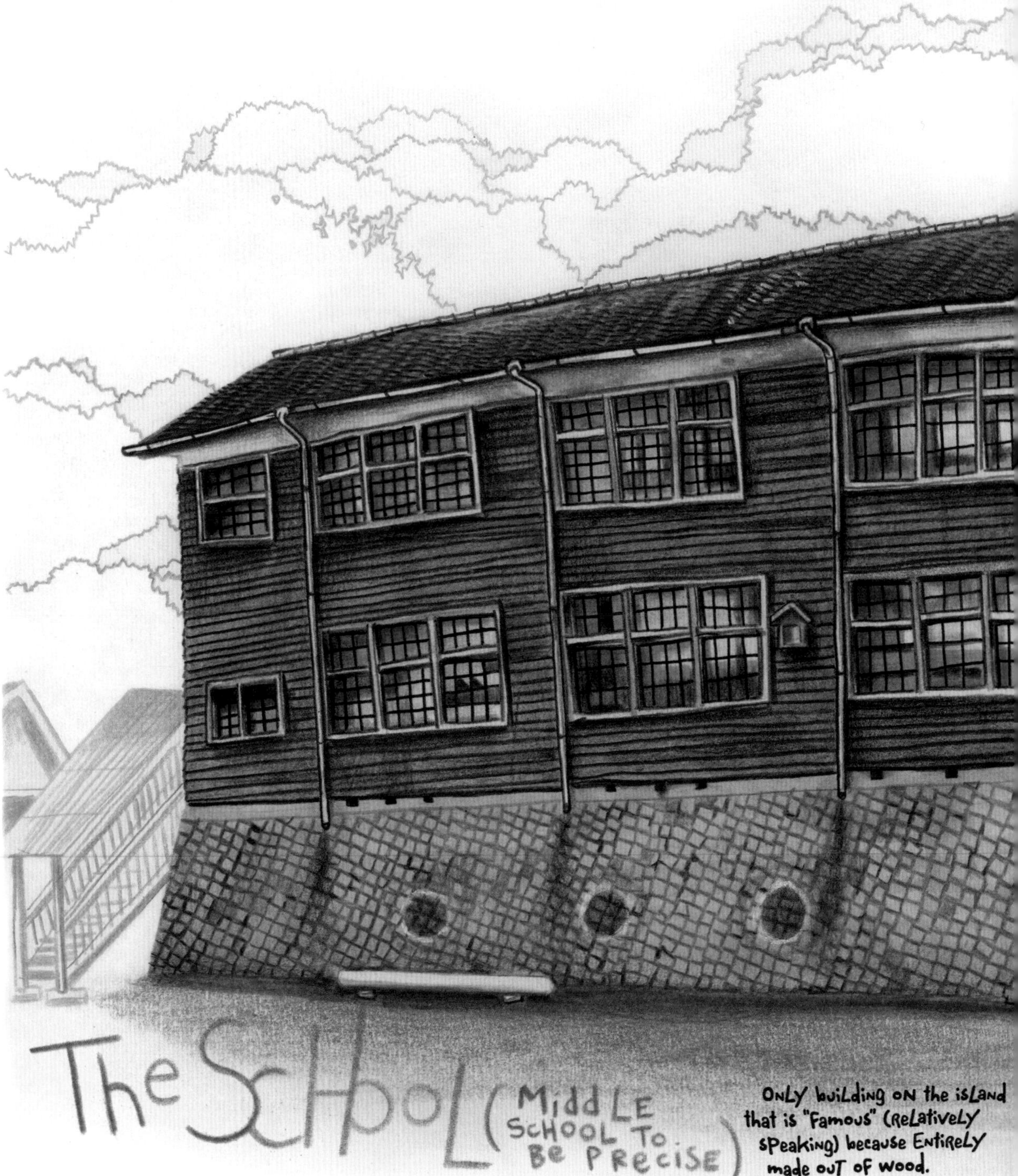

The School (Middle school to be precise) Chūgakkou

Only building on the island that is "Famous" (relatively speaking) because entirely made out of wood.

The elementary school building is that way.

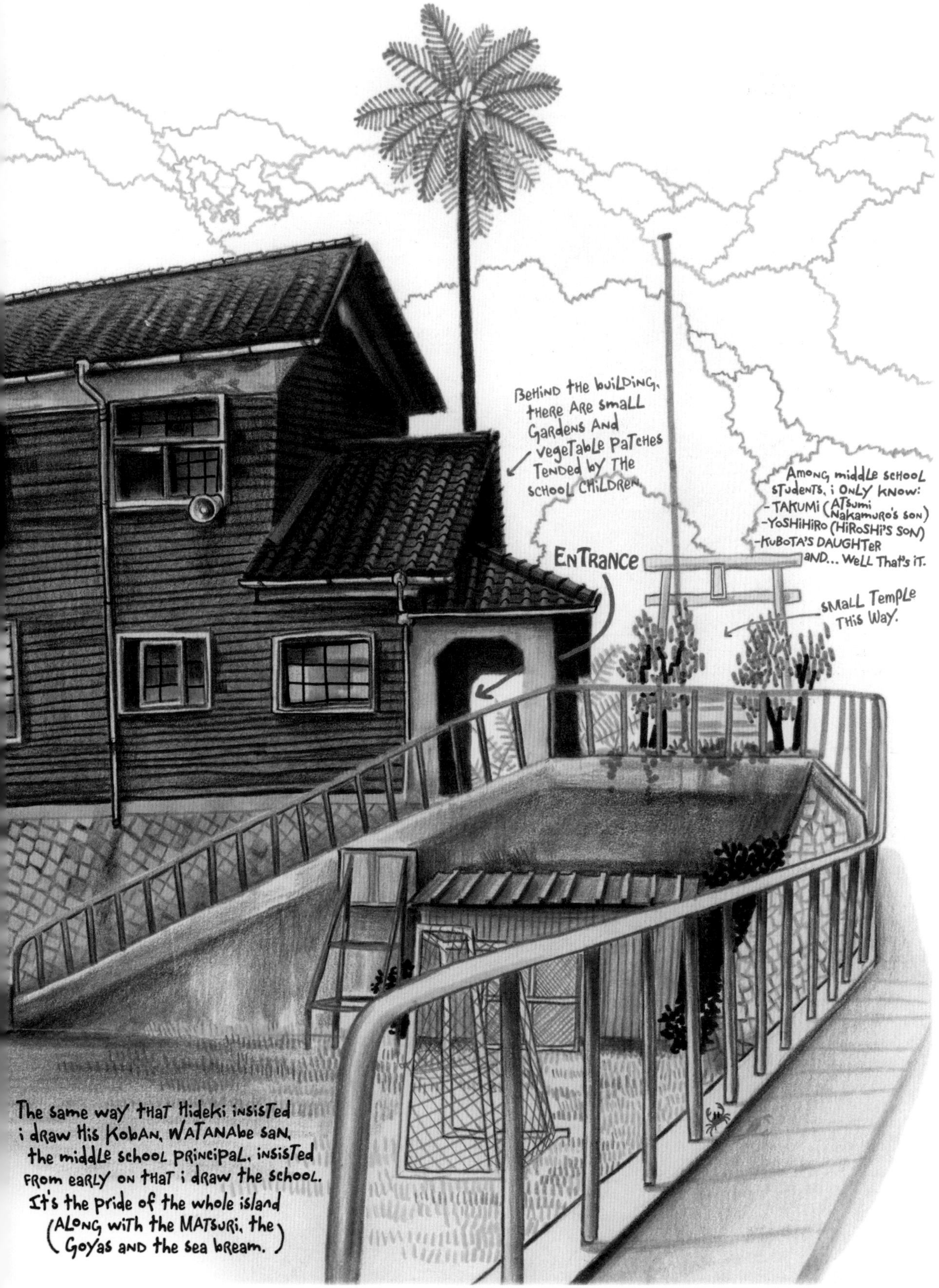
BEHIND THE building, THERE ARE small GARDENS AND VEGETABLE PATCHES TENDED by THE SCHOOL CHILDREN.
ENTRANCE
AMONG middle school STUDENTS, i ONLY KNOW:
-TAKUMI (ATSUMI NAKAMURO'S SON)
-YOSHIHIRO (HIROSHI'S SON)
-KUBOTA'S DAUGHTER
AND... WELL That's iT.
SMALL Temple THIS Way.
The same way THAT Hideki insisTed i draw His Koban, WATANAbe SAN, the middLe school PRiNcipaL, insisTed FROM earLY ON THAT i draw the school. It's the pride of the whole island (ALONG with the MATSURi, the Goyas AND the sea bream.)

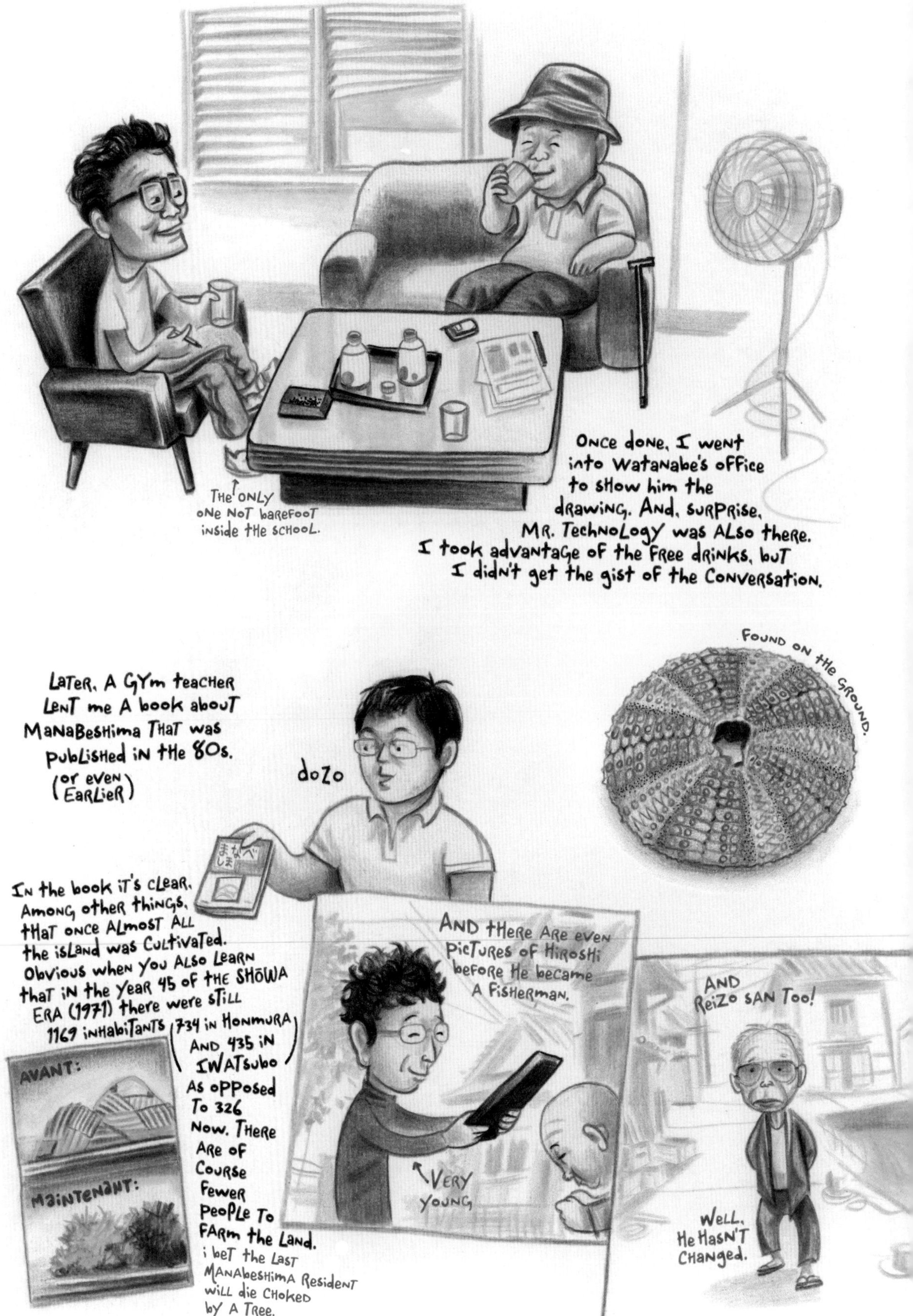
THE ONLY ONE NOT BAREFOOT INSIDE THE SCHOOL.
ONCE DONE, I WENT INTO WATANABE'S OFFICE TO SHOW HIM THE DRAWING. AND, SURPRISE, MR. TECHNOLOGY WAS ALSO THERE. I TOOK ADVANTAGE OF THE FREE DRINKS, BUT I DIDN'T GET THE GIST OF THE CONVERSATION.
LATER, A GYM TEACHER LENT ME A BOOK ABOUT MANABESHIMA THAT WAS PUBLISHED IN THE 80S. (OR EVEN EARLIER)
DOZO
まなべしま
FOUND ON THE GROUND.
IN THE BOOK IT'S CLEAR, AMONG OTHER THINGS, THAT ONCE ALMOST ALL THE ISLAND WAS CULTIVATED. OBVIOUS WHEN YOU ALSO LEARN THAT IN THE YEAR 45 OF THE SHŌWA ERA (1971) THERE WERE STILL 1169 INHABITANTS (734 IN HONMURA AND 435 IN IWATSUBO) AS OPPOSED TO 326 NOW. THERE ARE OF COURSE FEWER PEOPLE TO FARM THE LAND.
I BET THE LAST MANABESHIMA RESIDENT WILL DIE CHOKED BY A TREE.
AVANT:
MAINTENANT:
AND THERE ARE EVEN PICTURES OF HIROSHI BEFORE HE BECAME A FISHERMAN.
VERY YOUNG
AND REIZO SAN TOO!
WELL, HE HASN'T CHANGED.

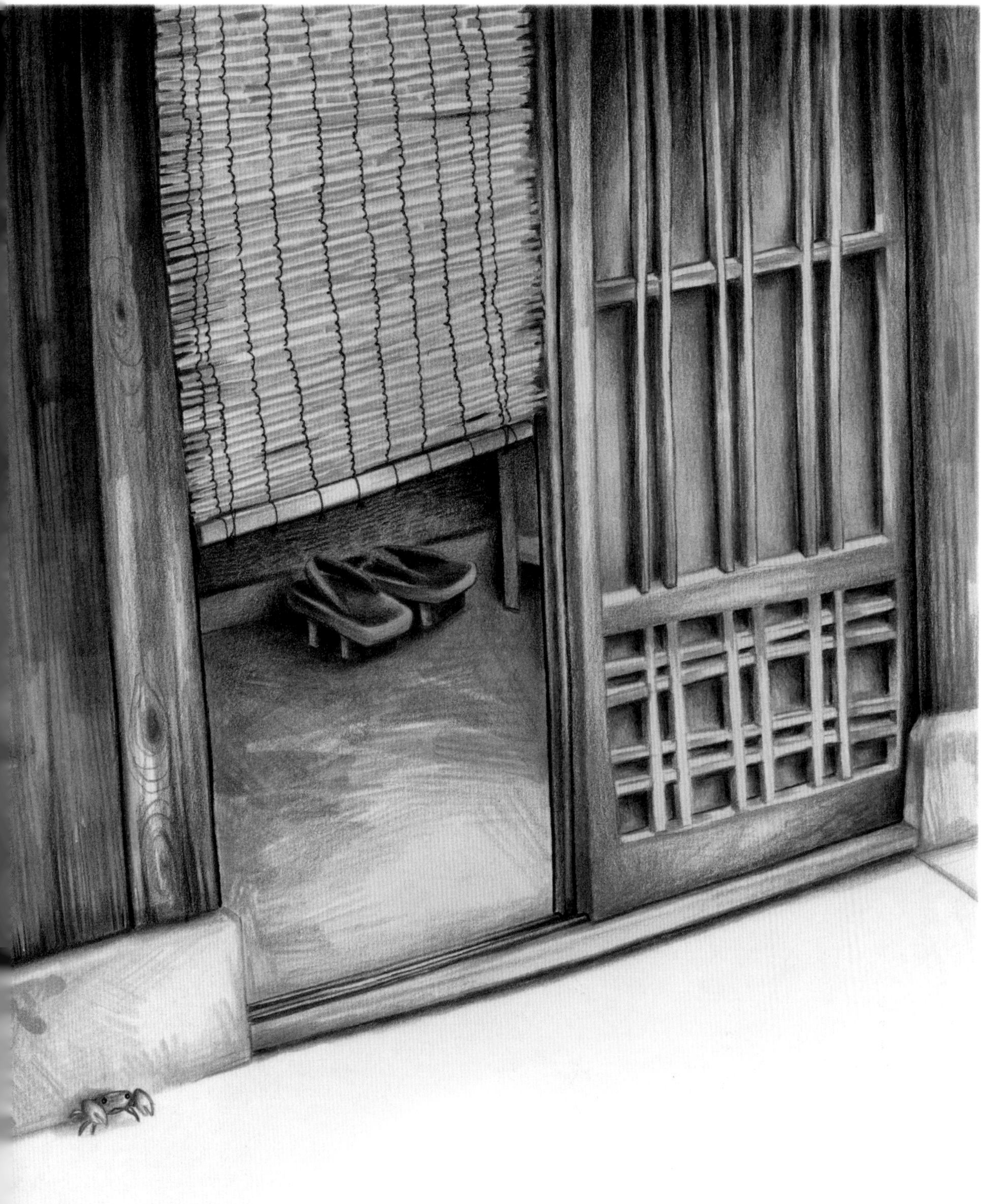

LOOKING INTO THE INN.

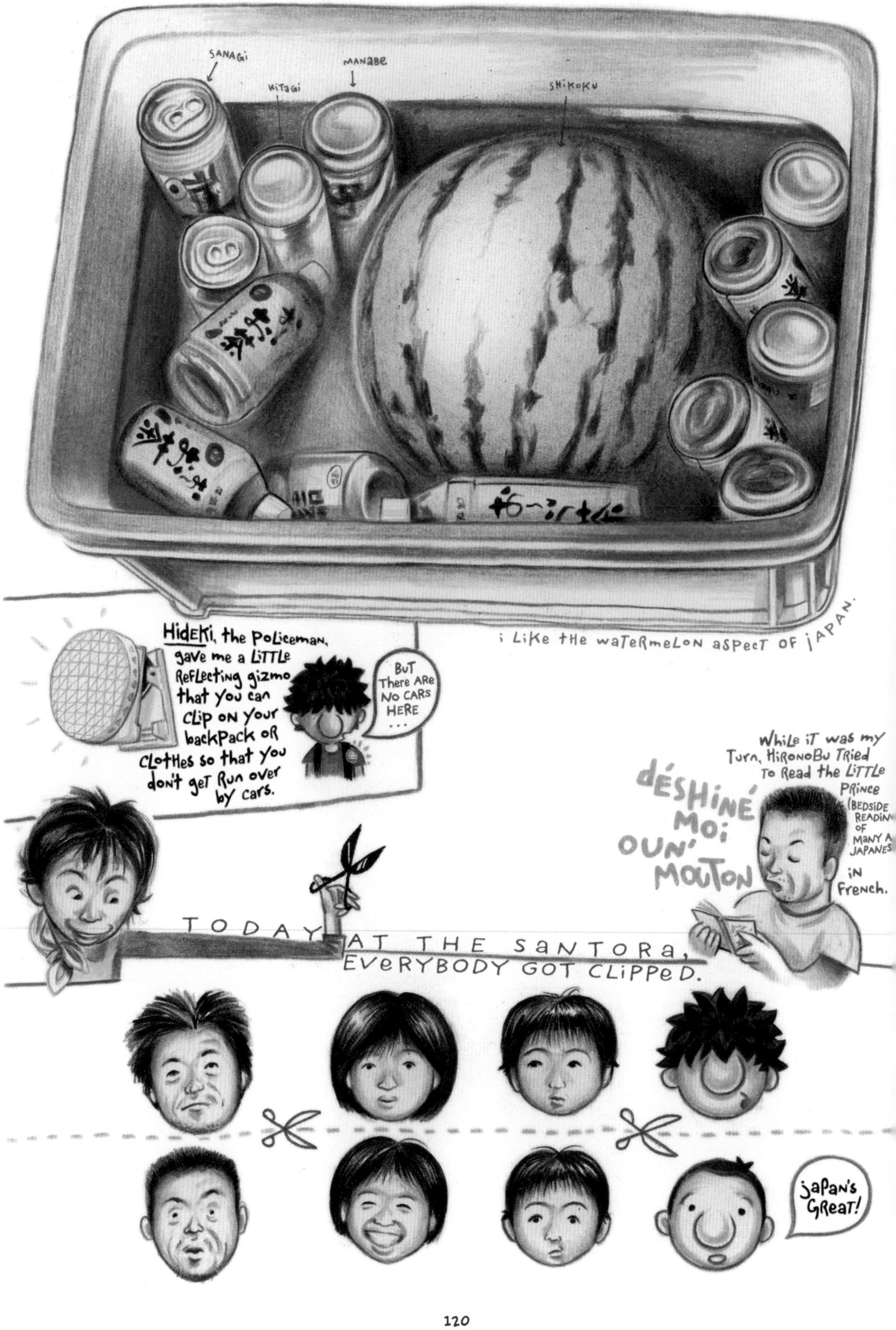
SANAGI
KITAGI
MANABE
SHIKOKU
i Like the watermelon aspect of japan.
Hideki, the Policeman, gave me a Little Reflecting gizmo that you can clip on your backpack or clothes so that you don't get Run over by cars.
But There Are No Cars Here ...
While it was my Turn, Hironobu Tried To Read the Little Prince (Bedside Readin of Many A Japanes in French.
déshiné moi oun' mouton
Today at the santora, everybody got clipped.
japan's Great!

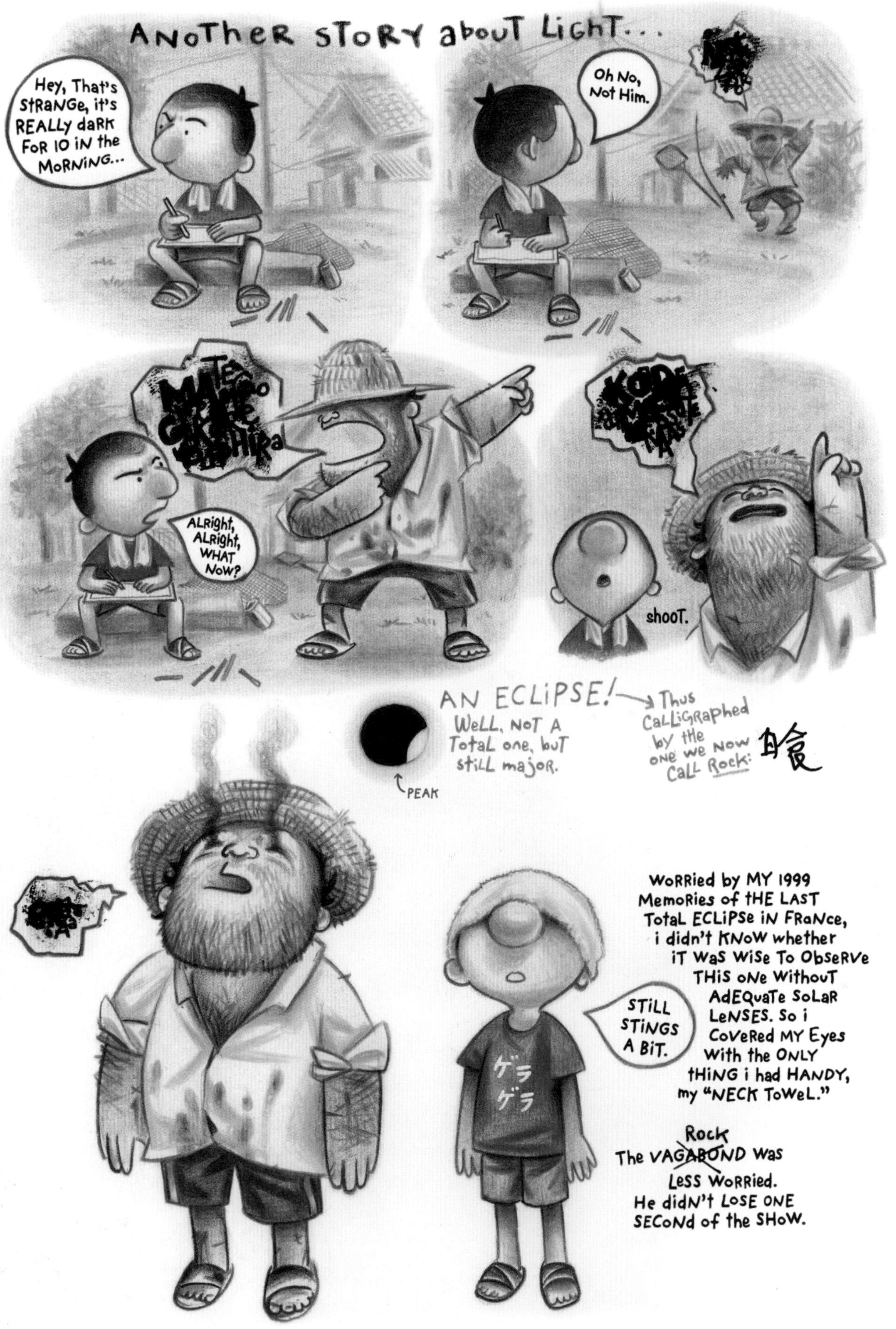

ANOTHER STORY about LIGHT...
Hey, That's STRANGE, it's REALLY dark FOR 10 IN the MORNING...
Oh No, Not Him.
ALRight, ALRight, WHAT NOW?
shooT.
AN ECLIPSE!
Thus CaLLiGRaphed by the one we Now CaLL Rock:
WeLL, NOT A TotaL one, buT still major.
PEAK
STiLL STiNGS A BiT.
ゲラゲラ
WoRRied by MY 1999 Memories of tHE LAST TotaL ECLiPSe iN FRaNce, i didn't KNOW whether iT WaS WiSe To ObSeRVe THIS oNe WithouT AdEQuaTe SoLaR LeNSES. So i CoVeRed MY Eyes With the ONLY tHiNG i had HANDY, my "NECK ToWeL."
The ~~VAGABOND~~ Rock Was LeSS WoRRied. He didN't LOSE ONE SECoNd of the SHoW.

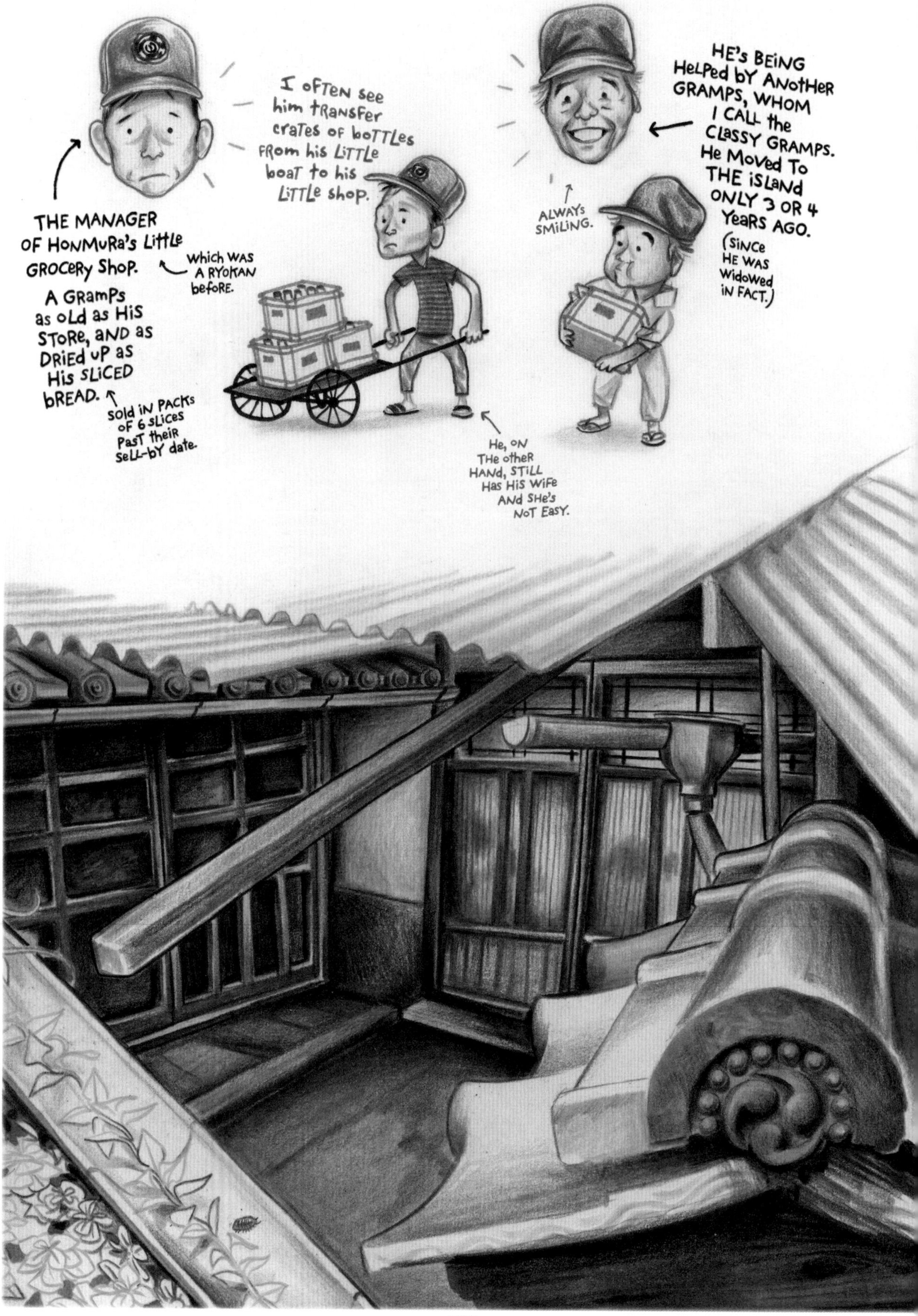
THE MANAGER OF HONMURa's Little GROCERY ShoP.
Which WAS A RYOKAN before.
A GRAMPS as oLd as HIS STORE, aND as DRIED UP as HIS SLICED bREAD.
Sold IN PACKS of 6 sLices Past their seLL-bY date.
I oFTEN see him TRANSFER crates of boTTLes FROM his LITTLE boat to his LITTLE shop.
HE'S BEING HELPED bY ANOTHER GRAMPS, WHOM I CALL the CLASSY GRAMPS. He Moved To THE iSLand ONLY 3 OR 4 YEARS AGO.
(SINCE HE WAS Widowed iN FACT.)
ALWAYS SMILING.
He, ON THE other HAND, STILL Has HIS WIFE AND SHE's NOT EASY.

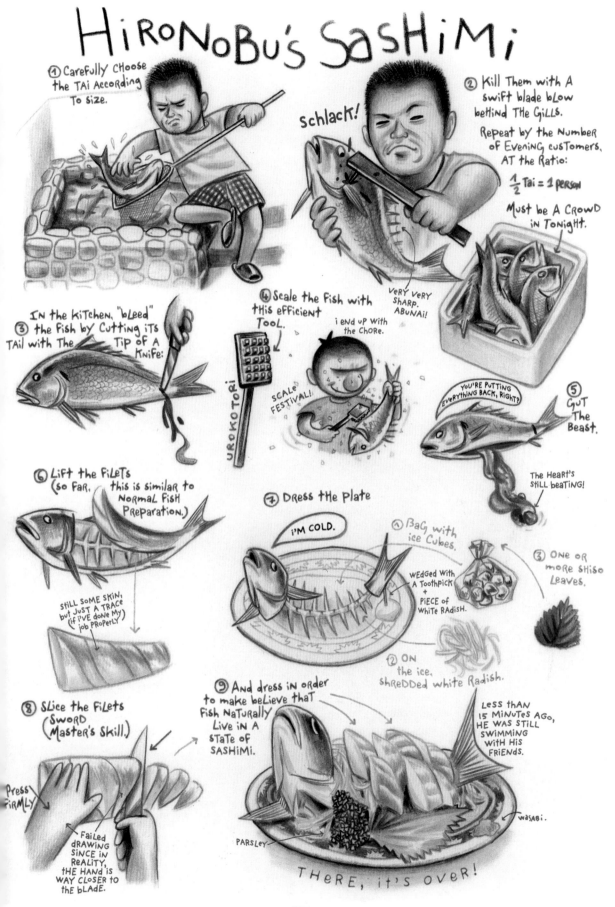

HIRONOBU'S SASHIMI

① Carefully Choose the TAI According to size.

Schlack!

② Kill Them with A swift blade blow behind The Gills.

Repeat by the Number of Evening customers, AT the Ratio:

$\frac{1}{2}$ Tai = 1 person

Must be A Crowd in Tonight.

VeRY VeRY SHARP. ABUNAi!

③ IN the kitchen, "bleed" the Fish by Cutting its Tail with The Tip of A Knife:

④ Scale the Fish with this efficient Tool.

i end up with the Chore.

UROKOTORI

SCALE FESTiVAL!

YOU'RE PUTTING EVERYTHiNG BACK, RiGHT?

⑤ GUT The Beast.

The Heart's Still beating!

⑥ Lift the Filets (so far, this is similar to NORMAL FiSH Preparation.)

⑦ Dress the Plate

i'M COLD.

① BaG with ice Cubes.

③ ONE OR more SHiSO Leaves.

WEDged With A Toothpick + PIECE of WHiTe RAdish.

STILL SOME SKIN, but just a TRACE (if i'VE done My job properly)

② ON the ice, SHReDDed white Radish.

⑧ Slice the Filets (SWORD (Master's Skill.))

Press FiRMLY

Failed dRAWiNG SiNCE iN REALiTY, THE HAND iS WAY CLOSER TO the bLAdE.

⑨ And dress in order to make believe thaT Fish NaTurally Live iN A STaTe of SASHiMi.

LESS thAN 15 MiNuTes AGO, HE WAS STiLL SWIMMiNG WITH HiS FRIENDS.

PARSLEY

WaSABi.

THERE, it's OVER!

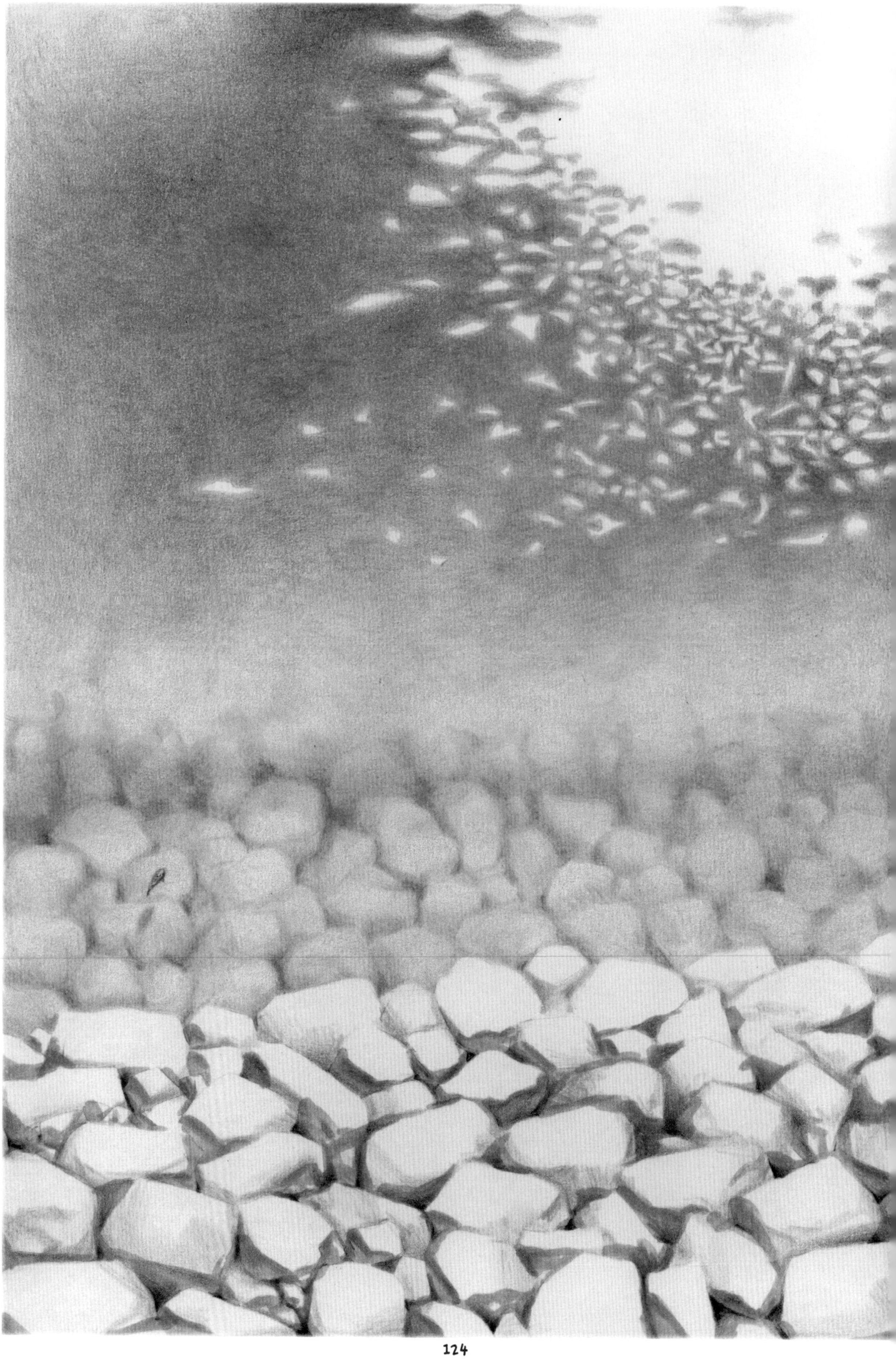

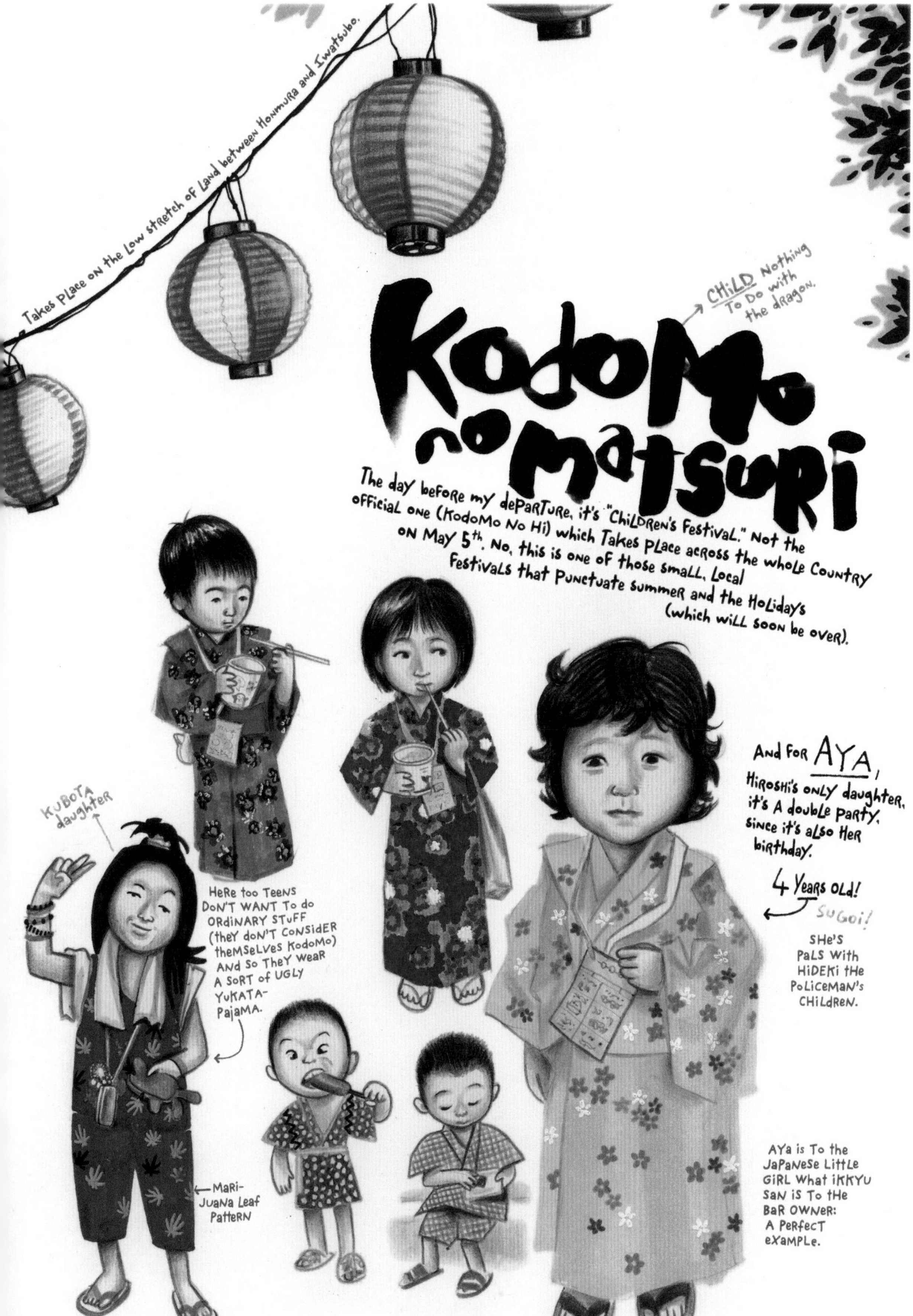
Takes Place on the Low stretch of Land between Honmura and Iwatsubo.
Kodomo no matsuri
CHILD Nothing To Do with the dragon.
The day before my departure, it's "Children's Festival." Not the official one (Kodomo No Hi) which Takes Place across the whole Country on May 5th. No, this is one of those small, Local Festivals that Punctuate summer and the Holidays (which will soon be over).
KUBOTA daughter
Here too Teens don't want to do ordinary stuff (they don't consider themselves Kodomo) And so They wear A sort of ugly Yukata-Pajama.
Mari-Juana Leaf Pattern
And for AYA, Hiroshi's only daughter, it's A double party, since it's also Her birthday.
4 Years old!
SUGOI!
She's pals with Hideki the Policeman's Children.
AYa is To the Japanese Little Girl What Ikkyu San is To the Bar Owner: A Perfect example.

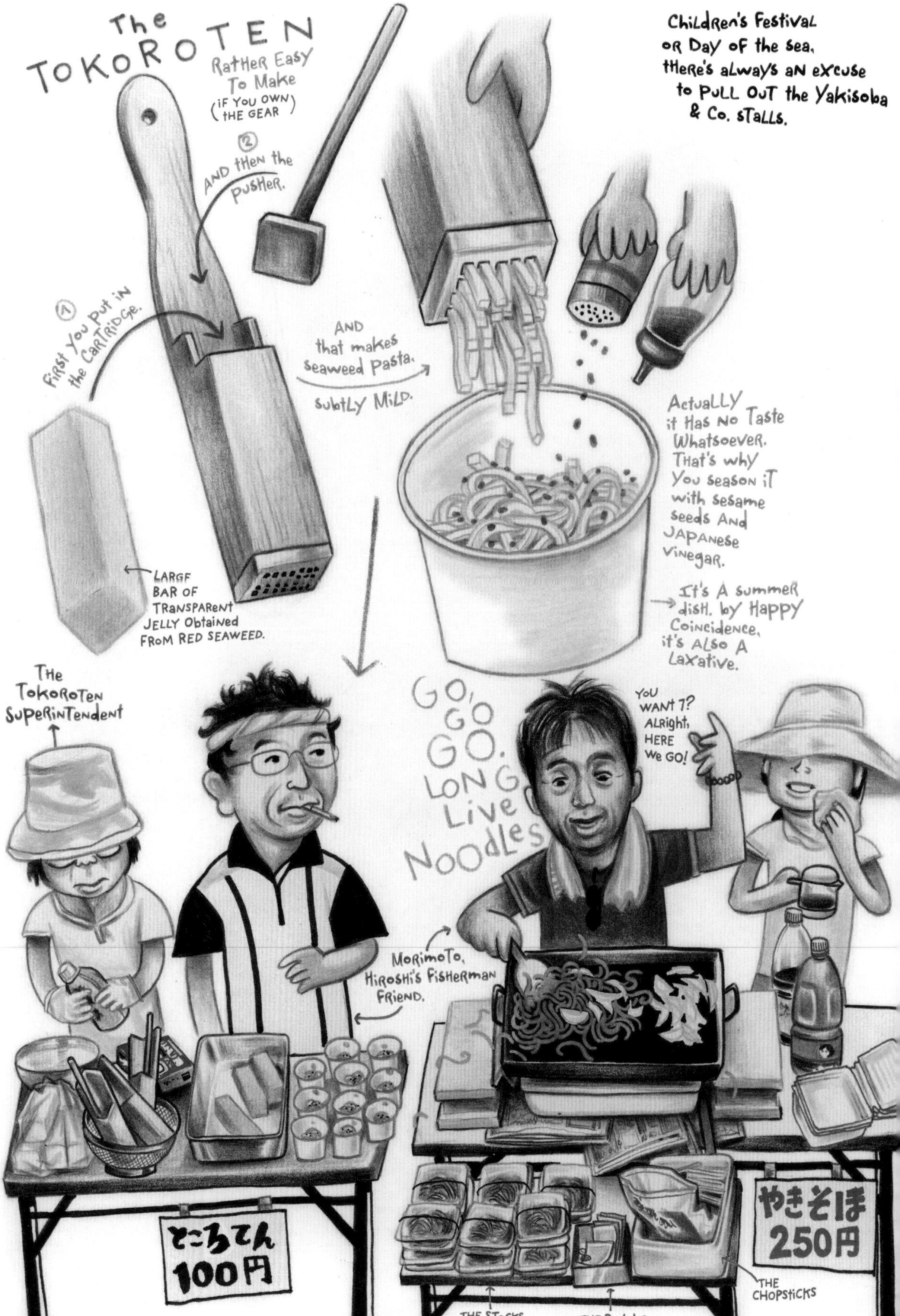
The TOKOROTEN
RatHer Easy To Make (iF YOU OWN THE GEAR)
① First You put in the CarTRidge.
② AND tHen the pusHer.
LARGF BAR OF TRANSPARENT JELLY Obtained FROM RED SEAWEED.
AND that makes seaweed Pasta.
subtLy MiLD.
Children's Festival or Day of the sea, there's always an excuse to pull out the Yakisoba & Co. stalls.
Actually it Has No Taste Whatsoever. That's why You season it with sesame seeds And JAPANESE Vinegar.
It's A summer dish. by Happy Coincidence, it's ALso A Laxative.
THe TokoRoTEN SupeRinTendent
GO, GO GO. LONG Live Noodles
YOU WANT 7? ALRIGHT, HERE WE GO!
MoRimoTo, HiRoSHi's FisHerman FRiEND.
ところてん 100円
やきそば 250円
THE STocks
THE Register
THE CHOPSTICKS

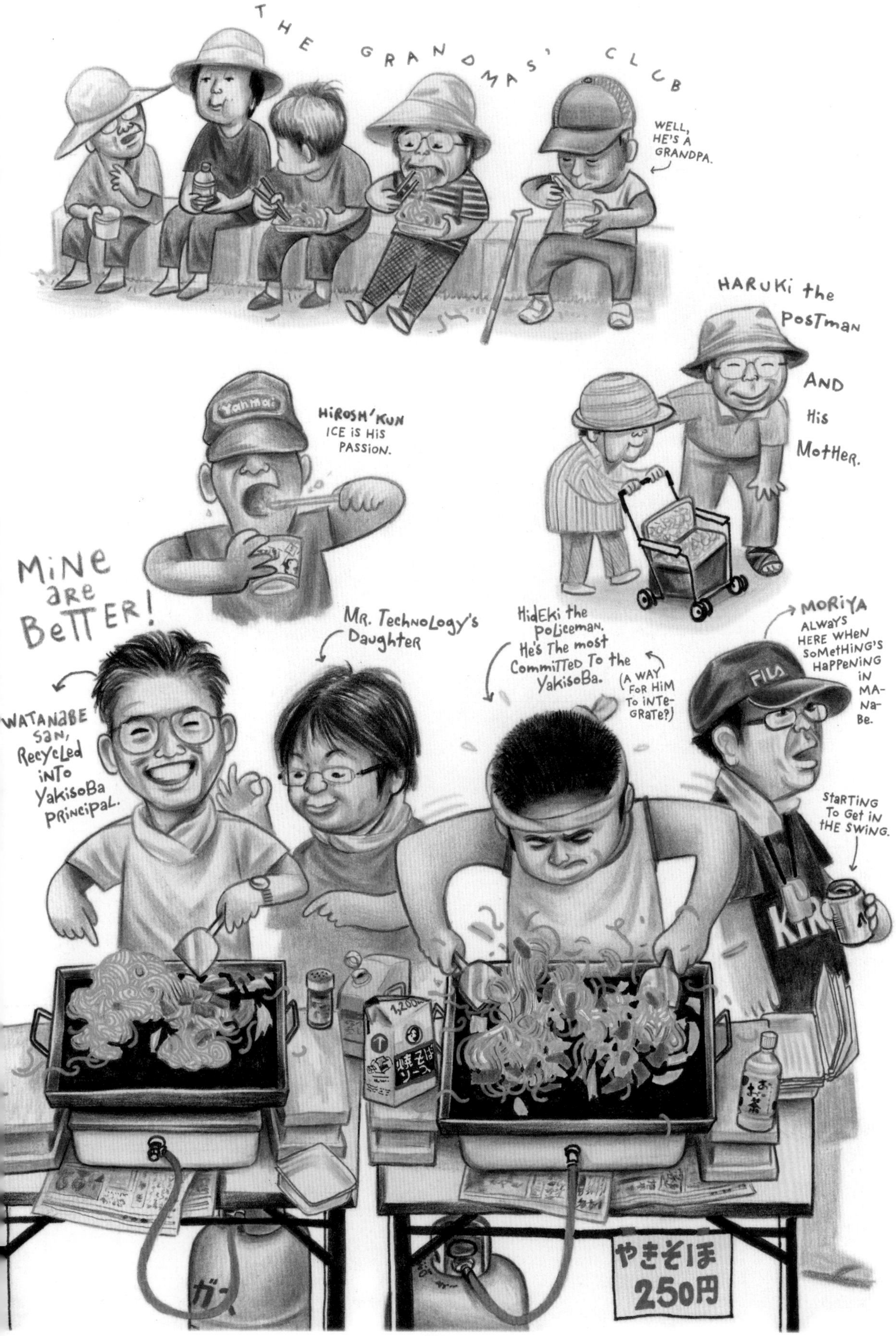
THE GRANDMAS' CLUB
WELL, HE'S A GRANDPA.
HARUKi the PosTman AND His MotHER.
HiROSHi'KUN ICE iS HIS PASSiON.
MiNE are BeTTER!
MR. TechnoLogy's Daughter
HidEKi the policeman. He's The most Committed To the YakisoBa.
(A WAY FoR HiM To iNTE-GRaTE?)
MORiYA ALWaYS HERE WHEN SOMeTHiNG'S HaPPeNiNG iN MA-Na-Be.
WATANABE SaN, Recycled iNTo YakisoBa PRiNcipaL.
STaRTiNG To Get iN tHE SWiNG.
FILA
KIR
焼そばソース
やきそば 250円
ガス
お茶

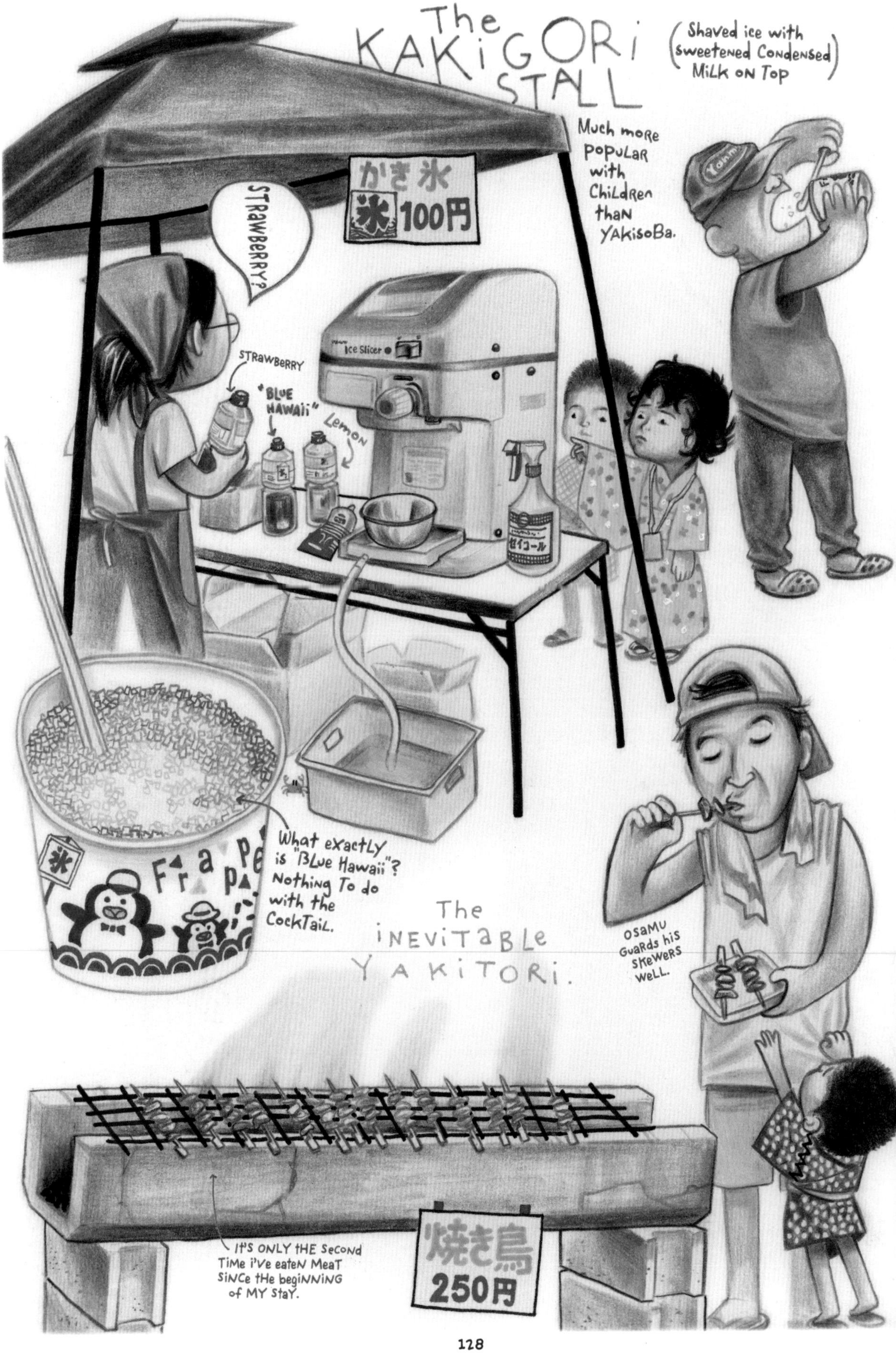
The KAKiGORi STALL
(Shaved ice with sweetened Condensed MiLk on Top)
Much more popuLaR with ChiLdRen than YAKisoBa.
かき氷
氷 100円
STRAWBERRY?
Ice Slicer
STRAWBERRY
"BLUE HAWAii"
Lemon
セイコール
What exactLy is "BLue Hawaii"? Nothing To do with the CockTaiL.
The iNEVITaBLe YAKiTORi.
OSAMU GuaRds his SKeWeRS WeLL.
iT'S ONLY tHE Second Time i've eaten MeaT SiNCe tHe beginNiNG of MY staY.
焼き鳥
250円

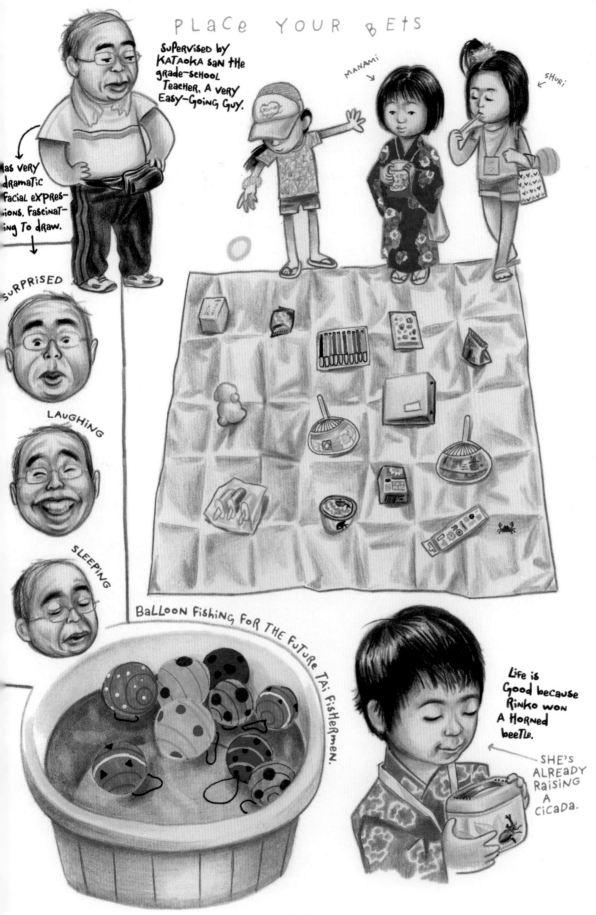

PLACE YOUR BETS

SUPERVISED by KATAOKA SAN the grade-school Teacher. A very Easy-Going, Guy.

Has very dramatic Facial expressions. Fascinating To draw.

MANAMI

SHURI

SURPRISED

LAUGHING

SLEEPING

BALLOON FISHING FOR THE FUTURE TAI FISHERMEN.

Life is Good because Rinko won A HORNED beeTle.

SHE'S ALREADY RAISING A CICADA.

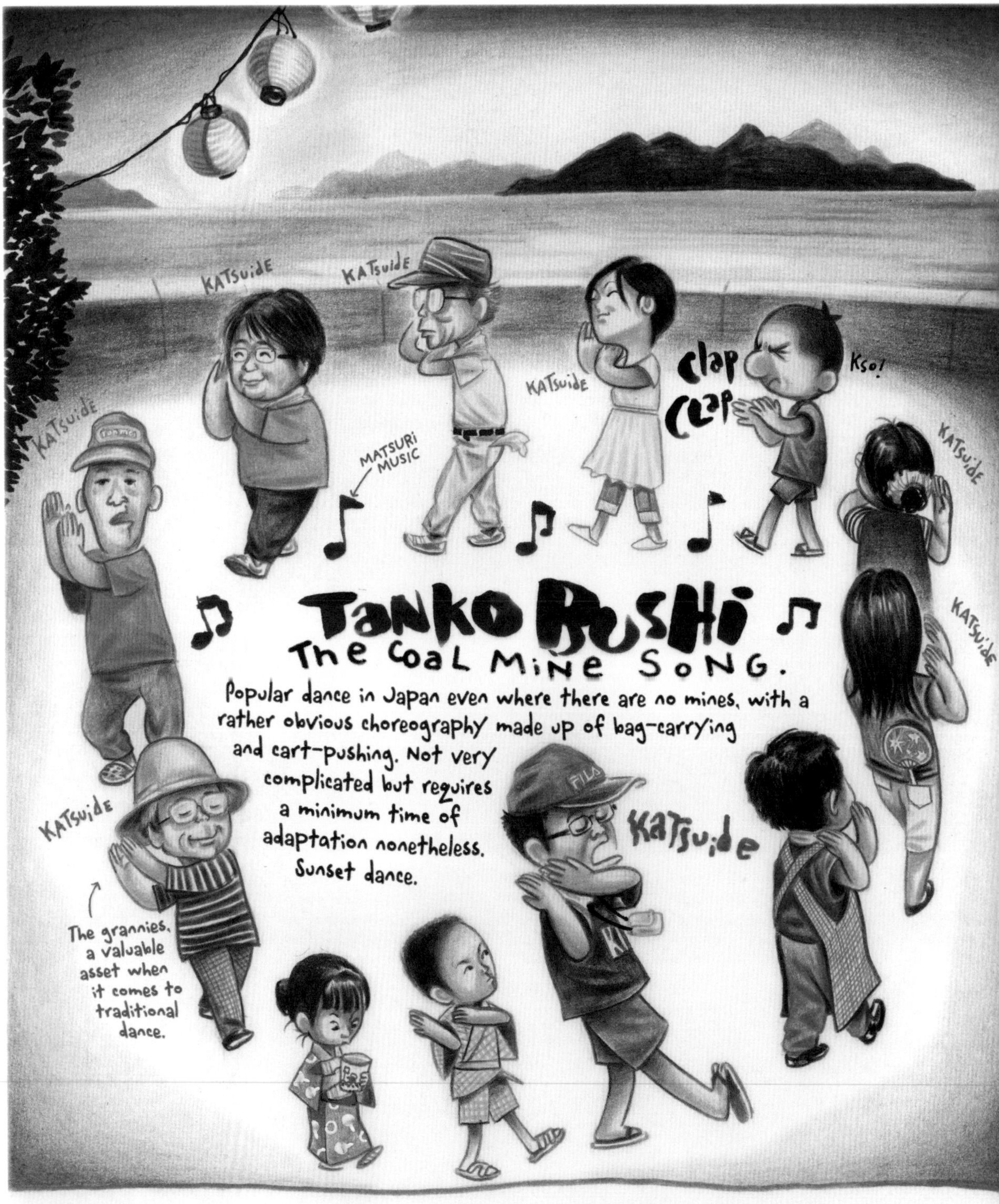
KATSuide
KATSuide
KATSuide
Clap
Clap
Kso!
KATSuide
MATSURI MUSIC
KATSuide
KATSuide
TANKO BUSHi
The CoaL MiNe SoNG.
Popular dance in Japan even where there are no mines, with a rather obvious choreography made up of bag-carrying and cart-pushing. Not very complicated but requires a minimum time of adaptation nonetheless. Sunset dance.
KATSuide
Katsuide
The grannies, a valuable asset when it comes to traditional dance.

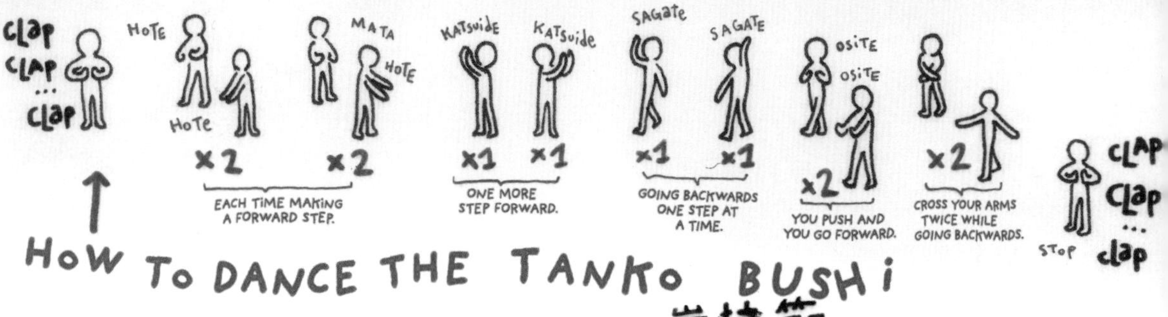
Clap
Clap
...
Clap
HOTE
HoTe
MATA
HOTE
×2
×2
EACH TIME MAKING A FORWARD STEP.
KATSuide
KATSuide
×1
×1
ONE MORE STEP FORWARD.
SAGATE
SAGATE
×1
×1
GOING BACKWARDS ONE STEP AT A TIME.
OSiTE
OSiTE
×2
YOU PUSH AND YOU GO FORWARD.
×2
CROSS YOUR ARMS TWICE WHILE GOING BACKWARDS.
STOP
CLAP
Clap
...
clap

HOW TO DANCE THE TANKO BUSHi
炭坑節

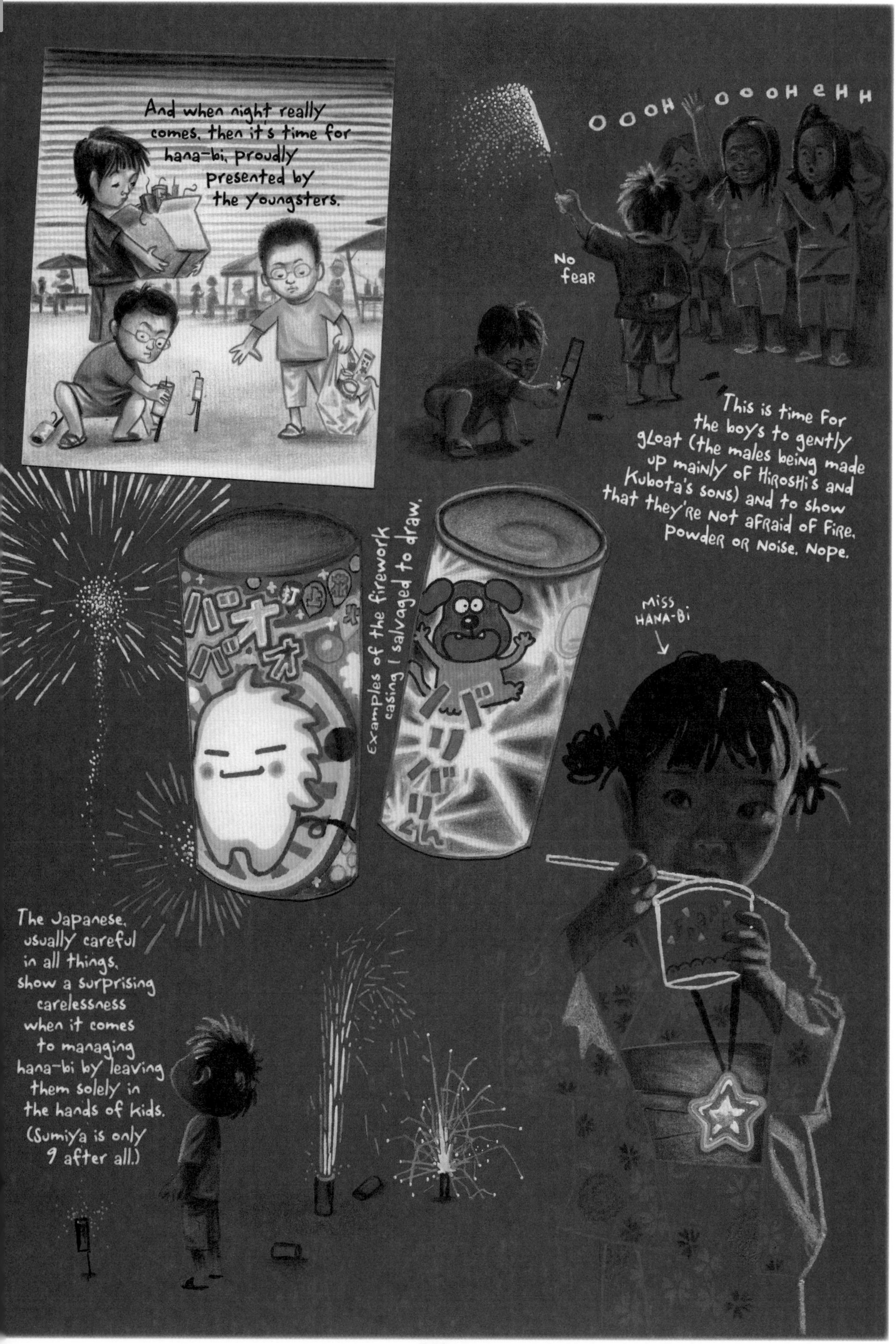

And when night really comes, then it's time for hana-bi, proudly presented by the youngsters.
OOOH OOOH EHH
No fear
This is time for the boys to gently gloat (the males being made up mainly of Hiroshi's and Kubota's sons) and to show that they're not afraid of fire, powder or noise. Nope.
Examples of the firework casing I salvaged to draw.
Miss HANA-BI
The Japanese, usually careful in all things, show a surprising carelessness when it comes to managing hana-bi by leaving them solely in the hands of kids. (Sumiya is only 9 after all.)

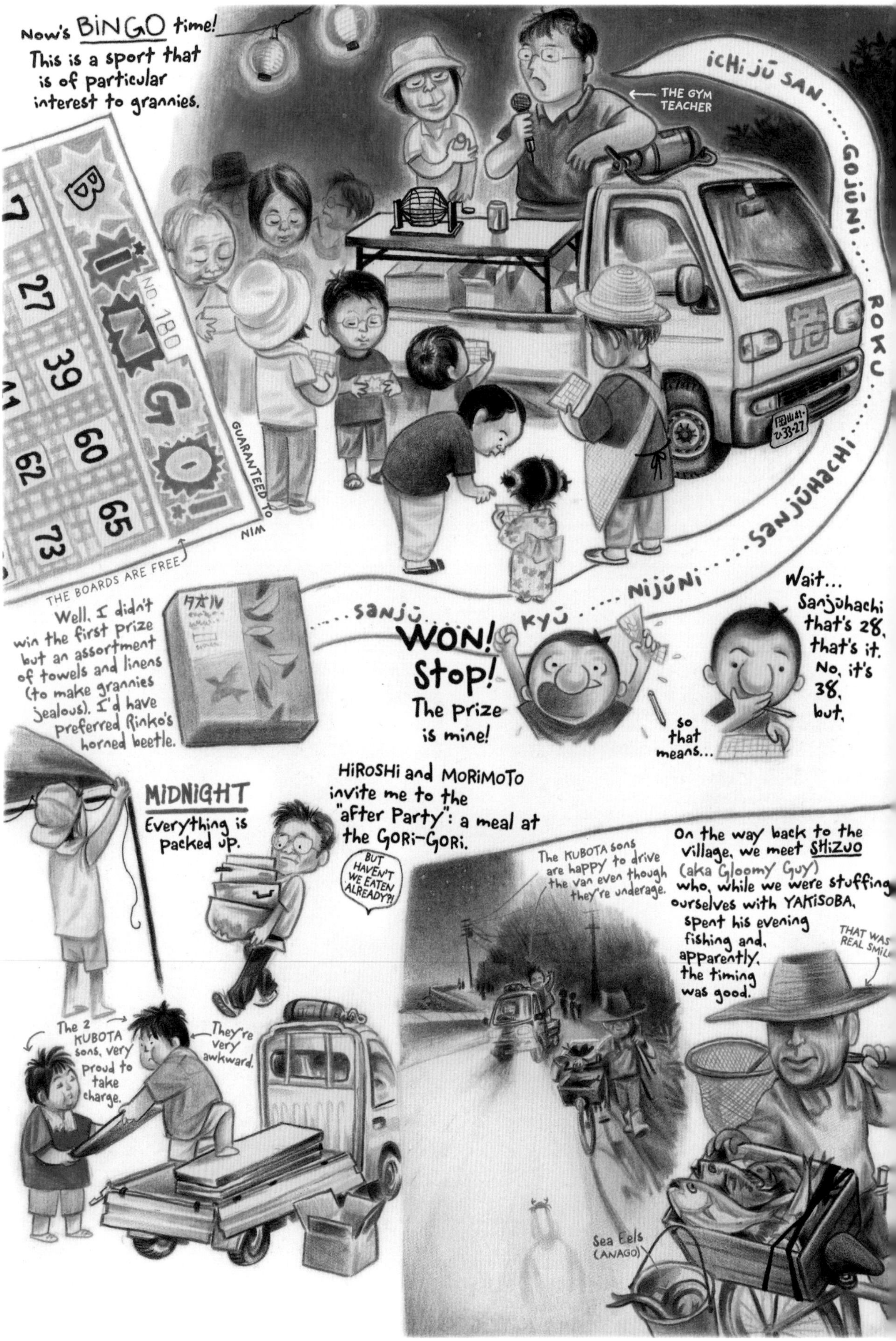
Now's BINGO time!
This is a sport that is of particular interest to grannies.
THE GYM TEACHER
ICHIJŪ SAN...... GOJŪNI...... ROKU...... SANJŪHACHI......
BINGO
NO. 180
GUARANTEED TO WIN
THE BOARDS ARE FREE
Well, I didn't win the first prize but an assortment of towels and linens (to make grannies jealous). I'd have preferred Rinko's horned beetle.
タオル
......SANJŪ...... KYŪ...... NIJŪNI
WON! Stop! The prize is mine!
Wait... Sanjūhachi that's 28, that's it. No, it's 38, but,
so that means...
MIDNIGHT
Everything is packed up.
HIROSHI and MORIMOTO invite me to the "after Party": a meal at the GORI-GORI.
BUT HAVEN'T WE EATEN ALREADY?!
The 2 KUBOTA sons, very proud to take charge.
They're very awkward.
On the way back to the village, we meet SHIZUO (aka Gloomy Guy) who, while we were stuffing ourselves with YAKISOBA, spent his evening fishing and, apparently, the timing was good.
The KUBOTA sons are happy to drive the van even though they're underage.
THAT WAS A REAL SMILE
Sea Eels (ANAGO)

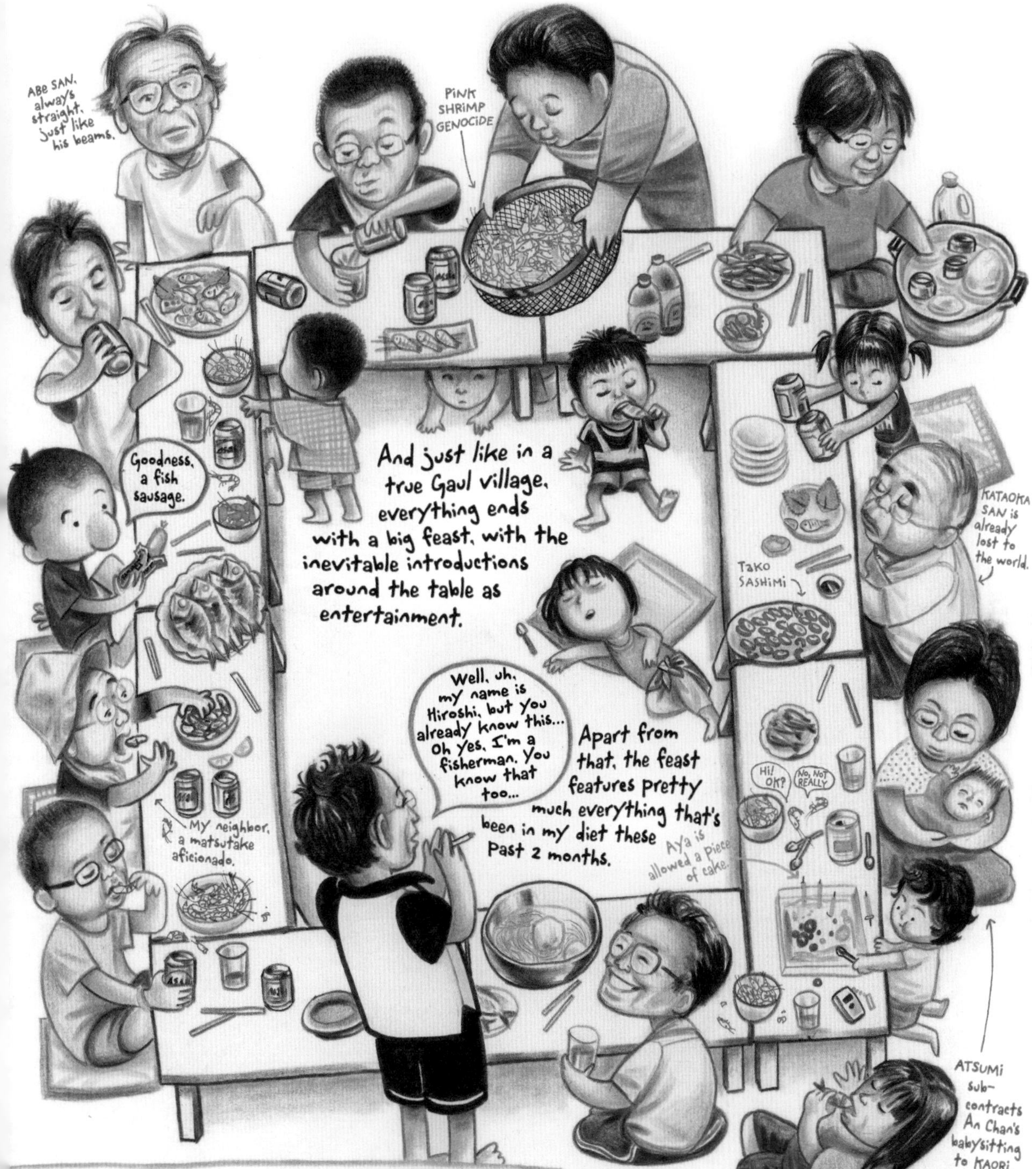
ABE SAN, always straight, just like his beams.
PINK SHRIMP GENOCIDE
And just like in a true Gaul village, everything ends with a big feast, with the inevitable introductions around the table as entertainment.
Goodness, a fish sausage.
KATAOKA SAN is already lost to the world.
TAKO SASHIMI
Well, uh, my name is Hiroshi, but you already know this... Oh yes, I'm a fisherman. You know that too...
Apart from that, the feast features pretty much everything that's been in my diet these past 2 months.
HI! OK?
NO, NOT REALLY
My neighbor, a matsutake aficionado.
Aya is allowed a piece of cake.
ATSUMI sub-contracts An Chan's babysitting to KAORI.

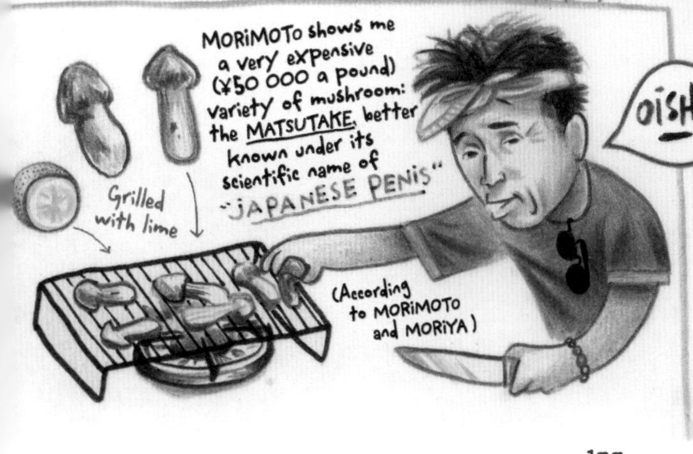
MORIMOTO shows me a very expensive (¥50 000 a pound) variety of mushroom: the MATSUTAKE, better known under its scientific name of "JAPANESE PENIS"
OISHI!
Grilled with lime
(According to MORIMOTO and MORIYA)

Even Never-ending Feasts come to a conclusion.
Moriya invited me to sleep at his parents' house and since his house is also on the way, Kubota comes along.
It's fun except that we're ALL more or less drunk and Moriya has trouble finding his own house.
(even though he organizes visits of the island for the tourists.)

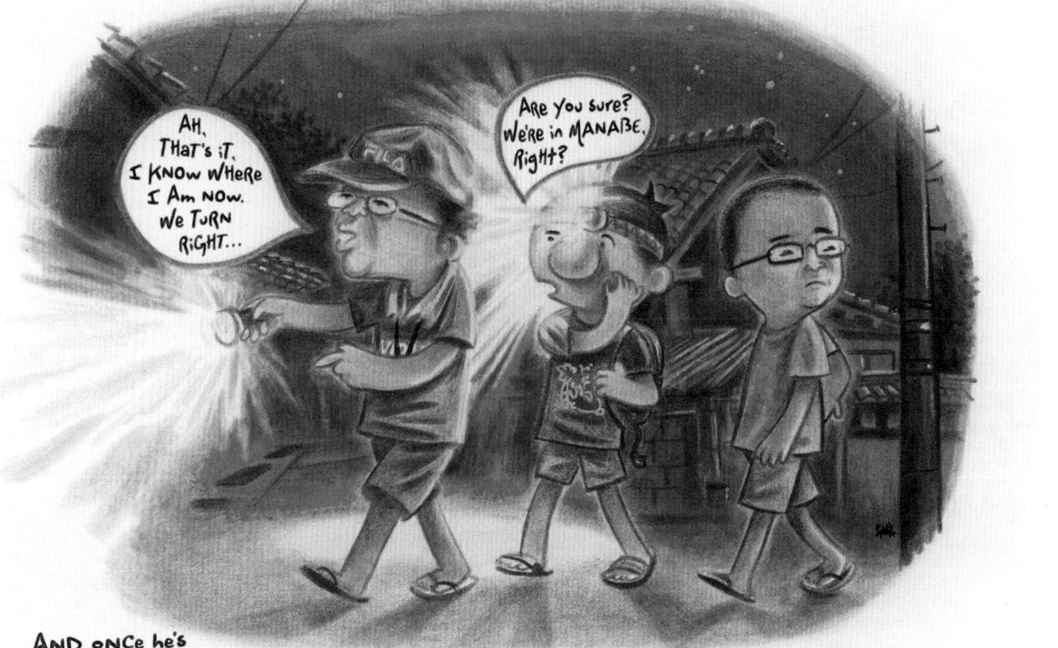
Ah, That's it, I know where I am now. We turn right...
Are you sure? We're in Manabe, right?

And once he's found the way again, Moriya loses his keys. In the end, Kubota puts us up at his.
And not completely satisfied with their state of drunkenness, our two friends continue their high-flying discussion started earlier over a plate of shrimps.
Me, I've had it.

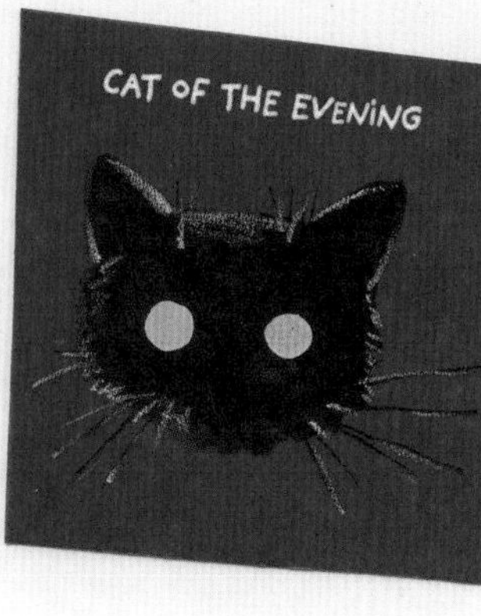
CAT OF THE EVENING

So for my last night on the island I could have wished for something softer and more comfortable, or else a poetic moment, sleeping on the Santora's pontoon, under the stars and lulled by a gentle tide.

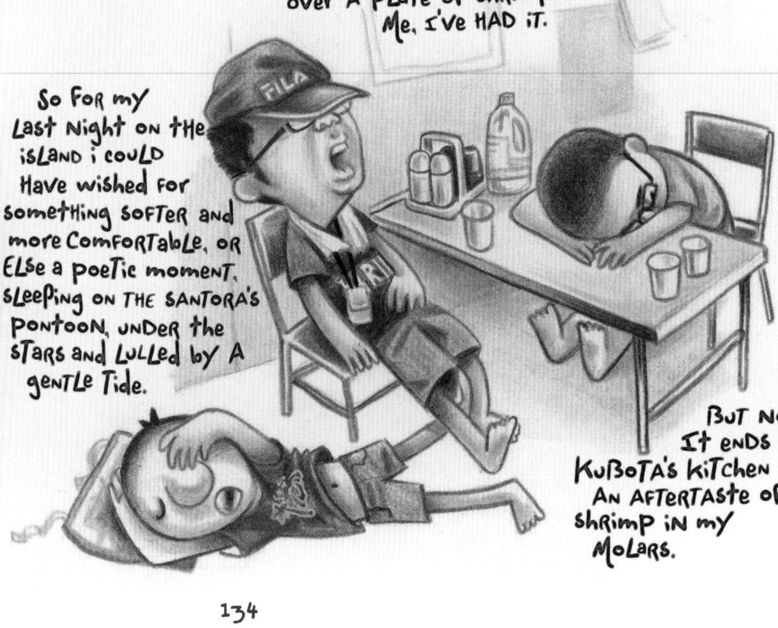

But no. It ends in Kubota's kitchen with an aftertaste of shrimp in my molars.

THe DaY After

Looks Like any other day of Departure. i go back to the hoteL, Gather my beLongings, give Away my Fishing Rod and pet my Last Octopus.

Before Leaving, i pay one Last visit to the person who's FoLLowed me the most during my isLand stay, but who, come to think of it, Has Never invited me to His House.

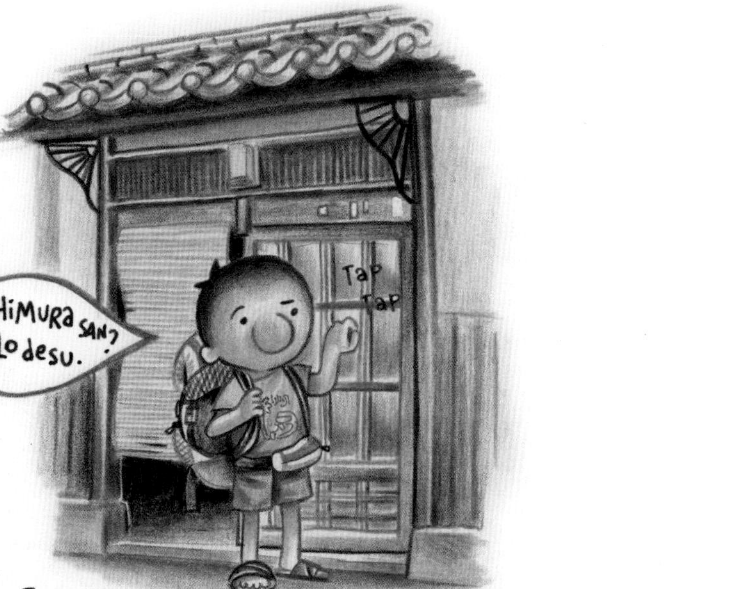

SHIMURA SAN? FLO desu.
Tap Tap

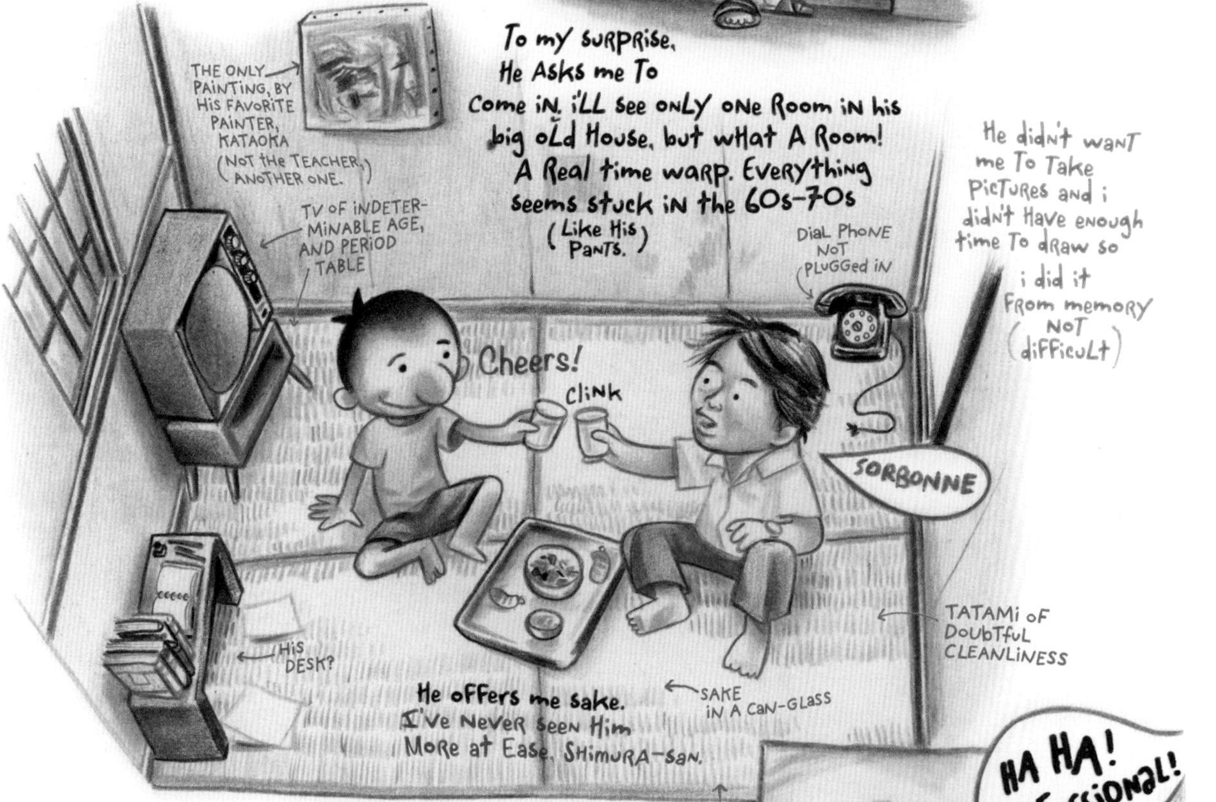

To my surprise, He Asks me To come in. i'LL see onLY one Room in his big oLd House, but wHat A Room! A Real time warp. Everything seems stuck in the 60s-70s (Like His Pants.)
THE ONLY PAINTING, BY HIS FAVORITE PAINTER, KATAOKA (NOT THE TEACHER, ANOTHER ONE.)
TV OF INDETERMINABLE AGE, AND PERIOD TABLE
DiaL PHONE NOT PLUGGed iN
He didn't want me To Take Pictures and i didn't Have enough time To draw so i did it From memory NOT (difficuLt)
Cheers!
CLink
SORBONNE
HIS DESK?
TATAMi oF DOUbTfuL CLEANLiNESS
He offers me sake. I've Never seen Him More at Ease, SHimuRA-san.
SAKE IN A CaN-GLASS
ENTRANCE

He ALSo shows me pHotos of wHen He was A student in OSAKA.

NO WAY! You were A ReaL HooLigan!

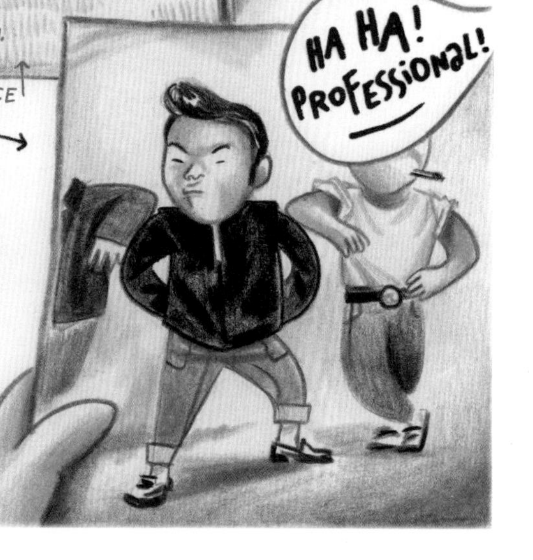

HA HA! PROFESSIONAL!

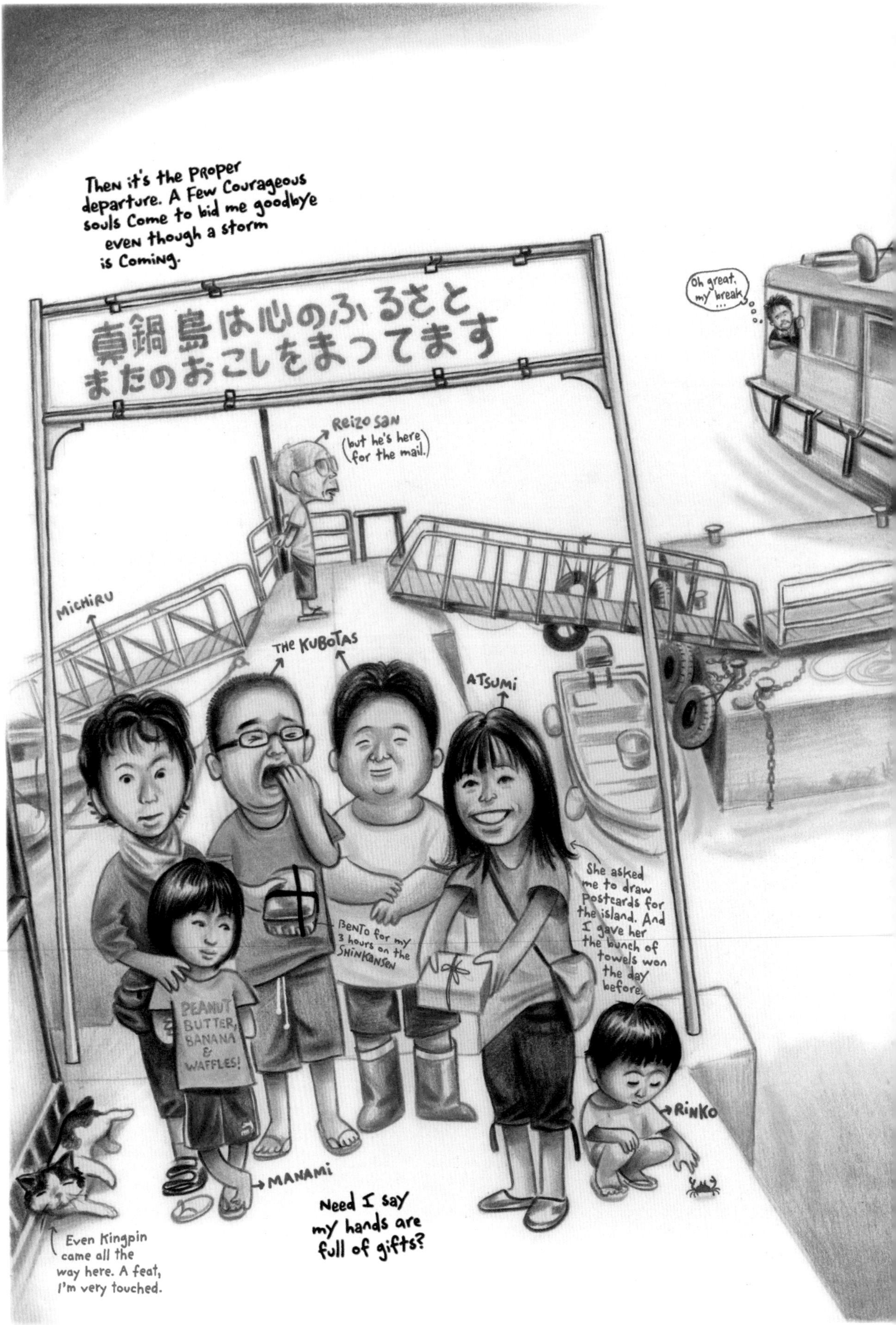
Then it's the Proper departure. A Few Courageous souls Come to bid me goodbye even though a storm is Coming.
真鍋島は心のふるさと
またのおこしをまってます
Oh great, my break...
Reizo San (but he's here for the mail.)
Michiru
The Kubotas
Atsumi
Bento for my 3 hours on the Shinkansen
She asked me to draw Postcards for the island. And I gave her the bunch of towels won the day before.
Peanut Butter, Banana & Waffles!
Rinko
Manami
Need I say my hands are full of gifts?
Even Kingpin came all the way here. A feat, I'm very touched.

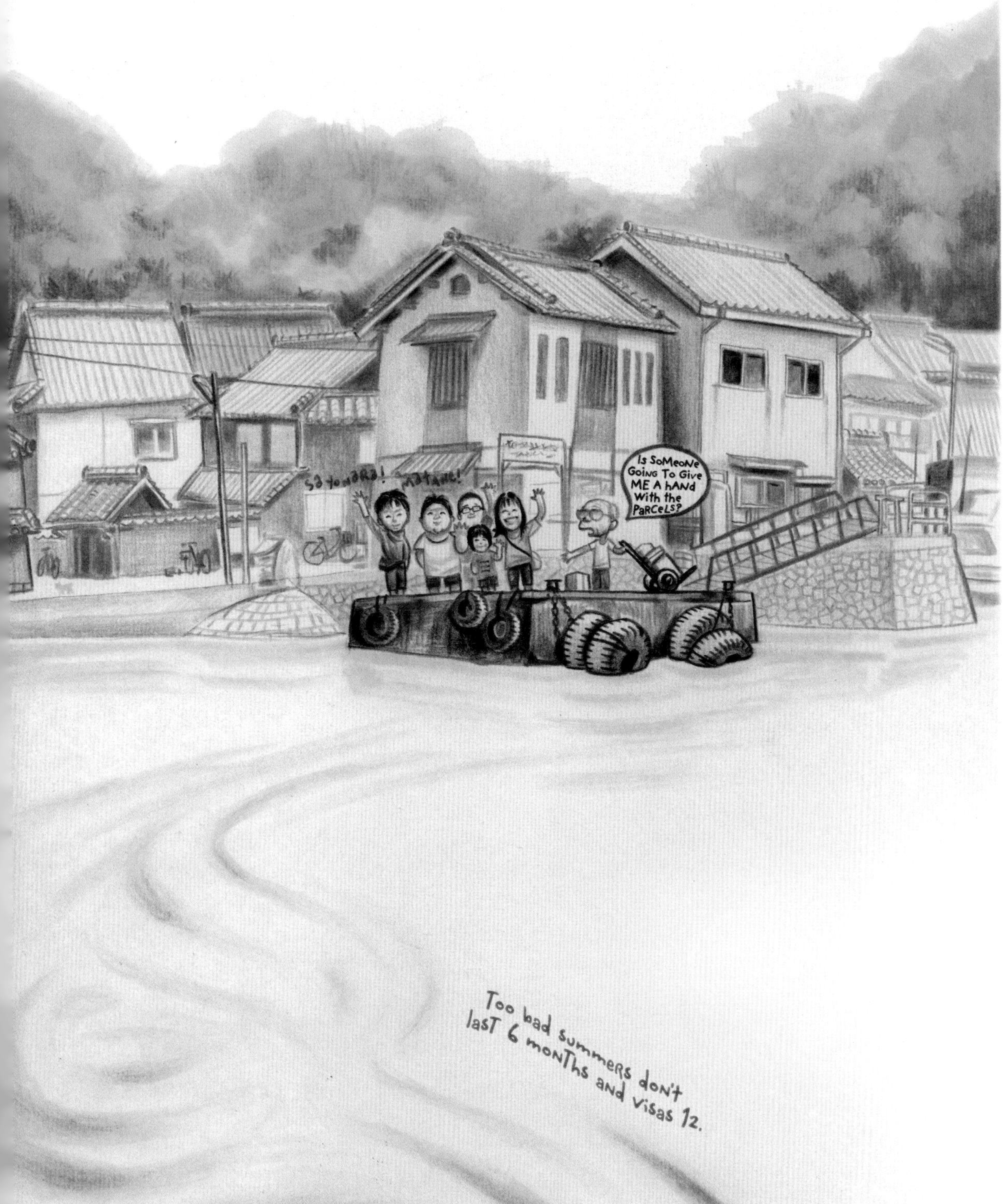
Sayonara!
Matane!
Is someone going to give me a hand with the parcels?
Too bad summers don't last 6 months and visas 12.

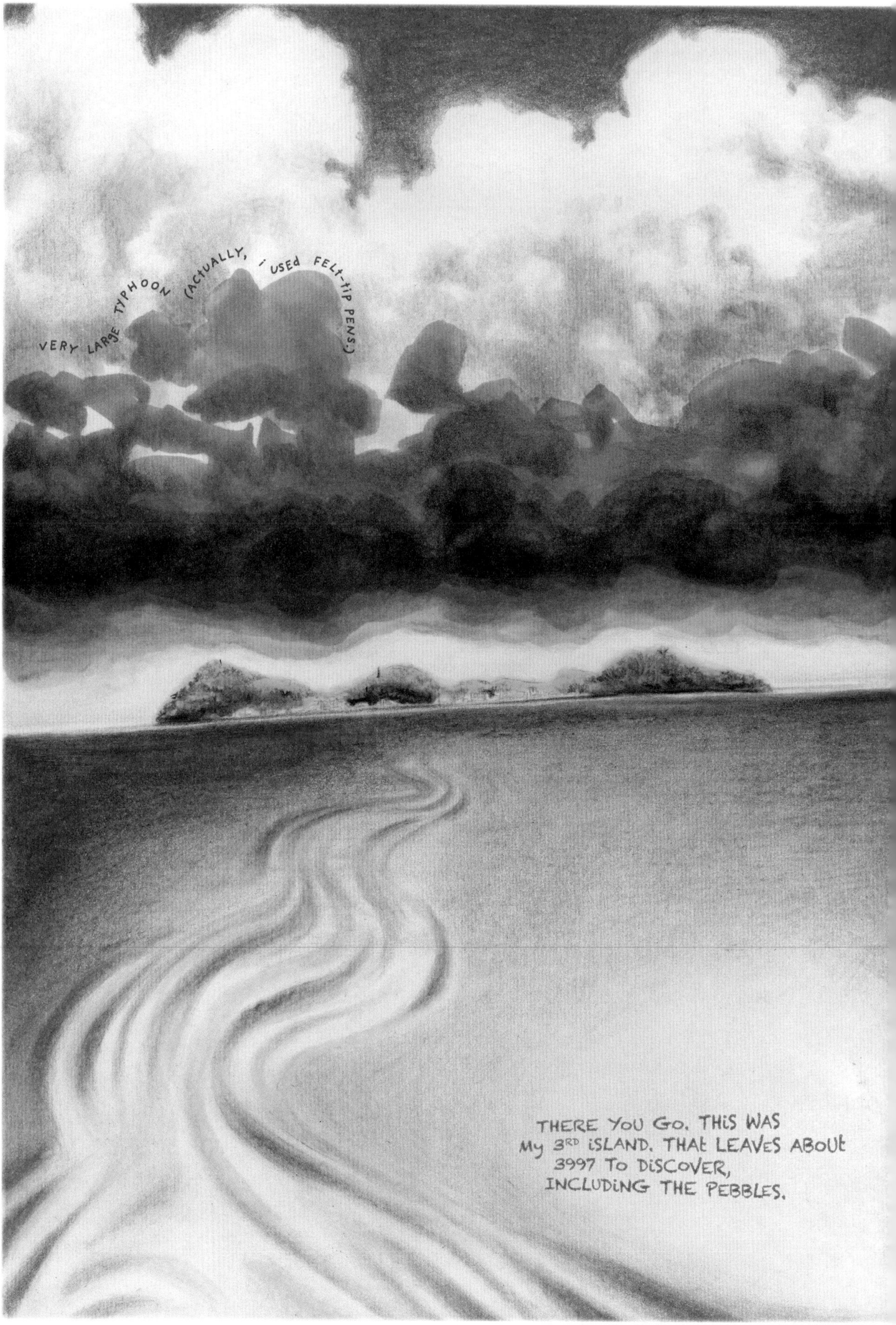
VERY LARGE TYPHOON (ACTUALLY, i USEd FELT-tip PENS.)
THERE YOU GO. THIS WAS
My 3RD iSLAND. THAT LEAVES ABOUT
3997 TO DISCOVER,
INCLUDING THE PEBBLES.

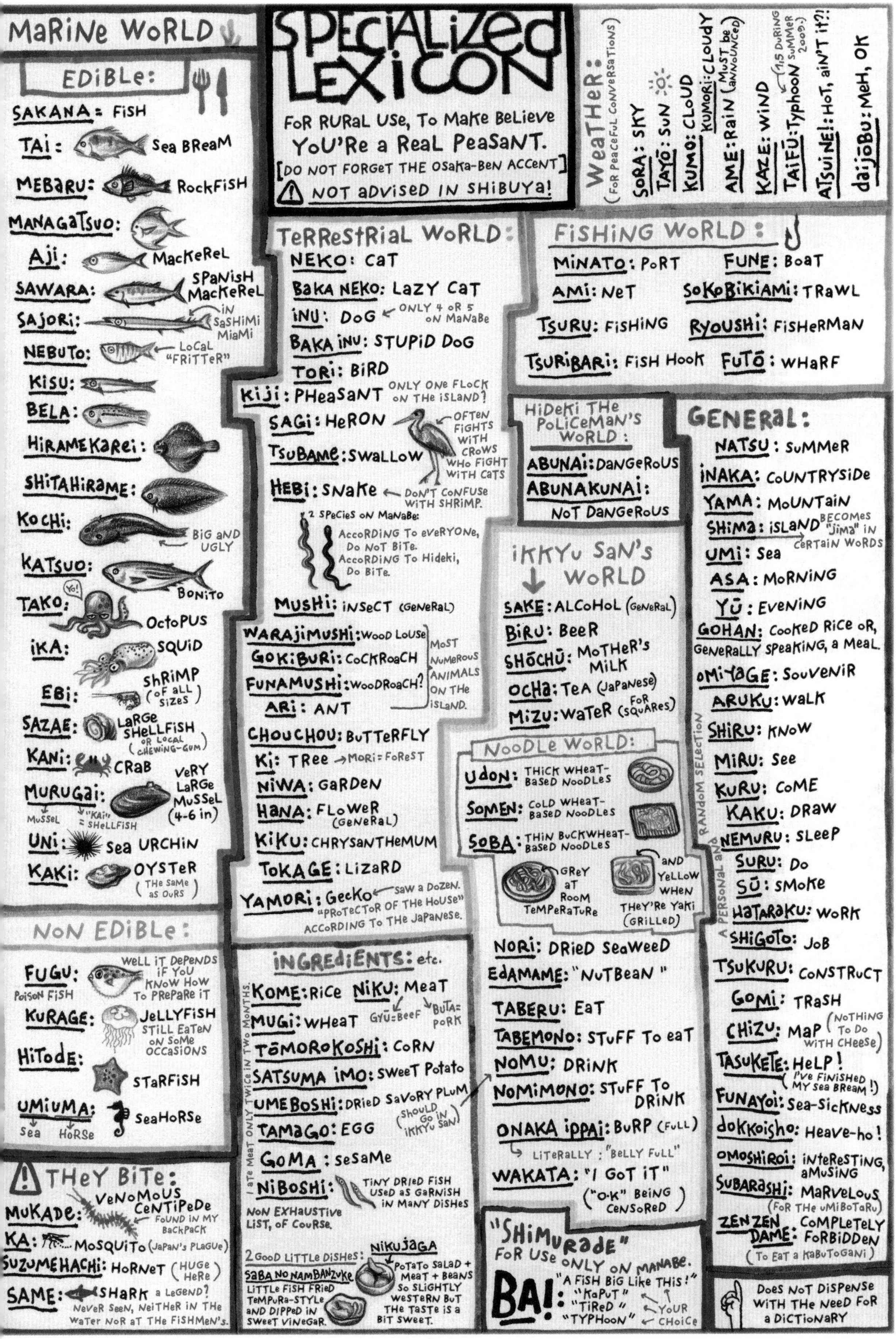
MaRiNe WoRLD
EDiBLe:
SAKANA = FiSH
TAi: Sea BReaM
MEBaRU: RockFiSH
MANAGaTSUO:
Aji: MacKeReL
SAWARA: SPaNiSH MacKeReL
SAjORi: iN SaSHiMi MiaMi
NEBUTO: LoCaL "FRiTTeR"
KiSU:
BELA:
HiRAMEKaRei:
SHiTAHiRAME:
KOCHi: BiG aND UGLY
KATSUO: BoNiTo
TAKO: Yo! OcToPUS
iKA: SQUiD
EBi: ShRiMP (oF aLL SiZeS)
SAZAE: LaRGe SHeLLFiSH (oR LocaL cHeWiNG-GuM)
KANi: CRaB
MURUGai: VeRY LaRGe MuSSeL (4-6 in)
MuSSeL "KAi" = SHeLLFiSH
UNi: Sea URCHiN
KAKi: OYSTeR (THe SaMe aS OuRS)
NoN EDiBLe:
FUGU: WeLL iT DePeNDS iF YoU KNoW HoW To PRePaRe iT
PoiSoN FiSH
KURAGE: JeLLYFiSH STiLL EaTeN oN SoMe OCCaSiONS
HiTodE: STaRFiSH
UMiUMA: SeaHoRSe
Sea HoRSe
THey BiTe:
MUKADE: VeNoMoUS CeNTiPeDe FouND iN MY BacKPacK
KA: MoSQUiTo (JaPaN'S PLaGUe)
SUZUMEHACHi: HoRNeT (HUGe HeRe)
SAME: SHaRK a LeGeND? NeVeR SeeN, NeiTHeR iN THe WaTeR NoR aT THe FiSHMeN'S.
SPeCiALiZeD LeXiCON
FoR RURaL USe, To MaKe BeLieve YoU'Re a ReaL PeaSaNT.
[Do NoT FoRGeT THE OSaKa-BeN ACCeNT]
NOT adViSeD iN SHiBUYa!
WeaTHeR: (FoR PeaceFuL CoNVeRSaTioNS)
SORA: SKY
TAYŌ: SuN
KUMO: CLoUD
KUMORi: CLOUDY
AME: RaiN (MUST be ANNOUNCED)
KAZE: WiND
TAiFŪ: TyphooN (1,5 DURiNG SUMMeR 2009.)
ATSUiNE!: HoT, aiN'T iT?!
daijoBU: MeH, OK
TeRReStRiaL WoRLD:
NEKO: CaT
BaKA NEKO: LaZY CaT
iNU: DoG ← ONLY 4 oR 5 oN MaNaBe
BAKA iNU: STUPiD DoG
TORi: BiRD
Kiji: PHeaSaNT ONLY ONe FLocK oN THe iSLaND?
SAGi: HeRON ← OFTeN FiGHTS WiTH CRoWS WHo FiGHT WiTH CaTS
TSUBAME: SWaLLoW
HEBi: SNaKe ← DoN'T CoNFuSe WiTH SHRiMP.
2 SPeCieS oN MaNaBe:
AccoRDiNG To eVeRYONe, Do NoT BiTe.
AccoRDiNG To Hideki, Do BiTe.
MUSHi: iNSeCT (GeNeRaL)
WARAjiMUSHi: WooD LouSe
GOKiBURi: CoCKRoaCH
FUNAMUSHi: WooDRoaCH?
ARi: ANT
MoST NuMeRouS ANiMALS ON THe iSLaND.
CHOUCHOU: BuTTeRFLY
Ki: TRee → MORi = FoReST
NiWA: GaRDeN
HaNA: FLoWeR (GeNeRaL)
KiKU: CHRYSaNTHeMUM
TOKAGE: LizaRD
YAMORi: GecKo ← SaW a DoZeN. "PRoTeCToR OF THe HouSe" ACCoRDiNG To THe JaPaNeSe.
FiSHiNG WoRLD:
MiNATO: PoRT
FUNE: BoaT
AMi: NeT
SoKoBiKiAMi: TRaWL
TSURU: FiSHiNG
RyOUSHi: FiSHeRMaN
TSURiBARi: FiSH HooK
FUTŌ: WHaRF
HiDeKi THe PoLiCeMaN'S WoRLD:
ABUNAi: DaNGeRoUS
ABUNAKUNAi: NoT DaNGeRoUS
iKKYu SaN'S WoRLD
SAKE: ALCoHoL (GeNeRaL)
BiRU: BeeR
SHŌCHŪ: MoTHeR'S MiLK
OCHa: TeA (JaPaNese)
MiZU: WaTeR (FoR SQuARes)
NooDLe WoRLD:
UdON: THiCK WHeaT-BaSeD NooDLes
SOMEN: CoLD WHeaT-BaSeD NooDLes
SOBA: THiN BuCKWHeaT-BaSeD NooDLeS
GReY aT RooM TeMPeRaTuRe
aND YeLLoW WHeN THeY'Re Yaki (GRiLLeD)
GENeRaL:
NATSU: SuMMeR
iNAKA: CoUNTRYSiDe
YAMA: MoUNTaiN
SHiMa: iSLaND BeCoMeS "Jima" iN CeRTaiN WoRDS
UMi: Sea
ASA: MoRNiNG
YŪ: EveNiNG
GOHAN: CooKeD RiCe oR, GeNeRaLLY SPeaKiNG, a MeaL.
OMiYAGE: SouVeNiR
ARUKU: WaLK
SHiRU: KNoW
MiRU: See
KURU: CoME
KAKU: DRaW
NEMURU: SLeeP
SURU: Do
SŪ: SMoKe
HaTARaKU: WoRK
SHiGoTO: JoB
TSUKURU: CoNSTRuCT
GOMi: TRaSH
CHiZU: MaP (NoTHiNG To Do WiTH CHeese)
TASUKETE: HeLP! (i'Ve FiNiSHeD MY Sea BReaM!)
FUNAYoi: Sea-SicKNeSS
dOKKOiSHO: Heave-ho!
OMOSHiROi: iNTeReSTiNG, aMuSiNG
SUBARASHi: MaRVeLouS (FoR THe uMiBoTaRu)
ZENZEN DAME: CoMPLeTeLY FoRBiDDeN (To EaT a KaBuToGaNi)
A PERSoNaL aND RaNDoM SeLecTioN
DoeS NoT DiSPeNSe WiTH THe NeeD FoR a DiCTioNaRY
iNGREdiENTS: etc.
i aTe MeaT ONLY TWiCe iN TWo MONTHS.
KOME: RiCe
NiKU: MeaT
GYŪ = BeeF
BUTA = PoRK
MUGi: WHeaT
TŌMOROKOSHi: CoRN
SATSUMA iMO: SWeeT PoTaTo
UMEBOSHi: DRieD SaVoRY PLuM (ShouLD Go iN iKKYu SaN)
TAMaGO: EGG
GOMA: SeSaMe
NiBOSHi: TiNY DRieD FiSH USeD aS GaRNiSH iN MaNY DiSHeS
NoN EXHAuSTive LiST, oF CouRSe.
2 GooD LiTTLe DiSHeS:
SABA NO NAMBANZUKE: LiTTLe FiSH FRieD TeMPuRa-STYLe aND DiPPeD iN SWeeT ViNeGaR.
NiKUJAGA: PoTaTo SaLaD + MeaT + BeaNS So SLiGHTLY WeSTeRN BuT THe TaSTe iS a BiT SWeeT.
NORi: DRieD SeaWeeD
EDAMAME: "NuTBeaN"
TABERU: EaT
TABEMONO: STuFF To eaT
NOMU: DRiNK
NOMiMONO: STuFF To DRiNK
ONAKA iPPai: BuRP (FuLL)
LiTeRaLLY: "BeLLY FuLL"
WAKATA: "I GoT iT" ("O.K" BeiNG CeNSoReD)
"SHiMurade" FoR USe ONLY oN MaNaBe.
BA!: "A FiSH BiG Like THiS!" "KaPuT" "TiReD" "TYPHooN" YouR CHoiCe

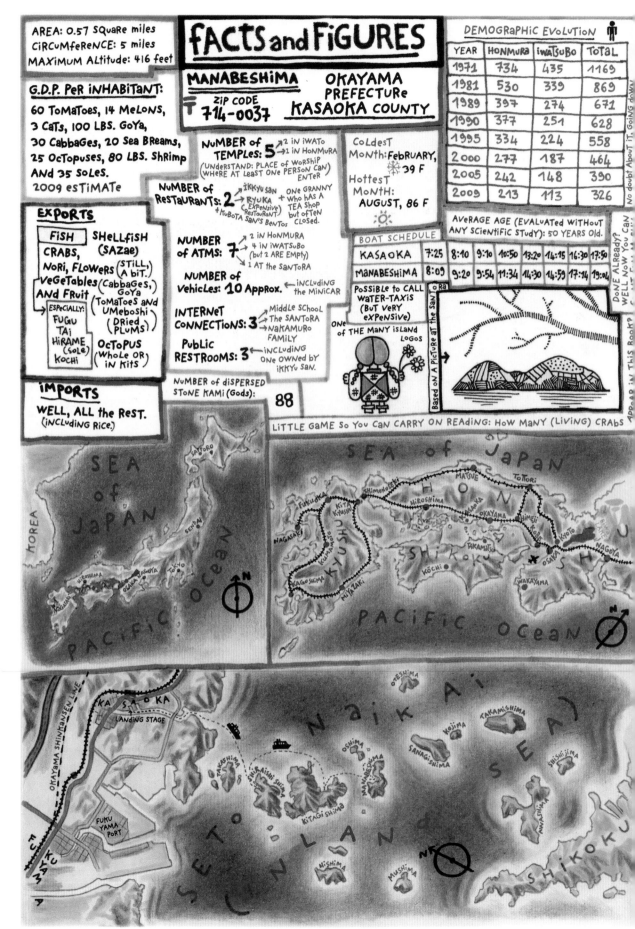

FACTS and FIGURES

MANABESHIMA — OKAYAMA PREFECTURE, KASAOKA COUNTY

〒 ZIP CODE 714-0037

AREA: 0.57 SQUARE miles
CIRCUMFERENCE: 5 miles
MAXIMUM Altitude: 416 feet

G.D.P. PER INHABITANT:
60 Tomatoes, 14 Melons, 3 Cats, 100 LBS. Goya, 30 Cabbages, 20 Sea Breams, 25 Octopuses, 80 LBS. Shrimp And 35 Soles.
2009 estimate

EXPORTS
- FISH
  - ESPECIALLY: FUGU, TAI, HIRAME (SOLE), KOCHI
- SHELLFISH (SAZAE)
- CRABS,
- NORI, FLOWERS (STILL, A BIT.)
- VEGETABLES AND FRUIT (Cabbages, Goya Tomatoes and Umeboshi (Dried Plums))
- OCTOPUS (Whole or in Kits)

IMPORTS
WELL, ALL the Rest. (including Rice.)

NUMBER of TEMPLES: 5 → 2 in IWATO → 1 in HONMURA
(Understand: place of worship where at least one person can enter)

NUMBER of RESTAURANTS: 2 → IKKYU SAN → RYUKA (Expensive restaurant) + KUBOTA SAN'S Bentos + One granny who has a tea shop but often closed.

NUMBER of ATMS: 7 → 2 in HONMURA → 4 in IWATSUBO (but 2 are empty) → 1 AT the SANTORA

NUMBER of Vehicles: 10 Approx. ← including the minicar

INTERNET CONNECTIONS: 3 → Middle School → The SANTORA → NAKAMURO FAMILY

Public RESTROOMS: 3 ← including one owned by IKKYU SAN.

NUMBER of dispersed STONE KAMI (Gods): 88

Coldest Month: FEBRUARY, 39 F
Hottest Month: AUGUST, 86 F

DEMOGRAPHIC EVOLUTION

YEAR	HONMURA	IWATSUBO	TOTAL
1971	734	435	1169
1981	530	339	869
1989	397	274	671
1990	377	251	628
1995	334	224	558
2000	277	187	464
2005	242	148	390
2009	213	113	326

No doubt about it. Going down

AVERAGE AGE (EVALUATED WITHOUT ANY SCIENTIFIC STUDY): 50 YEARS Old.

BOAT SCHEDULE

KASAOKA	7:25	8:10	9:10	10:50	13:20	14:15	16:30	17:50
MANABESHIMA	8:09	9:20	9:54	11:34	14:30	14:59	17:14	19:04

POSSIBLE to CALL WATER-TAXIS (BUT VERY EXPENSIVE)

One of THE MANY ISLAND LOGOS

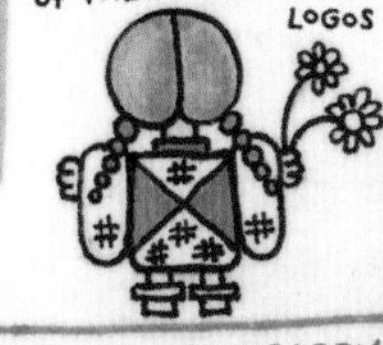

Based on A Picture at the SANTORA

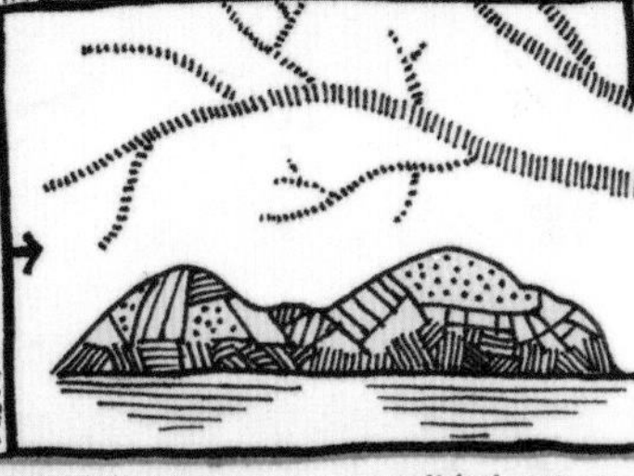

DONE ALREADY? WELL NOW YOU CAN

LITTLE GAME So You Can CARRY ON READING: HOW MANY (LIVING) CRABS APPEAR IN THIS BOOK?

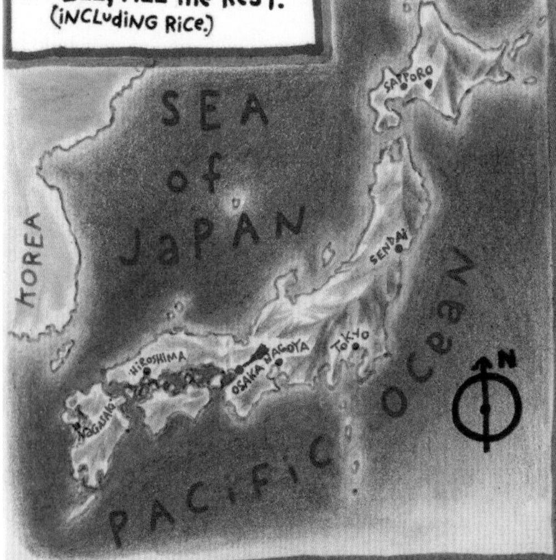
SEA of JAPAN
KOREA
SAPPORO
SENDAI
TOKYO
NAGOYA
OSAKA
HIROSHIMA
PACIFIC OCEAN
N

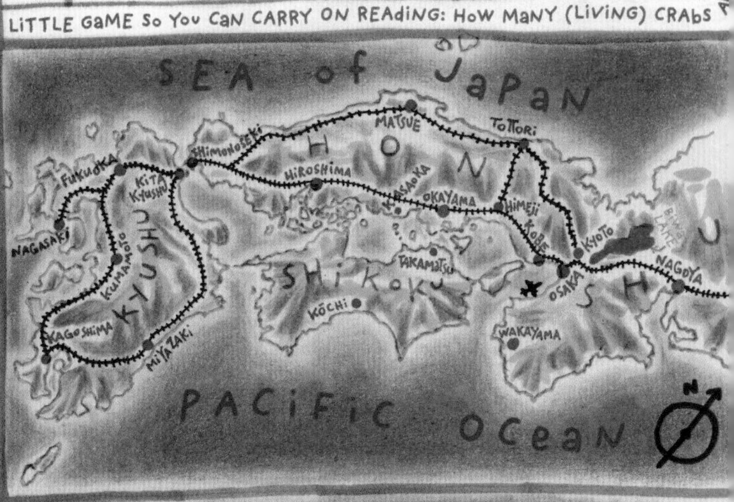
SEA of JAPAN
HONSHU
MATSUE
TOTTORI
SHIMONOSEKI
HIROSHIMA
KASAOKA
OKAYAMA
HIMEJI
KOBE
KYOTO
BIWA LAKE
NAGOYA
OSAKA
FUKUOKA
KITA KYUSHU
NAGASAKI
KUMAMOTO
KYUSHU
KAGOSHIMA
MIYAZAKI
SHIKOKU
TAKAMATSU
KOCHI
WAKAYAMA
PACIFIC OCEAN
N

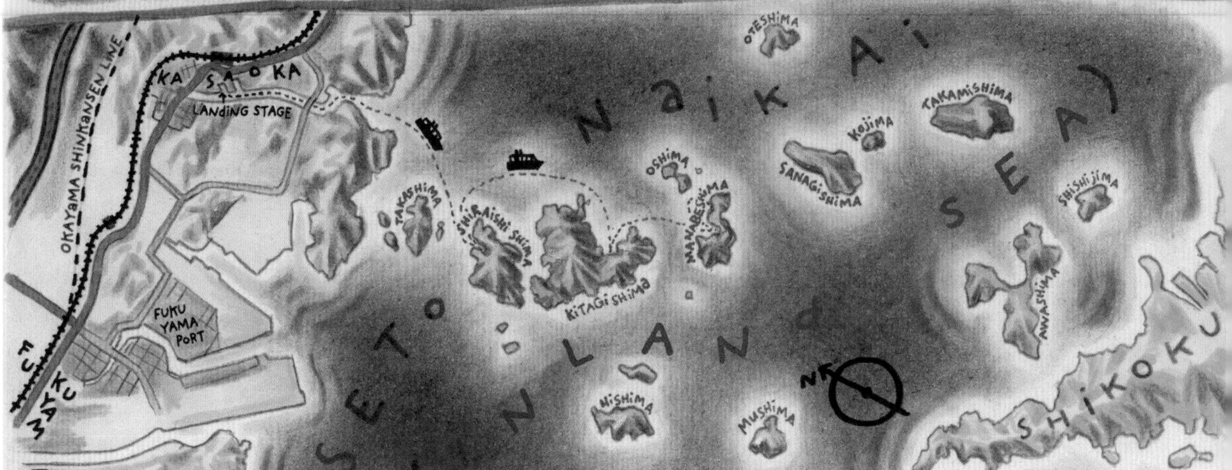
KASAOKA
LANDING STAGE
OKAYAMA SHINKANSEN LINE
FUKUYAMA
FUKU YAMA PORT
OTESHIMA
TAKAMISHIMA
KOJIMA
OSHIMA
SANAGISHIMA
MANABESHIMA
TAKASHIMA
SHIRAISHI SHIMA
KITAGI SHIMA
SHISHIJIMA
AWASHIMA
MUSHIMA
SETO NAIKAI (INLAND SEA)
SHIKOKU
NE

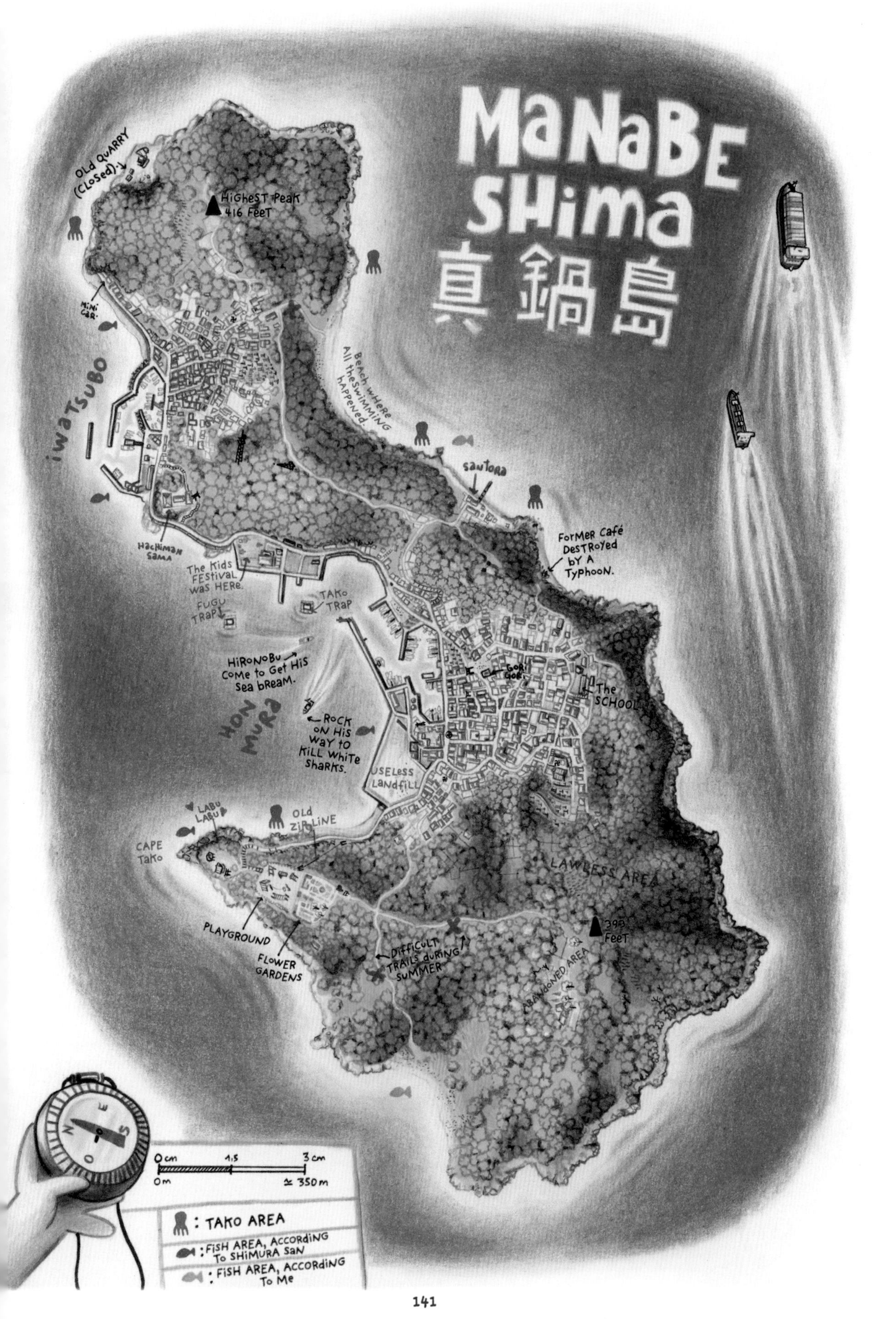
MaNaBE SHima
真鍋島
OLd QUARRY (CLoSed)
HiGheST Peak 416 FeeT
MiNi CaR
iwaTSUBO
Beach wHeRe All theSwimmiNG happeNed
SaNTORa
FoRMeR Café DesTRoYed bY A TyphooN.
HachiMaN SaMa
The Kids FESTivaL was HERE.
TaKo TRaP
FUGU TRaP
HiRoNoBu come to Get His Sea bReaM.
GORi GORi
The SCHOOL
HON MURa
ROCK ON HIS WaY To KiLL WhiTe SharKs.
USELess LaNdFiLL
LaBU LaBU
OLd ZiP LiNE
CAPE TaKo
LAWLESS AREA
PLAYGROUND
FLOWER GARDENS
DiFFiCULT TRAiLS duRiNG SUMMER
393 FeeT
ABANdONED AREA
0 cm
1.5
3 cm
0 m
≃ 350 m
TAKO AREA
: FiSH AREA, ACCORdiNG To SHiMURA SaN
: FiSH AREA, ACCORdiNG To Me
N
E
S
O

NO FUGU WaS HURT DURING tHE MAKING of THiS BooK.

However, the SaME cannoT be stated About TAKo, SHRiMP, OR UMiboTaRu...

SoME MORE NoodLes?

HO
2009-2010